How I Succeeded
In Retirement
and
The BiWay Story

An Autobiography by **MAL COVEN**

How I Succeeded
In Retirement
and
The BiWay Story

BPS
books

Toronto and New York

Published in 2012 by
BPS Books
Toronto & New York
www.bpsbooks.com
A division of Bastian Publishing Services Ltd.
www.bastianpubserv.com

ISBN 978-1-926645-85-8

Cover: Gnibel
Text design and typesetting: Daniel Crack, KD Books www.kdbooks.com

Printed in Canada

**You are invited to comment on this book,
using the email address feedback@biwaybook.com**

This book is dedicated to my grandchildren
Miriam, Nomi, Daniel, Isaac, Samuel,
Ruby, and Pearl,
who have given me the supreme compliment
– they think their Zaida is cool

CONTENTS

Me and Tony, a relative of Tom Mix's horse.

PREFACE

LEAVING a written legacy for my children, grandchildren, and great-grandchildren is something I've been pondering for some time. Now that I've lived over 80 years, the time has come.

I am not sure where the journey back through my life and times will take me, but I am sure that I want my loved ones to know and understand their heritage directly from me: where and how I grew up, how I got to where I did, what influenced my decisions along the way … and the people who were a part of it.

I hope I will have the courage to tell the story as it really was – sharing my loves, successes, failures, and most important, my determination to succeed, whether at Biway or in my many original entrepreneurial ventures since Biway. My determination to face the challenges that came my way along with some good advice from others helped to make it happen.

If I could succeed, so can those who follow me.

This is my story.

At Marblehead Harbor, about to board a fishing boat.

PART ONE

BERESHEET –
IN THE BEGINNING

In this cast of thousands that's my father and me, upper left,
Aunt Mary, lower left, and my mother holding my sister.

1

MATTAPAN, MASS.

I was born on April 8, 1929, at the Forest Hills Hospital in Boston, about a ten-minute ride from where I would grow up: 53 Westmore Road in Mattapan, a section of Boston situated between Dorchester and the town of Milton. This was to be my home with my parents until I married in May 1957. My dad had bought the house when he and my mother were married in the early 1920s.

Mattapan was a middle class area and mostly Jewish. Westmore Road is in the Wellington Hill area. The two main streets crossing near there are Morton Street and Blue Hill Avenue, the latter being the main shopping area. Morton Street was the major thoroughfare going south in the direction of the South Shore and north in the direction of Boston proper.

Our house was on a very small lot. The kitchen had a table and six chairs and a gas stove that was modern for the times. Not many years into my life, my prize accomplishment at carpentry class in elementary school – a smoking stand, a little wobbly, with a hexagonal top sanded and shellacked to the best of my ability – stood in a corner next to the sink. Years later I wanted to claim my prized work of art but unfortunately it was lost when the family moved to Milton.

Off the kitchen was a pantry containing our icebox. Mr. Goldstein delivered a 10¢ piece of ice each week and the icebox would have to be emptied before the ice could be put in – an inconvenience we were glad to be free of when we were able to replace it years later with a proper refrigerator.

The pantry was where Dad kept his vishniac (an alcoholic drink made with cherries) safely out of harm's way. Off the kitchen was a stairway to the backyard. The back porch was where the laundry was hung out to dry and where the milkman left the milk, delivered daily. On a few occasions in the winter, the snow was so deep he came in a horse-drawn sled. On freezing days, the cream, which was at the top of the bottles, rose out over the top with the cap perched on top – an unusual sight. Dad loved sour milk, or, as it is known today, buttermilk, but I couldn't stand the smell of it.

Next to the kitchen was the dining room, outfitted with a table, eight chairs, and three additional matching pieces – an expensive set bought by Dad when his business prospered. This furniture so filled the dining room that there was very little room to pass between the pieces. My mother did Dad's bookkeeping on the dining room table.

Dad

Next to the dining room was the parlour. It was many years before I actually laid eyes on the parlour sofa as it was always covered with sheets to keep it dust-free and clean. I discovered what it really looked like when my mother replaced the sheets with see-through plastic, a modern advancement at the time. The only exception to the coverings was Dad's reading and snoozing chair.

Next to the parlour was the sunroom – which later became my bedroom – furnished with wicker furniture except for my bed.

The master bedroom was next to the kitchen. I spent time there when I was not well. It was here that Mom kept me company when I had an asthma attack. We played cards or checkers and ate sunflower seeds.

Between the master bedroom and my sister Bea's bedroom was the one bathroom for the family. It was bedlam at school time with Mom evicting Dad who was usually reading his beloved *Forward*, a daily newspaper in Yiddish. First came my turn and then my sister Bea's, with Mother directing traffic. There was a bathtub and in later years a shower connected to the faucet. The tub was used once a year to kosher some of Mom's dishes before Passover as well as every week for our Saturday-night bath.

Bea's bedroom had twin beds and I slept in her room when I was very young before I was moved to the sunroom. I remember listening to my favourite evening programs on my radio – *I Love a Mystery* and *Inner Sanctum* – hiding under the covers to mute the sounds.

—

Our house had a screened-in front porch where we often sat in the summertime. If the breeze was blowing in the right direction, you could smell the Baker's Chocolate Factory in Milton not far away. My beautiful cousin Marilyn lived upstairs. She went steady at various times with Benny Diamond and Jay Long, among others. They made good use of the porch.

The front garden was surrounded with a hedge about four feet high. There were also hollyhocks, a rose trellis, and a lilac tree. Dad took care of trimming the hedges. I remember seeing his hand shake from the strain of using the scissors. This bothered me more than it did him. He never stopped until he was finished.

The backyard was a jumble of weed and rocks, as Uncle Fritzy found out when he dug it up for our wartime Victory vegetable garden. People took much pride in the produce from their gardens, particularly the tomato plants. Uncle Dave (mother's brother) had his own Victory garden on a lot in Newton.

A great tomato rivalry ensued between Dave and Fritzy as they compared the taste, size, and quality of their crop of tomatoes. (I learned one thing about farming during that time. If you plant just one row of corn, you get very high stalks and no corn. You need at least two rows. I've never made use of this information but am passing it along to my descendants in case they might want to take up farming.)

The streets of our neighbourhood were lined primarily with two-family clapboard houses, most of them owned by one of the occupants. We owned ours.

The upstairs of our house was usually rented out. Before I was born we rented it to

Mom

my uncle Morris Coven along with his wife Bessie, son Danny, and daughter Bea, and later on to the Spurber family. After that it was occupied by Fritzy and Sally Furman and their children Marilyn and Howard – my uncle, aunt, and cousins, respectively. Later, my sister Bea and her husband Harry Richman lived there for many years until my dad sold the house and moved to Milton. My sister and brother-in-law took up similar digs just past Mattapan Square in Milton.

~

My father Isaac, known to everyone as Ike, was born in 1891 in the town of Daugai, Lithuania – 54°22' Longitude: 24°20' – in the province of Vilna (now Vilnius). At that time it was part of the Russian Empire and later became the separate country of Lithuania. His parents were Israel Kovensky (1862–1924) and Bayla Gerstein. As I understand it, Dad lived on a farm with his parents and four brothers. There was a lake abutting their property, which, he said, had "the best fish in the world." In those days Jews could not own property so my guess is that they leased it in some way.

Israel's sons, as well as others, worked on the farm. All I know about it is that they had horses, cows, and chickens. My dad told me he used to ride the horses bareback with his arms around the horse's neck, something I found difficult to picture knowing him later in his life.

Dad also told me he was very proficient in giving haircuts to his brothers Morris, Louis, Sam, and Charlie. This skill was tested many years later in the backyard of my home on 44 Old English Lane in Thornhill, Ontario, when my brother-in-law Abe Fish wrapped a sheet around himself, sat down on a chair, and told Dad to start cutting. Dad giggled through the whole episode as our family looked on. He retired on his laurels after that episode.

My father arrived at Ellis Island, New York, on July 11, 1909, on the ship *Lapland*. The reason he gave Immigration for coming to America was that he was joining his older brother Morris in Boston. Morris had changed his last name to Coven, so Isaac Kovensky became Isaac Coven.

My mother, Eva Woronoff, came to America in 1903 from somewhere in the Russian Empire – exactly where, I do not know, but probably Russia proper. She came with her mother Rebecca (Stanetsky, born c. 1873) and her father Max (born c. 1871) along with her siblings Rose, David, Louis, and Israel (Issy).

They lived in the west end of Boston next to the Charles River, one of the first places that immigrants lived before eventually migrating to Dorchester, Mattapan, or Roxbury.

My sister Beatrice, always known as Bea, was three years older than I. I remember well the advice she constantly gave me as a kid, probably until the time of my Bar Mitzvah. She coded this advice in the immortal letters MYOB (mind your own business). It seemed that important things in my family were kept from me. Times were tough and my guess is that they were sheltering me from any bad news in the family.

With my sister Bea, on the back porch of 53 Westmore Road.

2

LIFE WITH MY PARENTS

Dad's first work that I know of was a stint in a restaurant/bakery with a cousin, Frank Gerstein, who eventually moved to Toronto. Dad said Frank went to Toronto to open a jewellery store. When I moved to Toronto many years later I learned that he had created Peoples Credit Jewellers, which eventually had over 50 stores in Canada.

Dad also told me of other early working days, on Salem Street in Boston, a popular shopping street for immigrants. The street was lined with clothing stores, looking somewhat as the Lower East Side of New York and Kensington Market in Toronto do to this day. Most of the signs were in Yiddish. For blocks you could see garments on racks in front of stores, pushcarts on the sidewalk, as well as kosher butcher shops and other stores.

On a few Sundays Dad was employed as a "puller." His job was to entice passersby into the store. He received ten cents for each customer he persuaded to enter the store. Once they were in the store, his job with them was done.

Some of the storekeepers, he told me, used unsavoury ploys to keep customers in the store. For example, they would sit a customer down for a shoe fitting and then hide one of his shoes. The missing shoe would not reappear until he was deemed a deadbeat. Another method was used in a suit try-on. A wallet with a $10 bill was placed in the pocket of the pants. Come try-on time for the pants, the customer found the wallet and its contents and closed the sale very quickly, thinking he was getting a bargain. (Of course the $10 was included in the price of the suit.)

Years later I purchased a photograph of Salem Street from that era at the Quincy marketplace and hung it in my library with other mementos of early years in Boston.

Soon Dad took up peddling, a common occupation of immigrants with little money and little English. Yiddish was the language commonly used by immigrants from Eastern Europe. Dad started by carrying the old piece of luggage he landed with on Ellis Island, knocking on doors in various parts of the city and selling needles and thread and other sundries. People liked him and requested other items such as house-dresses, shirts, socks, sheets, and blankets.

In order to serve them better, he acquired a horse and wagon. Because his customers could not pay him in full, he gave them credit. Typically they gave him $1 or $2 each week toward the full amount. This became known as custom peddling. From that start he built a route of customers whom he called on weekly, both collecting money and selling additional merchandise. In those days that was one of the few ways that credit was available. There was no such thing as credit cards issued by department stores.

Interestingly, many of the founders of large department stores, such as Macy's, Bloomingdale's, and Filene's, started as peddlers.

Dad's business was hurt in the Depression, which hit North America the same year I was born. At one point he was looking to move the family to a rental as the bank was threatening to take over our home. We didn't have to move, though, because his brother Louis bought the house and gave it to Dad.

Dad didn't have to be concerned about getting enough exercise: It was built into his work as he climbed two, three, or four flights of stairs every day to reach his customers. Starting when I was about 14 years old, I substituted for him on days when he wasn't feeling well, walking up the flights of stairs to collect what was owing. I had to hold my nose at the foreign-smelling odors that greeted me, from Italian cooking on one floor to Greek on the next to Eastern European on another.

In later years Dad had an office at 660 Washington Street near Essex Street. Many custom peddlers had their offices in that building, which was a wholesale clothing store. The peddlers paid no rent because they helped attract customers to the wholesaler.

This building gave us a great view of the Santa Claus Parade – a Jordan Marsh department store tradition. This was also where I would be fitted for my Bar Mitzvah suit. The proper colour, fabric, and fit had to pass the scrutiny not only of my dad but also of his brothers Sam, Louis, and Morris. (Dad's youngest brother, Charlie, a gambler, got sent back to Lithuania and died in the Russian army.)

On some Saturdays I volunteered to go collecting with Dad, knowing we would end the day back at his office and be treated at the Essex Delicatessen to a corned beef sandwich, potato salad, and all the pickles and coleslaw we could eat. These were the same pickles Dad blamed for his appendicitis attack. Sometimes I went to his office during the week, for example, when I had an orthodontist appointment at the Little Building. From there it was on to the Essex Delicatessen and then the RKO Theatre, where I watched two movies and a stage show for 35¢, usually compliments of Uncle Louis.

Dad (right) and his brothers Louis (left) and Sam.

My father was a soft and gentle man, rarely raising his voice. There was one exception. I can't remember what it was but I must have done something really bad. Dad pulled off his belt and chased me around the house. We both made sure he never caught up to me. Another typical punishment was having your mouth washed with soap and water for "lying" to your parents. Luckily, I received only the threat and not the actual punishment.

By the early 1930s, Dad did well enough to step up from a horse and wagon to a car. Our car was a very important part of our lives. It was not primarily for family leisure; it was the backbone of Dad's business.

I vividly remember going to the dealer with him to purchase a new 1941 Plymouth. It was a proud moment in our family back then as it still is for most families today. Jewish families never bought Ford cars because of the known anti-Semitism of the founder Henry Ford. Chrysler products were our norm, hence our new Plymouth. It took Dad awhile to get used to the gear shift on the wheel rather than on the floor, his new car being the first to be set up this way. That was the last time cars were made until after World War II because all production was shifted to the war effort.

During wartime many commodities were rationed and gas stamps were needed to buy gas. Dad received extra stamps because his car was used mostly for business – picking up and taking merchandise to his customers. The car was so important to him that its health was inquired after, along with that of his family, when his brothers called him on the phone. Most of the time Dad was able to say, "Running like a lily," a superlative of the times.

⁓

Dad collected only till noon on Sundays and joined all of us in the kitchen for lunch. Noontime was the major meal in our house on that day of the week. It usually consisted of lettuce and tomato salad, barley and bean soup, chicken, and dessert.

After the meal Dad retired to the living room to read the Sunday *Forward*. Although this newspaper was printed in Yiddish, I was able to enjoy the Sunday issue with Dad as we looked together at its rotogravure photos. Dad always puffed away on an El Producto cigar. Many times he dozed off, cigar in his mouth, ashes falling on his vest. Mom always seemed to know when it was time for her to enter from the kitchen to wake him. She scolded him gently, and he immediately apologized.

In the 1920s my father was also a diamond dealer, selling diamond rings. As a kid I played with his ring sizer, which, along with having all the finger sizes, had a magnifying loupe for determining the quality of diamonds. Once he lost a small bag of diamonds. Fortunately an honest man found the bag and returned it to him. Knowing Dad I am sure he rewarded the man suitably. On another occasion his nephew Danny Coven asked him to pick a diamond engagement ring for him. Danny was well-to-do and insisted that Dad make a profit on the ring. True to form, Dad would have none of that. He sold it to Danny at his cost.

~

If there was one thing that Dad taught me, it was ethics and honesty. He was a scrupulously honest man, not only in his business dealings but also in his personal life. He told it like it was. Sometimes that was not such a great idea and got him into trouble with the family. He passed that honesty trait on to me. He refused to deal in black market goods and gas stamps during World War II and he never overcharged when goods were scarce during the war, even when others did. If he promised a customer something, he delivered, even under difficult circumstances.

An expression that Dad used quite often was "to tell the honest truth." What he really meant was the whole truth.

His first cousin Leo Thall served in the army during World War II. Our family sent him huge salamis to supplement his diet. The more they aged, the better they were.

Leo had a good job as head cutter at the Lowell Knitting Mills, which was owned by another cousin, Frank Cohen. They paid Leo very well – over $100 a week. That was excellent pay in the Depression of the 1930s, equivalent to about $1,600 a week today.

Leo was single with no family responsibilities and gambled most of his money away either at the racetrack or Cutler's Pool Room with the bookies. One day he came to our house with $10,000 in cash. He told Dad to hold it for him and under no circumstance to give it back to him. He wanted to save it, probably to have a nest egg should he marry.

Some years later Leo drove up to our house in a big black sedan with two men. He came into the house and asked Dad for the money. Per Leo's instructions, Dad refused.

"Give me the money – otherwise those guys in the car are going to kill me!" Leo said.

"What could I do?" Dad told me later. "I had to give him his money."

Dad had two pastimes. One was playing cards; the other was making vishniac. He played Gin Rummy with Mom, Whist with his brothers-in-law, and poker once a week with other relatives. He played Mashi-Pashi, a card game similar to War, with me. Playing cards was a big part of my growing up years. I played Casino with my sister (as I did in later years with my own children). Mom played Bridge with the "girls" and Rummy 500 with us.

I loved it when Mom's Bridge game was at our home. She always made enough food so there were leftovers for me (oven-warmed rolls stuffed with egg salad, sweet mixed pickles, and for dessert, her apple pie or Dorothy Muriel cupcakes).

As for the vishniac, Dad delicately mixed cherries with Canadian Club whisky (my first introduction to anything from Canada), tasting his concoction as he went along to make sure the blend was proper.

Uncle Fritzy, who lived upstairs with his family, often came downstairs to sample Dad's delicacy. Fritzy was no stranger to liquor: He not only owned a store that sold liquor on Charles Street at the foot of Beacon Hill in Boston but he also was no stranger to its appeal. Fritzy's approval of the current batch of vishniac was very important to Dad. Of course, Fritzy had to try many samples before he could give it the thumbs up.

Dad, like the rest of the family, loved ice cream. If there had been a competition for fastest person to eat a pint of ice cream, he would have won it. He could down a pint in two minutes flat, all the while proclaiming that he really preferred a different flavour.

I remember two arguments between Mom and Dad in my presence because they were repeated often.

One was on the way home from the Sunday-night poker game, and included lines like, "Why did you fold so early?" or "I lost the pot because you stayed in the game too long."

The other blew up whenever they were trying to pinpoint a relative's age or weight; for example, of Great-aunt Anne, who weighed close to 200 pounds, they would say:

Mom: *"She needs a size 24 house dress."*

Dad: *"What are you talking about? She's only a size 16."*

Of another relative's age the dialogue went:

Mom: *"She's probably well into her 80s."*

Dad: *"Impossible – I think she's only 75."*

~

Mother kept a kosher home and ate out in the same manner. But Dad sometimes ate in kosher-style restaurants. At High Holiday services he never left his seat in shul or missed a word of the prayers. At home Mother always lit the Shabbat candles and made the traditional blessing over them. (When I moved to Toronto many years later, I followed the tradition of the Fish families, making Shabbat special. I made the blessing over the wine every Friday night along with the moitzi over the Chalah.)

The rest of Mom's siblings were born in Boston, bringing the family to ten children: Mother; my aunts Rose, Sarah, and Mary (teacher); and my uncles David, Louis Warren (school principal), Issy (lawyer), Abraham (died 1905), Moishe (doctor), and Joe (taxi driver).

Mother was the stalwart of the whole family. She was the confidante, peacemaker, and mediator, usually via the telephone. She was a very good listener, acting as a psychiatrist to her sisters and brothers. She was also very close to many of her nieces, in particular, Edith Levy, her sister Rose's daughter. She was like a second mother to her.

Mom mediated a dispute when her younger brother Joe was promised $5,000 for his daughter's wedding by their brother David. David died before the wedding and there was nothing in his will about the commitment he had made. Mom had to convince all of her brothers and sisters that giving Joe the money was the right thing to do.

Uncle Dave (Woronoff) was a cutter in a garment factory. He was a bachelor and took pride in declaring himself "the best uncle." He probably was. On many Sundays he planned an outing for his nieces and nephews, always to an interesting, surprise location. We went to see something historical or to a beautiful spot in the woods or to the seashore.

At some point he always asked if we were hungry and then brought out hot chocolate, sandwiches, or cakes.

He also took me fishing, his favourite pastime, at Marblehead Harbour. We went out in a little rowboat and each of us dropped a line about six or eight inches from the bottom of the harbour. We always came back with a large basket of flounders. The fish seemed to like his line better; he always caught most of the fish.

Before we left, an old man on the shore cleaned our catch and then we took it home to my mother to fry with potatoes and onions. For the most part I ate only the potatoes and onions. We typically ate in the kitchen except for holidays and company time, when we relocated to the dining room. Mom cooked an assortment of East European foods: brisket, flunken, chicken, cabbage rolls. Kugels were the mainstay of our meat meals. The only foods we ate at home that were not cooked at home were Morris & Scheff corned beef, salami, hot dogs, and those delicious knishes from the caterer at the foot of Wellington Hill.

Mom often sent me down the hill to pick up a dozen knishes. As I walked home I started eating – first one, then another. She always assumed I would eat two or three. One time I remember arriving home with only six – not the number my mother had accounted for. Well, it was a long walk up Wellington Hill and I must have been especially hungry that day.

According to Dad, Mom's dairy meals were far superior to her meat meals. She catered to his love of fish, lockshen (noodles), and kneidlach (dumpling) soups with side dishes of scallions in vinegar and slices of white radish.

One day Mrs. Slifky, a next-door neighbour, gave Mom her recipe for spinach latkes. They tasted terrible. I felt Mom would be insulted if I told her that, so I stuffed them one by one into my pockets and afterwards broke them into little pieces and flushed them down the toilet. We told Mom they were okay but that we preferred her traditional potato latkes. She never made the spinach ones again.

I was the only one in the family interested in spaghetti. Mom made it in her own inimitable way, with a heavy dose of ketchup and chicken fat, with some of noodles ending up being crispy. I loved it. This was my introduction to Italian food.

My introduction to Chinese food came once when I accompanied her shopping. As was her custom, she stopped for a coffee break at the local kosher cafeteria on Blue Hill Avenue, ordering coffee and dessert. On that one occasion she let me order Jewish chop suey – the only Chinese food I had until I was 17 and went with friends to Chinatown (no pork, of course).

Mom rarely sat down with us at mealtime, joining us only once we had almost finished eating. She ate anything of value that we had left on our plates, supplementing it with what was on top of the stove.

Dad had some unorthodox eating habits. Mom served him chicken thighs, potatoes, and vegetables. Dad ate the veggies, then the potatoes, but when it came to the thighs, he always broke off the pulka and returned the rest of the thigh to my mother.

"Please, Eva, I'm not that hungry," he always said. "Please, take it back."

Mom never gave up trying to refuse his offers. I used to think Dad preferred the pulkas. I found out years later that he really liked the white meat but in this instance we came first.

As many times as we wanted to help Mom with the dishes after meals, she always refused to accept it. The kitchen was her domain. She preferred to do everything herself. The only help she ever had in the house was from George, who came in every other week to do the heavy cleaning.

I can still picture Mom ironing in the kitchen with her transistor radio perched at the end of ironing board. This was usually when I arrived home from school, around 3:30 p.m. She actually liked to iron. She treated it as a sort of art form, and the results showed it. She gave me every detail of the baseball game she was listening to whether it was the Red Sox or the Braves who were playing – she was a fan of both teams.

As a child I was allergic to certain grasses, which brought on asthma attacks.

At the time a nebulizer was used to help a sufferer's breathing. This device was similar to a perfume-dispensing bottle. No matter how tired she was, Mom stayed with me, sometimes well into the night, squeezing the bulb-like ball at the end of the tube to spray moisture into my lungs. She kept at it for hours on end, squeezing first with her right hand and then with her left. Thank heaven medical science has improved on that procedure.

One day we had an afternoon appointment with Dr. Goldman whose office was at 520 Beacon Street. This was very close to Fenway Park, home of the Red Sox, and I convinced Mom to take me to the game. As much as she loved baseball, she did not enjoy watching the game in person. She had a difficult time following the ball. Listening to the radio announcer Jim Brett describing the action in great detail was better for her. She never went to a game again but did watch it on television, once we had one.

~

Our first television arrived when I was about 17 years old. Night after night we pulled our chairs close to the magical box and watched the evening shows. Jerry Lester was the host of the evening variety show, similar to the host of *The Tonight Show* today. One of the regulars on his show was Dagmar, a busty blonde who usually stole the show with her double entendres, which were racy for those times.

There was another show that began with a girl singing "Especially for You." Dad always assumed that she was singing to him personally.

Mom loved the soap operas and followed them on the radio. *The Romance of Helen Trent, Our Gal Sunday*, and *The Guiding Light* were her favourites. Dad's favourite TV programs were wrestling matches. He got so excited I was afraid he would have a heart attack. He mimicked the actions of the wrestlers and grunted with every slam. We didn't want to spoil his fun so we gave up telling him that it was only an act.

Dad rarely went to the movies. However, on one occasion I did get him to take me. Mom was playing Bridge at a house of one of the "girls" that evening. Dad and I went to the Franklin Park Theatre on Blue Hill Avenue to see *Of Mice and Men*, a great movie I could enjoy only many years later.

"Best Uncle" Dave and me at Marblehead Harbor.

I told Dad he should park around the corner from the theatre and he protested that the car might be towed. I somehow convinced him that there would be no problem and off we went to the theatre. Once we were seated, it dawned on me that there was a chance he might be right. It was probably a small chance, but the thought stayed with me throughout the movie. It was impossible for me to enjoy it because I was counting the minutes until it was over.

When we left the theatre it was pitch black. As we walked down the street I couldn't see the car. My heart was pounding a mile a minute. Finally I saw it: It was a good hundred yards farther down the street than I had remembered.

Lesson learned: Never try to convince your parents of anything unless you're well aware of the consequences if you're wrong.

3

MY FIRST SCHOOL DAYS

I went to elementary school at the Martha A. Baker Grammar School on Hazelton Street about a ten-minute walk from my home. The houses on our street were clapboard and those along Hazelton Street were more expensive, made with brick. Walking to school one day a bully named Luntini, one of the few non-Jews in the school, taunted me for no particular reason. I reasoned with him a few times and we eventually made peace. You might call it an early lesson in pragmatism.

In the second grade I came to school one day with my fly unbuttoned. The teacher, Miss Woolf, embarrassed me no end by buttoning it up as the whole class looked on laughing. My fourth grade teacher was Miss Connolly. She asked us to bring in some cheese for "show and tell" once when we were studying the country of Holland in our geography class. The only hard cheese we ate at home was kosher Munster cheese. Miss Connolly had never even heard of it. She thought it was delicious and thanked me for introducing kosher cheese to her and the class.

As kids we played boxball on the street in front of our house. First we lined off an infield with chalk. The batter hit a grounder with his fist, trying to place it between the infielders. As in baseball, he ran the bases, trying to beat the throw. If the ball did get through the infield, it was usually a home run because the fielder had to chase the ball down the street.

Another popular game was hitting the ball against the stairs for a single or double, depending on how far it bounced. If you were accurate enough to hit the point of one of the stairs, the ball could go all the way to the house across the street. That was a home run over the head of the fielders. It always seemed that I was the only one whose mother called him in to do homework or to get out of a light rain.

We also played marbles and pitched baseball cards. In the latter game we each pitched the cards against the wall. The one whose card came closest to the wall won the card. The ideal play was to get a leaner, where the card stood up against the wall. We waxed our shooter card so the cards slid better.

I chummed around with kids who lived on Westmore Road. Among them were the Kaplan brothers, Norman and Harold. They always impressed my mother as being quiet and polite. That was true but only in front of adults. With their peers they were mischievous troublemakers. Once in a while I had lunch at the Kaplan home. One time I told Mom what a wonderful meal I had there. She didn't take it too well. Professional jealousy, I assume. I never commented on lunches at the Kaplans again.

In 1938 the first hurricane to ever hit Boston felled a large tree in a vacant lot. It was there that our group took a stand against the marauding Wellington Hill gang in a snowball fight. We were out-manned and out-gunned as huge snowballs came thundering down on us. We surrendered after a long and bitter fight once the barrier of that fallen tree could protect us no longer.

My indoor activities were savouring my stamp collection and reading comic books. Hundreds of comic books eventually came to rest in our cellar. What happened to them I will never know. Around 5 p.m. my favourite radio programs were on: *Tom Mix, Lone Ranger, Don Winslow of the Navy,* and *Jack Armstrong the All-American Boy.* I listened intently, crowding close to the radio.

In fact, I was doing just that on the fateful Sunday, December 7, 1941, when the program was interrupted by the announcement that we had been attacked at Pearl Harbor by the Japanese. The war had begun for the United States.

The U.S. government needed to borrow money to support the millions of dollars it would take to defeat Germany and Japan. One of the ways it raised money was by selling war stamps and war bonds. Even grammar school kids were asked to help. We used some of our meager allowance to buy 10¢ war stamps. We bought as many as we could each week and stickered them in a book. When the book was filled there was enough to buy an $18.75 war bond. The bond was a loan to the government for ten years. During that time, interest accrued. After ten years, the government would redeem the bonds and pay $25. The difference was the interest earned from our investment in the government.

~

Summer excursions with the family when I was very young were to Revere Beach for the day or to Houghton Pond in the Blue Hills, also known as Hoosic Woosic Pond – why, I have no idea.

We spent a week some summers deep in the countryside at "Cohen's Pleasant Hotel," in Millis, Massachusetts. Both sides of the road leading to the hotel were lined with trees so thick that they darkened the way. Anytime I am in the country, I am reminded of Millis. I'm sure somewhere under Cohen's property are the bottle caps that I collected and buried.

Dad always said it was less expensive to stay there than at home because they served three wonderful meals to all of us and fresh baked cookies and milk to the children in the afternoon, all for the price of $38 a week for the whole family.

Years later, when I was a teenager, Uncle Fritzy and Aunt Sally took me there for a week where I met my first love, Laura, from Providence, Rhode Island. After the holiday the romance ended when we each went home.

For a few summers we spent a week or two near the lake in Sharon, living in a little shack next to the Octagon House. One evening, to my dismay, Dad shooed away a skunk using my bat and glove, which became useless for obvious reasons.

4

LAST DAYS

OF CHILDHOOD

I graduated from grammar school and went on to junior high at the Solomon Lewenberg School for the seventh and eighth grades. I attended with the same friends that I had played with on the streets. Most of them did quite well at school and later in life.

Norman Kaplan went on to the Massachusetts College of Pharmacy, becoming a pharmacist and owning his own drug store. Harold Kaplan, his brother, went to Harvard and became a doctor. For Arnie Goldsmith it was Boston University, after which he became a university professor. Stanley Cohen went to Lowell Textile School and eventually owned a knitting Mill. George Katz went to MIT and became a business executive. Phil Barack attended Harvard and later became the CEO of the U.S. Shoe Corp.

We called our group the Rangers, which was also the name of our baseball team. I was not a great player either at bat or in the field. I had little confidence in my ability and prayed that the ball would not be hit to me. I was exhilarated when I did make the occasional good hit or catch.

I did shine at stickball, however. I often went with two of my friends to the Solly (Solomon Lewenberg school) with a stick or bat and a tennis ball or pimple rubber ball. We found an appropriate wall to pitch against and chalked it off with a square representing home plate. The pitcher used the square as his target. The batter tried to hit the ball to the fielder, who tried to catch it on the fly. Balls and strikes were called and we took turns in each position as the game progressed.

Good pitchers could make the ball do funny things and put us off stride by throwing first a curve ball and then a fastball. We batted the opposite way – righty to lefty and vice versa – to keep the ball from going out of the playground too often.

We were all baseball fans in those days, mostly of the Red Sox but of the Boston Braves, too. I was a great defender of the Braves. I felt sorry for them because they usually finished in next to last place. They did have their time, however, when they won the National League pennant in 1948.

Not only did we save and play with baseball cards, but we also knew every statistic of each player by heart, from batting averages to fielding averages and everything in between. We even knew their minor league records. We argued intensely over the merits of our favourite team, particularly in 1948 when the Braves were a better team than the Red Sox, in my opinion at least. Our heroes at various times ran from Jimmy Foxx to Ted Williams to Warren Spahn and Johnny Sain. Some of their pictures adorn the walls of my apartment.

In the summertime we tailed the ice truck, gathering slivers of ice to suck on. Mr. Goldstein also came with his ice cream truck selling Popsicles, Fudgsicles, and Hoodsies. These last consisted of a Dixie cup filled with chocolate and vanilla ice cream. Inside the lid were photos of famous Hollywood stars. Cowboys were my favourites, but I saved them all.

The truck we saw in the winter was Mr. Goldstein's coal truck. He wore a cap with union pins that covered most of the cap and from time to time he gave me one of them.

Going out for ice cream was a big treat in our family. We went to Howard Johnson's, famous for their 28 flavours of ice cream. With friends we walked to Mattapan Square to Brigham's or sat at the counter at Charms Pharmacy and had sundaes, ice cream sodas, frappes (a New England specialty: a milkshake with ice cream mixed in), or frappe floats (a frappe with a scoop of ice cream on top).

When it came to sundaes, the best were at Bailey's, downtown on Temperance Street. Bailey's was an old-fashioned ice cream parlour with a marble counter and a tiled stone floor. We sat on wireback chairs that were not too comfortable, but who cared about that?

Picture two huge scoops of ice cream with lots of hot fudge overflowing to the plate below, then a generous layer of marshmallow, then lots of chopped walnuts and a maraschino cherry on top. My mouth is watering as I write this – Pritikin, Weight Watchers, and Jenny Craig would not approve.

When I was older, and after a late date when the G&G was closed, we often went to Erie Street where they baked bagels all night. We bought a dozen hot bagels and a side of cream cheese and ate a couple and took the rest home. On weekends we sometimes walked to Mattapan Square. We made one or two stops before or after the movie at the Oriental Theatre. It was either Brigham's for ice cream or Simcoe's on the Bridge for a hot dog. Simcoe's served the most delicious foot-long hot dogs grilled to perfection on a toasted bun. Who could ever forget the brand – Essem, Yiddish for "eat them."

My ritual on rainy Saturday afternoons was going to the Morton Theatre on Blue Hill Avenue. A walk down Wellington Hill and we were practically there. For the princely sum of 35¢ I saw a feature film, another full length B-movie, and then one segment of a serial that continued for seven or eight weeks. Each segment was about 15 minutes and culminated with the hero – Tom Mix, Superman, Flash Gordon, Roy Rogers, or Dick Tracy – going over a cliff or trapped in a burning house. It always seemed that the hero in question was a goner, but lo and behold, the following week he had survived in some miraculous way for another 15-minute adventure.

After three hours of entertainment I came out of the theatre, my eyes blinking away as I tried to accustom myself to the daylight. I trudged my way up Wellington Hill and home.

One thing I definitely did not enjoy was getting my hair cut. It's still true now that I am in my 80s. The barber shop was near the corner of Blue Hill Avenue and Morton Street at the foot of Wellington Hill. I sat down in the chair as it was raised to the proper height in readiness for what would be a dreadful ordeal. The sheet was never tied tight enough to prevent hair from going down my neck.

I gave the barber the same instructions that I give to anyone who cuts my hair today: "Not too short and not too long."

When the barber finished cutting, he applied Slickum, a thick perfumed gel liquid used to plaster hair in place. I can still remember the awful smell of shaving lotion on my neck. Then came the powder. I always tried to stop it but the barber was too fast for me. Before I knew it I was engulfed in a cloud of powder dust.

I was happy to leave and walk back home, although as I walked up Wellington Hill my hair started to dry and strands of hair began to stand up one by one. By the time I was home I looked like a freak (not unlike some teens with a similar type of haircut today). I always wore a knitted toque indoors and outdoors for a day or two to keep my hair down.

Unfortunately, once another month had rolled along, it was time for me endure the same ordeal.

For my Bar Mitzvah party, in 1942, my parents rented a long plywood table stretching from the dining room through the parlour into the sunroom. It was covered with a linen cloth and accommodated seating for my friends and our family. We all sat down to a meal of corned beef and all the things that go with it because Mom knew that was my favourite meal.

5

BOSTON

LATIN SCHOOL

Dad, like my mother, never pressured me to greater academic heights. Both of them accepted my marks and suggested that I do better on my next report card.

After completing the eighth grade I had to make the first big decision of my life. Where was I to take my high school education? I pondered this for some time and decided to go to Boston Latin School, not only because I was seeking a superior education but also because two of my closest friends in the neighbourhood were going there. It turned out to be one of the best decisions of my life.

Boston Latin School, which includes junior high and high school grades, is the oldest public school in North America. It was founded in 1635, a year before Harvard. It had a great tradition of famous graduates, including the likes of Arthur Fiedler and Leonard Bernstein as well as Benjamin Franklin and 16 other signers of the Declaration of Independence. Unlike other high schools, you had to pass an exam to enter.

It was fall of 1942. I was only 13 years old when I started class four (ninth grade) there. The practice in Boston in those days was to start school with kindergarten at age four.

Boston Latin School is situated on Avenue Louis Pasteur in the Fenway area across the street from Harvard Medical School and next to Simmons College, an

BLS BULLETIN

Published by the Boston Latin School Association

Vol. 12, No. 2

Spring, 1985

exceptionally fine girls' school. Boston Latin School was a boys' school; most of the schools in Boston then were not co-educational. The dress code was shirt, tie, and jacket at all times.

It took me over an hour to get there from my home. I had to walk to the streetcar line, then take the elevated train, and then board a bus, followed by a ten-minute walk to the school. For the first time I felt great pride in going to school.

Boston Latin School had strict Rules of Conduct. Teachers used misdemeanour marks and a censure system to keep students in line. You could get a misdemeanour for running in the corridor, not dressing properly, getting caught looking at someone else's test papers, or even being late for class. If you accumulated 12 marks you could be censured and thrown out of the school.

There was a place on our report card each month for our approbation mark. Receiving approbation for the month required no marks below a B, not missing a day of school, and not being late for class. If you received approbation for every month of the school year, you got an approbation with distinction prize. I never reached that lofty goal.

Boston Latin was a different world from Mattapan. The curriculum consisted of Latin, French, Greek (not mandatory), history, economics, math, physics, and chemistry. It also included military drill, which was unique to the Boston school system. We marched around with disabled Springfield rifles from World War I. I was promoted to captain and company commander and I'm proud to say that one of my friends who served under me, Larry Mintz, went on to attend West Point and become an officer in the army.

My best subjects were math, history, and physics. My worst were Latin, English, and French.

Public declamation was an actual subject, on which we were graded. Each student had to speak in front of the whole class periodically and once a year to the school assembly, reciting from memory a famous speech from history.

Sports were also a part of the tradition. Like most schools we supported our school at an annual Thanksgiving game, in our case against arch-rival English High School, the oldest high school in the U.S., founded in 1821. After the morning game, I went home for the traditional turkey dinner. On that my mother particularly excelled.

I usually went to the game with my Uncle Fritzy and others in the family.

Uncle Fritzy was my hero when I was that age. He was a wonderful uncle. He was a professional boxer when he was young, before owning a liquor store on Charles Street with his brother.

Uncle Fritzy was a very strong man. He met his match, though, in a test of strength with my great-uncle from Providence, R.I. Both were able to lift a heavy kitchen chair by the base of one leg from the floor up over their head, but my great-uncle did it just as well even though he was Fritzy's senior by 30 years.

It was Uncle Fritzy who introduced me to the steam baths, taking me there on the occasional Sunday. Other Sundays we rented bicycles to ride in Franklin Park. Once in a while we went to see the Red Sox play at Fenway Park. On those days I got up early to check the sky for dark clouds, fearing that the game might be postponed.

Twice a week Uncle Fritzy took me and some of my friends to school, cutting our travel time in half. We had to leave at the crack of dawn in his 1937 Buick, the same car he would let me use when I was 16 and learning to drive. Besides the early hour, a downside to riding with him was his habit of clearing his throat and expectorating out his window. If you were sitting directly behind him, you had to quickly lean to the right to avoid the spray. The fellow in that seat usually did.

On an outing with Uncle Fritzy, Marilyn, and Bea at Franklin Park.

~

The students at Boston Latin School came from all over the city. All of them had chosen not to go to the high school in their district close to home. Some came from as far away as Brookline or Newton; because they lived outside Boston they were charged a tuition fee. Boston Latin School kids came from all walks of life, rich and poor alike, mostly middle class and poor.

Joey Albert came to school the whole year wearing rubbers over his shoes because his family couldn't afford to repair the holes in the soles of his shoes. He also had a severe acne problem, which I am sure had something to do with his decision to become a dermatologist. Frankie Weiner lived in a very poor part of Roxbury. His father had a truck and collected junk for a living. Frankie became a transportation lawyer.

Other classmates of mine included Archie Sherman, who went to Boston College and Harvard Law School and became a judge; Sheldon Seevak, Harvard, partner at Goldman Sachs; Pat Roache, Boston College, founder of a chain of supermarket stores; Larry Mintz, West Point, businessman in Colombia; Norman Cohen, Boston University, psychologist; Paul Miller, Yale, corporate lawyer in Chicago; Bobby Franklin, who became a psychiatrist; and Herman Weisman, who became a pharmaceutical executive.

Aaron Gordon was one of my favourite teachers; he made ancient history interesting. Max Levine taught us French and was a fixture at Latin School for 50 years. Mr. Wilbur taught us Latin. (We studied Caesar and Cicero; however, this teacher was more famous for his apple orchard.) Mr. Pierce taught us civics and economics and convinced me to always read the *New York Times* to educate myself. Mr. Dobbyn taught us algebra and geometry and had a son who followed him as a teacher at the same school.

~

My first paying job, when I was about 13 years old, was with Mr. Rubin, a neighbour who lived across the street on Westmore Road. It was wartime and Mr. Rubin had barrels of assorted metal nuggets. My job was to pick out the shining metal, which was copper and more valuable. I did that for three days and was paid 40¢ an hour, collecting $10 for my work. It was important because I really earned it. I bought war saving stamps with some of the money and saved the rest.

The Simon and the Barash families were good friends of Mom. The Simons were very wealthy because they had the food concessions at the Boston Garden, Boston Arena, and the Rockingham Park and Suffolk Downs racetracks. When I was 14 or 15 years old Mr. Barash, who lived very close to our home, came by and took me to work every day in the summer to Suffolk Downs in Revere.

I was assigned to a stand where they sold coffee, cheese sandwiches, and, of all things, brownies – how lucky can you get? The customers gave me tips. One guess where the tips went. Right – I spent them on brownies. They were not in Mom's class but they were darn good. (Coincidentally, while I was working at Suffolk Downs, my schoolmate-to-be and partner-to-be at Biway, Russ Jacobson, was selling ice cream in the stands.)

When the season closed at Suffolk Downs, Mr. Barash and I went on to Rockingham Park Racetrack in New Hampshire.

—

The first job I received on my own was when I was 15 years old, in the middle of World War II. I rode to the end of the subway line, climbed the stairs to the street, and approached the first store I saw. It was a hardware store owned by an elderly Jewish couple. Their stock boy had taken off so they hired me on the spot.

They treated me no differently than if I was their son, making sure I didn't lift anything too heavy. I did have one mishap, however. I was filling some bottles with alcohol from a large container. My instructions were to fill the bottles, leaving about an inch of space at the neck. With one bottle I filled the neck and used my finger to flick out the excess. The alcohol went right into my eye. Luckily, soaking my eye in water prevented any harm.

A few weeks later, the couple's full-time, year-round stock boy returned. I then found a job next door in a stationery shop. My parents and I assumed this would be an easier job, but I soon discovered that there is nothing harder than lugging around reams of paper.

On one occasion I had to carry two stacks of rolls of theatre tickets to a customer via the elevated subway. The two stacks were three feet high and tied with rope. As I climbed the stairs to the elevator the ropes loosened and I had to rush around picking up the rolls, which were strewn all over the steps. I did finally make it to my destination, though my hands were bleeding because I had to keep tightening the rope.

One summer I worked as a waiter at Fritz's Camp, a family hotel in New Hampshire. I remember waiting on the tables of some nice Jewish families. This job was important because the experience got me another one the following summer, this time at the Lafayette Hotel in Old Orchard Beach, Maine. It was kosher and for the most part attracted Jewish families. Many of the families there were from Montreal as this was the closest resort to the Atlantic Ocean.

The tips were good except for those from the Canadians. Some of them told me they were restricted in how much money they could take out of Canada. A fine excuse for being cheap. We worked three meals a day but had one day off. We could spend time on the beach and at the amusement park, both of which were a few steps away.

My uncle Louis Coven had been there as a guest the previous year. One of my tables had four single ladies. Evidently Uncle Louis, who was single, had been very nice to them, taking them in his car to see the sights. They had their sights on him and wanted to know if he would be back.

We served the meals using a large metal tray. I was a very good waiter, if I do say so myself. I catered to the diners' every wish, from prune juice to pudding. I always gave them extra food and in some cases I received above-normal tips.

There was, however, one embarrassing moment. We left the kitchen holding a tray full of food by kicking the door to the dining room open and walking through. On this occasion I slipped and came crashing down, tray and all. As was the custom, everyone applauded.

Forming a good relationship with the cooks was very important. I was told that if they didn't like you, they could throw a few knives around. I made sure they liked me. It was fun working there. Not only was I earning money but I was also able to spend time at the beach and at the amusement park, where I met some ladies from

Quebec. They couldn't speak English and I couldn't speak French, but I still got along well with them.

All that said, when the season ended on Labour Day, I was happy to go home.

—

A great time in my life was turning 16 and learning to drive. As mentioned, Uncle Fritzy was my instructor. I learned on his 1937 Buick, which had a floor shift. You had to let the clutch pedal out very slowly as you pressed down on the gas pedal. If you didn't, the car jerked forward in spasms.

After many lessons I was ready for the driving test, or so I thought. I took the test using Uncle Fritzy's car. He was allowed to sit in the back seat to observe his protégé. It seemed that I started a tradition that would carry on to my children Robin and David years later. I did not pass. On a left-hand turn I let the clutch out too quickly and the car jerked back and forth, scaring the daylights out of the instructor and my uncle, too. I did pass the next time.

Very shortly thereafter I persuaded my mother to persuade my father to let me take the car on a date. Frankie Weiner and I were invited to a house party some 30 miles away in Framingham. The girls must have been very special for us to want to go that distance for a party.

A tremendous rainstorm blew up as we drove home on Route 9. About halfway home, I sideswiped a car that was parked on the shoulder without its lights on. It was a stolen car. All I can remember is feathers from a pillow flying all over. Fortunately, we were not hurt.

As you can imagine, I was heartbroken. Dad had given me the car reluctantly after telling me how important it was to the family with his whole business built around it.

Dad was playing his evening card game with Fritzy when I called. The first thing Dad asked was if we were okay. Obviously everyone was relieved that we were. Uncle Fritzy came to get us and took care of taking the car in for repair. I overheard Dad telling Mom that he had taken out extra insurance in case of such an event. To his great credit, he knew my confidence was shot and offered me the car as soon as it was returned. The only stipulation was that I not take it to Framingham.

I had just turned 16 when Mother noticed a lump on my right leg just above the knee. The doctor told us to have it removed immediately, which we did, at the Hahnemann Hospital in Brighton. Thankfully, it was benign. I walked around on crutches for a few weeks. The operation left a zipper-like scar on my leg. At the time, mid-August 1945, everyone was celebrating victory over Japan (VJ Day). Years later, when my children were very young, I told them that during the war I kept secret messages in my leg. Did they believe me? I doubt it.

Speaking of medicine, a landsman of my dad was our family doctor Dr. S.Z. Bell. He was a very nice fellow and a good doctor, but he had an impediment. He stuttered. You had to help him get the word out. He might say, "Asssssparrr" and you would contribute "aspirin" to save both his time and yours. The walls in his office were very thin and if you sat in the waiting room next to the wall that backed onto the office, you could hear every word of his conversations with his patients. Those seats always filled first.

My sister Bea was a good student, much better than I was. She graduated high in her class at the Jeremiah E. Burke High School and went on to secretarial school, the practical thing for a girl to do in those days.

She always had a good job. For many years she worked for the government and then as a legal secretary for Ropes & Gray, a prestigious law firm in Boston. Over the years her closest friends were Mickey Weisman and Barbara Barack. Barbara's brother Phil Barack went on to become the youngest chairman and CEO of the U.S. Shoe Corp. He held those positions for many years.

Bea married Harry Richman, a war veteran. Harry found his niche being a superior salesman of men's clothing at Filene's. He was also very active in the union there and was well liked by both his fellow employees and a loyal following of customers, of which there were many.

As well as being a good and thoughtful husband, he was a handy person to have around. Harry could repair most anything that needed fixing at 53 Westmore Road and in later years in Milton. After Hurricane Hazel hit Boston we had no electricity for a few days. True to form, handy Harry had some power in the trunk of his car, and we used it for our electric razors, shaving out on the driveway in the windy aftermath of the storm.

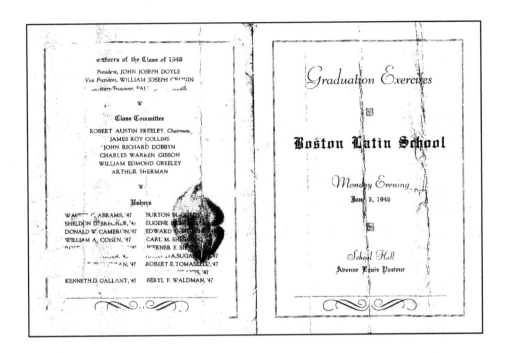

Officers of the Class of 1946

President, JOHN JOSEPH DOYLE
Vice President, WILLIAM JOSEPH CRONIN
Secretary-Treasurer, PAUL ... ...R

Class Committee

ROBERT AUSTIN FREELEY, *Chairman*
JAMES ROY COLLINS
JOHN RICHARD DOBBYN
CHARLES WARREN GIBSON
WILLIAM EDMOND GREELEY
ARTHUR SHERMAN

Ushers

WALTER C. ABRAMS, '47   BURTON M. ...
SHELDON D. BRECHER, '47   EUGENE ...
DONALD W. CAMERON, '47   EDWARD ...
WILLIAM A. COHEN, '47   CARL M. SH...
...   WERNER E. SI...
...   ... A. SUGA...
... ...N, '47   ROBERT E. TOMASELLO, '47
... ...S, '47
KENNETH G. GALLANT, '47   BERYL F. WALDMAN, '47

Graduation Exercises

Boston Latin School

Monday Evening
June 3, 1946

School Hall
Avenue Louis Pasteur

BIOGRAPHICAL NOTES FOR BLS CLASS OF 1946 50TH ANNIVERSARY

Please type or write neatly:

NAME: **MAL COVEN**   TITLE:

HOME ADDRESS: 17 Old Forest Road, Toronto, Canada M5P2P6

HOME TELEPHONE: (416) 484-4407

SEASONAL ADDRESS (if applicable):   3100 South Ocean Blvd. Palm Beach, FL 33480

SEASONAL TELEPHONE: (407) 547-0886   DATES OF RESIDENCY: January - March

BUSINESS ADDRESS:

BUSINESS TELEPHONE:

COLLEGE(S), DEGREE(S), YEAR(S):   Boston College B.S.B.A. 1951

MARITAL STATUS: Married   WIFE'S NAME (if applicable):   Barbara

CHILD(REN)'S NAME(S):   Robin Gofino, David Coven, Adam Cooper

GRANDCHILD(REN)'S NAME(S):   Miriam, Niomi, Daniel

In the space provided below, please share with us biographical information on you, your family, career, interests, anecdotes...anything goes! You may add a page if you need more space.

1951 - 1961 - Filene's Boston

1962 - 1990 - Founded BiWay Stores Ltd., Senior Executive Vice President and Chief Executive Officer for part of the time

1991 - Investor in retail ventures

My kids and grandchildren live close by in Toronto. Robin is a lawyer, David is an importer, Adam is a nickel trader. My first wife passed away thirteen years ago. I have been happily married to Barbara for ten years. My hobbies include cycling, travel, theatre, and swimming.

BOSTON LATIN SCHOOL 50TH REUNION 1996
Together again: Archie Sherman (left), me, Sheldon Seevak,
Leo Karas, Larry Mintz, and Irwin Shostack.

6

BOSTON COLLEGE

I graduated from Boston Latin School in 1946, the school's first peacetime gradu-
ating class after World War II.

Four years' worth of veterans were coming out of the service and were entitled to
many benefits for their service to the country, including free tuition, books, a monthly
living allowance, and even extra academic credits. The competition for places at
universities was therefore very keen for kids coming out of high school.

At the time I thought I might want to be a dentist. Luckily for me, Tufts University
rejected me. I was accepted to both the University of Massachusetts and Boston
College. I chose the latter because U of M was located in the western part of the state.
Going there would have meant living there, an additional expense for my parents.

Although Boston College was a Jesuit University, it did have some Jewish
students. There were probably not more than 50 in the Arts & Sciences school and
a handful in the Business School. There are many more today, probably in the same
ratio of Jews to the general population of Boston.

I decided to enter the Arts & Sciences school to earn a bachelor of education
degree and become a teacher. My first day in class I realized that most of the school's
athletes were seeking the same degree. BC was most famous at the time for its football teams and athletes.

Academically, I was the star of the class – I even tutored some of the athletes,
particularly before exam time. Some of them went on to professional football careers,

among them Butch Songin, who quarterbacked the Hamilton Ticats to a Grey Cup victory, Ernie Stautner, a Hall of Fame linesman for the Pittsburgh Steelers, and Artie Donovan, a Hall of Fame star for the Baltimore Colts. As I will describe later, some of my relationships with the athletes would be a great help to me in the future.

After one semester I saw no future for me in Arts & Sciences and transferred to the Business School, where I made some enduring friendships.

One of them was with Russ Jacobson, who became my lifelong friend and was to join Abe Fish and me in Toronto as a partner in Biway. When Russ came to Toronto he added a new dimension of expertise to that chain's retailing. For sure we would not expanded so successfully without him.

Jerry Levinson was the athlete in our group. He won Letters in three sports. He was a star pitcher on the baseball team and went on to have a professional career, signing a contract with the Boston Braves.

Our first victory ever over Notre Dame.

Bobby Woolf, although he was a year ahead of us, was on the basketball team with Jerry and went on to become a high-profile agent with clients the likes of basketball's Larry Bird.

Also in our group was Arthur Ezrin, who went on to a business career, though he could have been a professional concert pianist, and Mel Silverman, who became a successful retailer but died at a very early age.

Another friend, this one from my Latin School days, was Archie Sherman. Archie stayed at Boston College for only one year and then transferred to Harvard, going on to become a judge. In his year at Boston College he talked his way into becoming track manager. The track coach at the time was Jack Ryder, a former Olympic coach. Archie anointed me as his assistant manager and when he transferred to Harvard I inherited his job.

The track manager was responsible for organizing the home track meets, travelling with the team on away meets, and taking care of financial matters. We travelled to New York many times for the invitational meets at Madison Square Garden. The team practiced outdoors year-round, on a cinder track in the spring and on the boards in the winter. Many times we had to shovel the snow off the boards to prepare for practice.

The most famous athlete we had at the time was Harold Connelly, who went on to become a two-time Olympic champion in the hammer throw. Some of the school's football players competed in the field events, notably Ernie Stautner, who could throw a 16-pound shot put without practice farther than others who practiced diligently.

Ernie was not interested in track and field. On the day of the home meets I had to look for him in the "barracks," where the athletes lived, to persuade him to participate. It was much easier to get him to do so when we were travelling to Madison Square Garden. On one occasion I walked into a bar with him and felt well protected.

As the team's money manager I found out that steak for breakfast was the order of the day when the team was travelling, which took a large bite out of my budget. Two great rewards for being track manager were a one-year scholarship that covered the $750 tuition fee and an award sweater, a heavy Shaker cardigan sweater with a big chenille B, which I wore very proudly.

On one occasion on a hot summer day I went to Revere Beach, the Coney Island of Boston, clad in that woolen sweater.

I was with Russ and Miltie Holtzman, who asked me if I was a little warm wearing a sweater. Although the temperature was close to 90 degrees, I nonchalantly said, as perspiration rolled down my forehead, "Not at all."

～

I majored in marketing and was a very average student, thinking more about what I would do after BC and wondering how I could earn a living than I did about my subjects. Because BC was a Roman Catholic school, there were some courses I had to take even though they had nothing to do with business. One in my freshman year was Bible study, with the textbook being both the Old and New Testaments. Dad was not too happy when he saw me with the King James Version of the Bible. I lied and told him it was the Old Testament.

We also had to take Catholic philosophy. The way it was taught went like this: We studied Thomas Aquinas, the famous Catholic philosopher, and were taught to refute anyone who didn't agree with Catholic philosophy. In my last year I paid so little attention to the subject that I literally never opened a book and only showed up to half of the classes. How I ever passed is a miracle in itself. I remember having nightmares about flunking my oral exam and not getting my degree.

The only steady girlfriend I had at university was Arlene Furman. We dated for two years, not exclusively on her part, and went to football games, dances, and school proms together. Until then she was the only love of my life. She was beautiful – a little buxom, it's true, but that was just fine with me.

For the first time I was really in love, but I was a kid and the last thing on my mind was getting married. It was not, however, the last thing on her mind. One day she broke the news to me that she was getting married, not to me but to a fellow from St. Louis.

Unbelievably, 50 years later she called me when she was visiting her husband's cousin in Toronto. They came to visit at our home and we all went out to dinner.

I said to my wife, Barbara, when I took the call, "I wonder what she looks like 50 years later?"

"She must look great or she wouldn't have called you," Barbara said.

She was right. Coincidentally, Arlene ran the Jewish Film Society in Columbia, South Carolina, doing the same work that Barbara did when she was chair of the Jewish Film Society in Toronto. Arlene wanted to meet my children. Later, both of our families got together in Hollywood, Florida, for just that reason.

Ad Majorem Dei Gloriam

The Seventy-Fifth

Commencement

of

Boston College

Wednesday, June Thirteenth

MCMLI

At Four o'Clock in the Afternoon

BOSTON

JOHN COUGHLIN, B.S.B.A.
253 George St, LaCrosse, Wisconsin
Service: Air Force
Major: Marketing

JOHN P. COURTNEY, B.S.
153 Homes Ave., Dorchester, Massachusetts
Major: Economics
Activities: N.F.C.C.S. 2; Heights 3, 4; Foreign Trade
Club 3, 4; Yacht Club 1; Senior Representative 4; Junior
Week Committee; Rifle Team 3, 4

MALCOLM COVEN, B.S.B.A.
32 Wentworth St., Mattapan, Massachusetts
Major: Marketing
Activities: Track Manager 1, 3, 4; Heights 3; Intramurals
1, 2; Student Council 3.

WARREN J. COX, B.S.
36 Plymouth Ave., Milton, Massachusetts
Major: Chemistry
Activities: Intramurals 2, 3, 4; Chemical Society 2, 3, 4.

PAUL A. CRANDELL, B.S.
109 McGreevy Way, Charlestown, Massachusetts
Service: Navy
Major:
Activities: Physics Seminar 2, 3, 4.

DAVID M. ___ HONORS
10 Dewey St., ___
Major: English
Activities: ___ Sodality 1; Intramurals 1, 3, 4; ___ Chemical Academy 2

JOHN J. CRIMMINS, JR., B.S.
69 Glen Rock Ave., Malden, Massachusetts
Service: Marine Corps
Major: Economics
Activities: Intramurals 2, 3, 4; Nocturnal Adoration So-
ciety 3, 4.

JAMES A. CRONIN, JR., B.S.
119 Union Ave., West Haven, Connecticut
Service: Marines
Major: Chemistry
Activities: German Academy 2, 3; Chemical Society 3, 4;
Connecticut Club 3, 4.

GEORGE S.
114 Albion St.
Service: Navy
Major: Physics
Activities: Ca___
President; 4; P___
ative 3.

ALB___
28 La___
Service:
Major:
Acti___
Academy
Pro___

EDWARD
410 Medford
Major: History
Activities: In___
Heights 2, 3.

JA___
33 ___
Se___
M___
Ac___
In___

GRADUATES

OF

84

PART TWO

LEARNING MY CHOPS

Merchandise Diploma

This Certifies That

Malcolm Coven

having satisfactorily completed

all the requirements for

graduation from the Filene

Merchandise Training Course

is awarded this Diploma by

Wm. Filene's Sons Co.

_By_ [signature]
VICE-PRESIDENT

Boston,
Massachusetts   3-24-53

7

GETTING STARTED AT FILENE'S

IT was 1951 and I was fresh out of Boston College with a Bachelor of Science degree in Business Administration and I was anxious to go out into the business world and earn some money. (I had to take an extra half-year of college because the classes I had taken in the Arts & Sciences School didn't count toward my business degree.)

Because I didn't have a lot of self-confidence, I thought I was better suited for a buying rather than a selling career. I applied to the executive training program of Filene's, as it was reputed to be the best such program. Filene's, a chain of seven department stores, had a great reputation and called itself "The World's Largest Specialty Store." It did not carry hard goods as other department stores did.

However, the little confidence that I had dissipated when I didn't make the cut.

I met with Danny Coven, my cousin, who was an accountant but also involved in many businesses. (He would later be a confidant of Paul Fireman, founder and CEO of Reebok and one of the founding investors of Staples.) He asked me what I wanted to do.

"To be a buyer at Filene's," I told him. "But they rejected me from their executive training program."

He then gave me advice that would have a lasting impact on my career and my life. I have passed his advice on to many young people since.

"If you want to work for a company, go there and take any job," he said. "You are better off on the inside looking in than on the outside looking in."

Thus it was that Mal Coven, armed with his shiny new degree, went to the Filene's employment office and applied for work. What I received was a temporary stock boy's position in the sporting goods department. My job was to move golf equipment from the store room to the selling floor, for which I was paid the princely wage of $8 per day.

After three days I got lucky. Mr. Bross, an executive on the seventh floor, was given the job of organizing a unit to comply with government directives from the Office of Price Stabilization (O.P.S.). He chose me to help him as we were fellow graduates of Boston Latin School.

At the time, inflation was rearing its ugly head. Prices of commodities were rising too quickly, eroding a family's buying power and standard of living. The O.P.S. was created to ensure that stores did not raise their prices too much. We had to set the standard to accomplish this.

The buyers at Filene's were told to create charts showing what they charged the previous year for each category of merchandise they bought. The chart was to make sure they did not raise their prices or their markup to more than an acceptable degree. It was my job, after the charts were completed, to police their prices and make sure they were in compliance. I had to meet with the buyers on an ongoing basis as they needed our permission to deviate in any way from those charts. The buyers wanted to make sure they got on my "right side" so they could get the maximum benefit from our office.

My salary was now $38.50 per week instead of $8 a day, but this was a permanent job, not a temporary one, and what prestige it was to work on the executive floor!

This went on for close to a year. Then the buyer of men's sportswear, Sam Maletz, who had taken a liking to me, took me aside and advised me to get into merchandising. In his opinion this was the only place in a department store where you could get ahead financially. He had no assistant in his men's sportswear department and asked me to join him. I did, but not as an assistant buyer. That job was kept open. I went there as what store management called a clerical.

As a clerical my job consisted of counting stubs, which were removed from the merchandise when it was sold, as well as being a stock boy and working on the selling floor when needed.

The merchandise in Department 219, men's sportswear, consisted of pants, sport coats, outerwear (winter jackets), rainwear, and men's robes. The price of sport coats started at $35, mostly from Mavest, the largest sports coat maker in the U.S. The most expensive were cashmere sport coats from Jackman of California, retailing at $75. These were typical retail prices of menswear in the 1950s at prestigious department stores.

I was told that the men's furnishings department agonized for a long time whether they should raise the Arrow and Van Heusen shirt prices from $3.95 to $4.25. They questioned whether that would hurt the shirt business.

～

Sam Maletz took me under his wing. In the two years I worked for him, first as a clerical and then as an assistant buyer, I received a lifetime of education in the menswear business. Some of the relationships I built during that time would have a profound effect on my career.

I had been in the department for only a few weeks when Plymouth Manufacturing, a rainwear maker, wanted to show us a new line of tweed raincoats they had developed. Although we usually were not allowed to carry topcoats, which were reserved for the men's clothing department, we would be allowed to carry these because they had a water repellent finish and were from a rainwear maker. They were to retail at $39.95 with a zip-out wool lining and came in an assortment of Donegal-type tweeds that were not only practical but also smart-looking, especially in their raglan sleeve model.

We purchased a substantial quantity for all the Filene stores. Because they were manufactured in Boston, we could get repeat deliveries quickly and efficiently. The following day I was filling in on the selling floor when a gentleman approached me. He said he was a friend of Sam and wanted to speak to him. Sam was out of the building so he engaged me in conversation.

"What's new in the men's sportswear business?" he asked.

5/16/70

DEAR MAL

YOUR WONDERFUL LETTER MADE MY
DAY FOR WHICH I THANK YOU FOR
BEING SO THOUGHTFUL — IN FACT
YOU ARE ONE OF THE VERY FEW
OF MANY I HELPED OVER THE YEARS
WHO STILL KEEP IN TOUCH —

FOR MY PART I STILL CALL LOUIS
MAIER WHO YOU REMEMBER WAS
HEAD OF MAUEST — HE IS NOW
IN HIS 80'S, IN BAD HEALTH AND
90% BLIND — AFTER ALL THE NICE
THINGS HE DID FOR SO MANY BUYERS
I'M THE ONLY ONE WHO STILL
CALLS — NUF SED —

ELLIE AND I ARE BOTH WELL,
MY EYESIGHT NOW 20/20 THANKS
TO CONTACT LENS —

NATURALLY I'M PROUD OF YOUR
SUCCESS AND LOOK FORWARD TO
HEARING MORE IN THE FUTURE —
BE SURE TO CONTACT ME
WHEN YOU NEXT VISIT BOSTON —
MY WARMEST REGARDS TO YOU
RUSS AND YOUR FAMILIES —
MY BEST ALWAYS

A note from Sam Maletz after retirement. He taught me the business.

Fresh in my mind was the session with Plymouth.

"Tweed raincoats," I replied, going on to describe our enthusiasm for the new Top-o-Tweed raincoats.

We also chatted about the other merchandise on the floor, which I was very familiar with even though I had been a clerical for only a couple of weeks.

The following week one of our suppliers, Milton Grayson of Congress Sportswear, came over to me with a newspaper in hand and congratulated me on the write-up about me he had just read in the local trade paper. I saw the headline, which I will never forget: "Filene's buyer's random thoughts on rainwear merchandising." Front page, two columns, continued on the back page, two more columns.

I came close to fainting. I knew I was in trouble. I had no idea this fellow I had spoken to was a reporter for the local trade paper. Not only was I not a buyer, I was not an assistant buyer but a lowly clerical stub counter at $38.50 a week.

When Sam found out, he was furious. He took me into a corner of our department shaking his fist and yelling.

"You are supposed to keep your big mouth shut and not speak to anyone about our merchandise, particularly a newspaper reporter. Wait until Mr. Fish finds out."

The men's merchandise manager was Abe Fish, coincidentally the same name as my future brother-in-law and partner-to-be at Biway.

"Your career at Filene's could be toast," Sam said.

I was called up to Mr. Fish's office and feared the worst. Luckily for me, Mr. Fish gave me only a light scolding. He told me to be more careful about the people I spoke to from then on.

The biggest beneficiary of the incident was my dad. In his custom peddling, he frequently did business on Kneeland Street, the centre of the jobbing trade in Boston. From that time on he was given a much different reception. He was not just the buyer of a few shirts and pants. Now he was the father of a Filene's buyer.

"I didn't know your son was such a big-shot buyer at Filene's," people said to him. "Bring him around one day. I have some things he would be interested in."

⌐

After close to two years, Sam was promoted to buyer of the men's furnishings department with a much larger volume than our sportswear department. I was an assistant buyer and too inexperienced to be considered for his job.

My new boss was Henry Allen, a very good Filene's Basement clothing buyer, who had come back to Filene's after an attempting to open his own store. He could size up a store full of merchandise and determine the prices at which Filene's Basement could sell in a very short time.

Mr. Allen was a friend of Abe Fish, who gave him my old boss's job. The new position was strange to him. Picking styles of men's robes or sport coats took patience, which he did not have. Buying assortments of colours and sizes was not his bag. Consequently, he always made sure I was with him when making purchases. He depended on me to do the detail work. Even though Mr. Fish was a friend and golf buddy of his at the Belmont Golf Club, he did not have much respect for Mr. Allen as a buyer and was aware that he depended a great deal on me.

On one occasion Mr. Allen planned to make a trip to Norwalk, Connecticut, to meet with Rabhor Robes and buy a robe promotion for Christmas. There was an old saying, "Robes sell like robes year-round except for Christmas when they sell like shirts." Mr. Allen preferred not to take me with him on this trip, which was not to my liking: I felt insulted because I had been selecting most of the men's robes for the department.

He came back the following day with a sample robe and swatches of different patterns. They were all wool and could be retailed for $10. He asked me to pick the patterns I liked best.

"I don't like any of them," I said.

They were what were called Ombre plaids and they looked terrible.

He then gave me the same pitch that they had probably given him about their intrinsic value and what they probably would have been worth at the regular price.

When I failed to fall for the pitch he said, "Okay, wise guy, what would you buy?"

"Tartan plaids – the same patterns we sell from higher-priced makers," I said.

"Impossible to get, and these are beautiful," he said and walked off to show them to his boss.

MR. MUIR HONORED

The head table with Mr. Ring, Mrs. Muir, Mr. Muir, Mrs. Walker and Mrs. Martin. (The last two named are Mrs. Muir's sisters and Mrs. Walker is also Mr. Muir's nurse.)

To have the affection and respect of those who work for you as well as those for whom you work must be a wonderful feeling. One such man is John Muir who was honored at a party Thursday, May 3. Mr. Muir is supervisor in the Basement Men's Clothing Departments and has been out with an operation. To let him know how much they miss him the party was given in his honor at Scituate Cabins.

Mr. Ring was a very able master of ceremonies. Mr. Hodgkinson sent a telegram which was read, as did Mr. Goldberg. Pete Cerrone of 052 spoke a few words as a representative of the salesforce. Mr. Ring presented the guest-of-honor with a present of money and a scroll inscribed with the signatures of his many Filene friends. All in all a very pleasant as well as heart-warming evening.

ANN KOSTANDIN PROMOTED

Ann Kostandin

Ann came to Filene's in 1951, having attended the Modern School of Fashion and Design. She started her Filene career by selling in our Men's Store; and her first promotion was to Merchandise Clerical in 360 (Children's Accessories and Underwear). Her next step up was to Assistant Department Manager, 651 (Bridal Shop); and her recent promotion has been to Department Manager and Bridal Consultant in this same department. Good luck, Ann, on your new job.

LOIS ROGGI PROMOTED

Lois Roggi

Lois graduated from Katharine Gibbs Secretarial School and spent the next few years doing secretarial work. Then last Christmas, having in the meantime moved to Boston, Lois came to Filene's to try Retailing. She liked it so much that in January of this year she entered Filene's as a Trainee for the main store. She started her retailing career as a main contingent but soon was promoted to Merchandise Clerical in Department 110. Her recent promotion moves her up to the Bridal Shop where she will be an Assistant Department Manager, Junior Grade. We wish her lots of success in her new department and with her new career.

MAL COVEN PROMOTED TO DEPARTMENT MANAGER

Malcolm Coven

Mal, a graduate of Boston College, has received most of his Filene training in 219 Department (Men's Sportswear). He entered the store in 1951; and shortly afterward was promoted to Merchandise Clerical in 219. Later he attained the position of Assistant Department Manager in this same department. Mal has now been promoted to Department Manager in 342 (Boys' 3-6 Apparel). Congratulations, Mal, and lots of luck.

PROMOTION FOR LORRAINE BARNES

Lorraine Barnes

Lorraine is a graduate of Smith College. During World War II as a Lieutenant in the Navy, Lorraine served as supply officer at the U. S. Naval Shipyard in Portsmouth. After the war, she worked at Kendall Mills as a merchandising assistant. In March of this year Lorraine decided to resume her merchandising career and came to Filene's as a Branch Trainee in our Chestnut Hill store. Now she has been promoted to Acting Department Manager at Chestnut Hill. Congratulations, Lorraine.

Store Management II will begi on Thursday, May 17th. A.M. in the Class Ro have not recei contact ment

An announcement in The Echo *of my promotion to department manager.*

I was told by Mr. Fish's secretary that the first question Mr. Fish asked was, "What does Coven think of them?"

Shortly thereafter Mr. Allen came back to the department with his tail between his legs and said, "We will be in New York next week. We'll look for something else."

The something else we found were authentic tartan plaid robes to sell for $12 but in desirable Black Watch, Mackenzie, and several other tartan plaids. This was one of the lessons I learned from Sam, who often said, "Intrinsic value is important, but desirable eye appeal is more important even though you have to pay a little more."

One innovation that I made in men's robes was suggesting to one of our suppliers to look for tartan plaid cotton material to manufacture into travel bag robes. We did carry a few bag robes in rayon polka dot patterns that sold very poorly. Every time I looked at that table of rayon polka dot bag robes I got dizzy. The tartan bag robes went on to be one of our bestsellers, not only at Christmas but for Father's Day, too.

I was responsible for other innovations in the sportswear department. We were the first to zero in on walking shorts, which were a fringe item in those days, and Chino pants, which till then had been sold mostly in Army/Navy stores.

After a few years as Henry Allen's assistant buyer, I felt I couldn't wait around to be promoted once another men's buyer died. The policy at Filene's was that any assistant buyer could apply for any buying positions that opened up. An applicant might know nothing about buying ladies' dresses, but that could be learned in just a few months. Being a good merchandiser was the predictor of success.

8

SELLING SNOWSUITS IN JULY

MY long-time friend Russ Jacobson was already a buyer of boys' wear in the famous Filene's Basement while I was still languishing as an assistant upstairs. Then a position opened up as boys' buyer, sizes 4-6x. It had been part of the responsibility of a woman who also bought all 2-3x and 4-6x. The new merchandise manager in children's wear, Bill McNamara, had decided make boys' 4-6x a separate buying category and was looking for somebody to fill that position.

I applied for the job and got it. It was a very small department with a volume of only $250,000 in the main store and less than that in all of the other branches combined. I was now a fully fledged buyer with much responsibility and prestige and was given a raise to $110 a week.

I usually had lunch with Russ, feasting on 10¢ hamburgers and hot dogs at Joe Nemo's. As executives we did not want to be seen there so we entered and left through the rear door. Once in a while we treated ourselves to sandwiches on Providence Street, where they served one and a half sandwiches. "If one is not enough, and two is too much, order one and a half," the shop's sign said. That was their motto.

We also lunched at the Essex Delicatessen on Essex Street where our favourite dessert was grapenut pudding, or at Warmouth's on Summer Street, where they served the best corned beef hash with a poached egg on top.

At one of my first meetings with Mr. McNamara, we discussed an upcoming promotion on children's winter coats, a preseason promotion in July. The ad was to be combined with 2-3x and 4-6x boys' and girls' and 7-14 girls'.

However, although the previous buyer had purchased them months in advance, they did not arrive on time for the July 4th promotion.

The boys' department was up against the grand total of 12 sales. Mr. McNamara asked me what we could do to replace them and make the figures of that day. I remembered seeing a rack of snowsuits in the stock room, around 25 of them, which were a carry-over from the previous season and whose last prices ranged from $14.98 to $19.98.

"Let's run snowsuits," I said.

"At what price?"

Seeing that I would not be responsible for the markdown because I had inherited the snowsuit merchandise, I thought for a moment and picked a number that I thought would move them quickly.

"$7.99," I said.

Over the July 4th weekend we ran a small two-column ad in the *Boston Post*: "Ready Monday, at 9:15 a.m. – boys' snowsuits – preseason sale – $7.99 – originally $14.98 to $19.98."

On that Monday I came to work at 9 a.m., with the 25 snowsuits hanging on two racks in my small department, ready to go on sale. The boys' 4-6x department was situated on the third floor at the top of the escalator. When the store opened, dozens of customers came charging up the escalator and filled my small department. The snowsuit racks were quickly emptied and the customers were screaming for more.

The phone rang. It was Mrs. Cantor, in charge of the mail and phone order department.

"I hope you have a lot of these $7.99 snowsuits," she said. "We're getting swamped with phone orders and the mail orders don't arrive for a few days."

I thought quickly. It was July and the customers certainly didn't need the snowsuits immediately. So I lined the customers up, took orders on sales slips and noted their size and colour preferences. Between the department orders and the mail and phone orders we had close to a thousand orders. The figure we were up against that day was a puny $200.

My next problem was finding snowsuits to fill the orders, and that meant a trip to New York. I had been there many times with Sam and Henry as an assistant buyer but this was my first trip there as a fully fledged buyer. This time I had a very specific and serious mission: acquiring close to a thousand snowsuits to fill the orders I had accumulated.

My plan was to pay no more than $5 per snowsuit. Although that meant I would be working at a few points lower than my average markup, it made sense because of the large volume. I had a big advantage and I played it for everything it was worth: I was a new buyer; the old suppliers wanted to keep me as a customer and new suppliers wanted in.

My first call was to the principal of a well-known manufacturer. He started to laugh at the price I wanted to pay.

"I have 250 snowsuits, all size 6x and mostly in blue," he said eventually. "I'll give you them at $5."

"I'll take them," I said, and on I went, knocking on doors, introducing myself to old and new resources. Finally I had accumulated the thousand pieces I needed, taking any size the suppliers had left over from the previous year.

We were the heroes of the store. We then planned snowsuit sales for Columbus Day, Veterans Day, and January Jumbo Day. Mr. McNamara decided that all of the other children's departments should join in.

I went to Jack Mates, one of our regular snowsuit suppliers. I raised the price to $10 and convinced him to give us a special promotional suit for future promotions. I don't remember the exact number but I'm sure all of the departments together sold close to eight thousand suits, almost half of which were ours. We even won the January Jumbo contest for the whole store with an increase in sales of 162%.

In another innovation we went to big boys' makers and traded up. The last buyer's 4-6x goods were offshoots of 2-3x – very babyish. I felt the need to go to big boys' styling. We bought Mighty-Mac winter jackets to sell for $25 when previously the highest-priced jackets sold for around $10. Mighty-Mac was the premier brand in boys' outerwear. We did similar things right across the board.

However, in the retail business you're a hero for no more than a year. If you took a

Grand winner is Department 342, Little Boys 3-6x. Pictured above, left to right in front row, are: Ethel Davis; Alice DeRoche; William McNamara, division manager; Mal Coven, department manager; Kay Santino and Gladys Wilson. In the back row are: Walter Dennis; Barbara McGrath, assistant department manager, and Mary Clarke. Not there when the photo was taken were Cecilia Katzeff and Paula Gullifa.

FINAL JUMBO WINNERS

The parade of Jumbo Winners has ended in a triumphant finale this week with the big news that the grand winner for the entire month is the Little Boys' Shop, 3-6x. As you may remember, this department gave a hint of things to come as they were the winners in the very first week's contest. They have made steady progress since then and step into the Jumbo spotlight by walking away with the 1st place honors for the en-tire month with a sales increase of 63.5% over quota.

They will enjoy the fruits of their efforts at a dinner in the near future. Everyone in the depart-ment is to be congratulated.

In addition to the grand prize winner, Mal Coven, Department 342, Little Boys 3-6x, winners for the entire month of January Jumbo in each division include: Department 100 (Gloves), Mr. Diamond, Department Manager, Mr. Matthews' division; Depart-ment 611 (Uniforms and Aprons), Mr. Baker, Department Manager, Mr. Malatesta's division; Depart-ments 620-621-622 (Millinery), Miss Seltzer, Department Man-ager, Mr. Gross' division; Depart-ment 451-625 (Sportswear), Mr. Levy, Department Manager, Mr. Bertman's division; Departments 470-471-474-480 (Junior Dresses and Coats), Miss Myers, Depart-

(Continued on page 2)

department from $1 million to $2 million and the following year you dropped down to $1,999,000, you were a bum.

Luckily for me, I was promoted to a much larger department, 8-16 boys', almost a year to the day that I was assigned to the 4-6x boys' department. In addition, I was responsible for the Varsity Shop, which catered to high-school and college students. The Varsity Shop was situated on the second floor right at the top of the escalator, as was the boys' department – a great location for both.

—

My business was going well in general but I definitely felt the pressure. At one point my inventory was too high and I remember at one point looking at the sprinkler in the stock room, hoping it would go off.

A big help to our department was the Davy Crockett rage. We took full advantage of it, selling everything from Davy Crockett coonskin hats to Davy Crockett pajamas. The only downside was the recording, "Davy Crockett, King of the Wild Frontier." We played it constantly, literally thousands of times, and it could drive you to drink. We did, however, earn thousands of dollars in extra business.

As was the custom, at the end of the season we sold our leftover merchandise to Filene's Automatic Basement. The Basement buyers came upstairs and made offerings for our leftovers. This year was different. My friend Russ Jacobson was the Basement boys' buyer and he came up to buy my remainders. I know he took it easy on me, quoting me higher than normal prices.

Then a setback. The powers that be decided that the Varsity Shop, a low-volume department, was in a location that was too valuable in the month of December before Christmas. We were forced to move it to the back of the floor and make room for Christmas decorations. I knew it would ruin the Varsity business but what to do?

At the time Filene's was a very promotional department store. There were five rectangular booths on the main floor. Each booth consisted of tables set in a very high traffic area of the main store with a salesperson in the centre. The merchandise in the booths could change daily. Any department with an appropriate high-volume item could apply to use one of them. You couldn't keep the booth for more than that day if the merchandise didn't sell fast enough.

I decided to find an item for a booth to try to make up for some of the business that the Varsity Shop move would cost. Varsity catered to high-school and college-age young men. The sizes we could carry were men's sizes, normally 36-44. We didn't carry 46 because usually that size was not appropriate for our customers, but we did have the right to do so.

I decided to put winter jackets on a booth on the main floor. One of my makers was William Barry of Lawrence, Massachusetts. I had a good relationship with them from my men's sportswear days. They were a very important menswear maker, not only for Filene's but for other department stores, including J.C. Penney. I drove to Lawrence to tell them of my problem. I needed jackets at a price that would sell well in a booth. I knew they could and would help me.

They let me select 150 winter jackets from their inventory. The assortment included some of their samples in leather, wool, and cotton, all regularly retailing from $25 to as much as $60.

We put them in the booth and in no time customers surrounded it two deep. We held on to the booth for three weeks because my friends at William Barry were carrying a large inventory for some of the chain stores they sold and they gave me a price to retail at $12. Here again the markup was low. However, one booth selling as much as $1,500 a day meant a good profit.

So what seemed a setback turned into an opportunity and success. Our sales at the Varsity Shop tripled for that month.

9

THE CONVERTIBLE
AND THE BLONDE

IT was August 1956. I had a week's holiday from my work at Filene's. My beautiful 1953 Dodge convertible was restless, having been confined to travelling the short distance back and forth from Mattapan to the subway that I took to work. What better thing to do than take it for a long drive?

I knew my classmate Jerry Levinson from Boston College was living in Montreal and decided to pay him a visit. Off I went. The scenery through New Hampshire and Maine were gorgeous. Riding along with the top down, I felt as free as the breeze. It was an adventure. I crossed into Canada and then crossed the Jacques-Cartier Bridge into the beautiful city of Montreal.

Once there, I called my friend's office and to my dismay found out he was in Winnipeg and would be there for a few days more. I was disappointed, but only for a moment, because I decided to see more of the country.

I saw a sign "To the Laurentian Mountains" and off I went again. The Laurentians were grand and beautiful, not exactly the Blue Hills near where I grew up in Mattapan. All of the signs were in French and I had no idea where to stop and sleep over until I reached Ste-Agathe, where I saw some signs in Yiddish. I asked downtown about accommodations and was directed to a resort called the Chalet. I checked in and to my delight found it had a very Jewish atmosphere. It was a family resort but had some single patrons, too.

I went to a dance that evening and saw a beautiful tall blonde, there with a girl-friend. I had gained some confidence in myself now that I was a buyer at Filene's but generally I was still shy socially. In spite of that, I went right up to her and asked her to dance. Her name was Miriam. We spent some quality time together and enjoyed each other's company. She told me she was spending the weekend at her family cottage in Val-David, a small village close by.

We left the dance and drove to another resort, the Castle des Monts, also a family resort. Miriam's brother Morris was working there as a bellhop. We met and chatted for a while. Morris had gone fishing that day and asked if I would be good enough to take the fish to their mother at their cottage in Val-David.

I wasn't too anxious to put smelly fish in my prized convertible but he finally convinced me. He reminded me that fish are lucky in the Jewish religion.

To flash forward: Fifty years later I came across a painting at the annual Art Show at Toronto City Hall. It was a painting of judges. Morris was now a Supreme Court justice. I bought the painting and sent it to him along with this note: "Fifty years ago this month you told me that fish are lucky. You were so right about that." Meeting and marrying Miriam and becoming a part of the Fish family changed my life.

Miriam was around 20 years old and was working in the garment trade as a receptionist and doing some modelling. Although she had good marks at Baron Byng High School, she didn't matriculate as she loved clothes and shoes more than taking the math exam in her final year. I am told there was a well-known shoe store in Montreal where some of Abe's friends worked. Abe gave them strict instructions to shun Miriam when she came in. He wanted to make sure she didn't blow her whole salary there.

During a stay at the cottage in Val-David a few years after I married Miriam, I met with her brother Abe. He told me of his plan to open a discount store in Toronto. I listened to his plan. Frankly, I was not impressed with his chances for success. I wondered how he could be successful without a retail background. I sure was wrong about that.

Miriam and I returned to Montreal. She invited me to stay at their home at 6066

Jeanne-Mance but made sure her girlfriend Dorothy slept over, too, to keep everything kosher.

To have a car in Montreal was not common among poorer Jewish families. The thought went through my mind that maybe my car was more of an attraction than I was.

Nevertheless I drove back to Boston feeling pretty good about myself even though I never did get to see Jerry Levinson. I had started a relationship with a beautiful, intelligent, and personable lady. We saw each other not too many times but we talked for hours on the telephone every day. Miriam kept a log of our telephone conversations. I know she did not miss a day right up to the day we were married.

That December Miriam invited me to Abe and Marci's wedding at the Primrose Club in Toronto. It was on Christmas Day and I had to get special permission to be away from my work. I took the train to Toronto and was placed at the head table at the reception dinner as Miriam's escort. Everyone assumed there was something between us. Frankly, we were a little embarrassed. They were right but just a little premature.

I believe it was not more than a few hours before the wedding that Miriam took me to Abe's apartment. I came to congratulate him and found him lying in bed in his underwear, just relaxing. I was impressed by his cool manner just before this great event in his life. I thought I would have been much different – as nervous as a cat. When the time came for me, I was.

Miriam's first trip to Boston was almost a disaster. I picked her up at the train station and took her downtown to Filene's. I had a job interview that day for a promotion to a much larger-volume department. I wrongly assumed that it would take no more than an hour and arranged to meet Miriam at noon for lunch.

What I didn't realize was that several people were being interviewed ahead of me. I had to wait two hours before mine. I couldn't leave to tell Miriam I would be delayed because I didn't know exactly when I would be called for my interview.

I felt terrible leaving the poor girl at the front of Filene's for what turned out to be an extra two hours. When I arrived she was in tears, alone in the city where she knew no one but me. Luckily she forgave me when I explained the circumstances.

I introduced her to my friends Russell and Sheila Jacobson and then to my parents at their home in Mattapan. She was very personable and hit it off with my Dad. He was impressed when he found out she could read his *Forwards* in Yiddish.

He took me aside and asked, "Where did you find such a beautiful blonde?"

~

Miriam and I were married May 19, 1957, in Montreal. I received a wonderful package in the deal: not only Miriam but two brothers-in-law and a wonderful mother-in-law and father-in-law. Miriam's wedding dress was the one Sheila Jacobson wore at

Miriam and Robin around the time of David's Bar Mitzvah.

סאנגרעגיישאן בית משה

Congregation Beth Moishe

DUROCHER and LAJOIE AVENUES
OUTREMONT, QUE.

OFFICE OF THE RABBI

Copy from the Register of the Congregation Beth Moishe of Outremont, Que.

On the nineteenth day of May, one thousand, nine hundred and fifty seven, there were married by the Authority of Banns and the usage of Israel, MALCOLM COVEN, buyer, of Mattapan, Mass., U.S.A., of legal age, bachelor son of Isaac Coven and Eva Woronoff, and, MURIEL FISH, stenographer, Of Montreal, of legal age, spinster daughter of Aaron Fish and Zlata Gruber. Marriage contract #5256 was made by Notary Samuel Senzilet. The witnesses were Isaac Coven and Aaron Fish. Act read.

Groom:	Malcolm Coven	(signed)
Witness:	Isaac Coven	(signed)
Bride:	Muriel Fish	(signed)
Witness:	Aaron Fish	(signed)

Rabbi J. J. Zlotnick, Minister   (signed)

This is to certify that the above is a true copy from the Register of Congregation Beth Moishe of Outremont, Quebec, of which the undersigned is Custodian.

Aaron J. Zlotnick
RABBI

her wedding. It was acquired from a Neiman Marcus lot that Filene's Basement had bought.

Miriam's mother Zlata was an extraordinary and courageous lady. When I came into the picture she was struggling to make ends meet. Her husband had lost one leg to diabetes and was later to lose the other. (When he had to have that second operation Abe was in Toronto and Moishe was overseas. Zlata herself was not well, so I had the task of taking Mr. Fish in an ambulance to the hospital for the operation.)

As the story goes, when the family was young they were renting a house on Main Street across from the synagogue near Rachel Street. Zlata took in boarders to help make ends meet. She came home one day to see a For Sale sign on the house and knew she would have to move. She approached the owner and asked to buy the house. He was not impressed; he didn't understand how she could even think of buying the house when she was always behind with her rent.

Well, she did it. She borrowed some money from relatives and the Free Loan Society and with her meager savings purchased the house. That gave her a start. She eventually sold the house at a profit and reinvested her earnings in a larger home at 6066 Jeanne-Mance. She went on to sell that house at a profit and bought another one at the corner of Ponsard and Circle Road to get a more prestigious address for Morris, who was going to law school at McGill University.

Eventually, when Moishe and Judy took over that home, Zlata rented a small apartment on Ponsard just down the street. In the meantime, she had bought two bachelor apartments that she personally looked after to make sure they showed a profit. Even though she was not well at the time, she took a bus instead of a taxi to the apartments, carrying all of the cleaning materials with her, keeping control of every nickel of her expenses. By this time her husband was bedridden and was her responsibility, too.

In spite of all her struggles, she was able to lend money to her sister-in-law who couldn't pay her own rent. Abe was in Toronto and Moishe was in residence at McGill or travelling to Russia and Cuba for the *Montreal Star*, where he worked while he was at school.

I was able to spend time with Moishe later on frequent trips with Miriam to Montreal and later when I moved my family to Toronto. I met some of his friends at McGill. Moishe was editor of the *McGill Daily*, one of the few daily college newspapers in North America. At that time he was living at McGill Commons.

I've always bragged about my ability to spot talent because Moishe was the best man at our wedding and went on to become a Supreme Court Justice. On one occasion when I was on a buying trip in Montreal, Moishe invited me to see him in action at court. He had just started practicing criminal law and was defending a young lady charged with a hit and run.

The judge ruled "guilty as charged." Then he turned to the Crown Attorney and said, "It is a good thing you weren't up against Mr. Fish in a case that wasn't so cut-and-dried. You would not be so lucky."

Was I ever proud to hear that.

*Jeep bought at an auction in Oakville for Moishe and Judy's
farm in Stukely, Quebec. Still running.*

In later years Moishe gave me a few challenges.

"There's an auction in Oakville of surplus army vehicles," he said once. "Buy me one. I need it for my farm."

Now the only thing I knew about cars was how to start the motor and drive.

"Go there early and you will learn about jeeps," Moishe said.

I arrived hours before the auction. There were almost 100 jeeps going up for auction and I asked questions of some of the people there. My strategy was to bid early because most of the bidders would probably lie back since there were so many to be sold. My strategy worked: I bought the second one that went up for auction for $1,500. Some 40 years later, as I write this in 2011, Moishe is still using it on his farm.

On another occasion I was visiting my son, David, in Paris, France. Moishe called me and asked me to buy a book at the Pompidou Centre that he needed at a trial in which he was defending *Penthouse* magazine. I bought the book and took it to FedEx because Moishe needed it in four days. FedEx, however, told me it would take a week to get it to him.

I called Moishe to tell him it was impossible to get the book to him in time. He said I would just have to figure out a way.

I knew that the father of my son's girlfriend, Michelle Barkley, was a supervisor at Air Canada and told him my problem. He directed me to go to the hotel where the pilots slept over in Paris and to use his name as a reference. He was sure one of the pilots would bring the book back to Toronto on the next flight.

I was just about to deliver the book when Moishe called to say he had found one in New York City. In spite of that, I was happy to know that I would have accomplished my goal.

⁓

The day after the wedding we packed all our wedding gifts and Miriam's belongings into my car and off we went on our honeymoon to New York City, where we had reservations at the Waldorf Astoria.

The ride from Montreal to New York was harrowing. Between Miriam weeping quite often because I was taking her away from her family in Montreal and the dark roads in the mountains, we didn't arrive at the hotel until midnight. I hadn't had the

LOUIS MAIER
3875 WALDO AVE.
NEW YORK 63. N. Y.

December 11, 1956

Dear Mal:

I do want to thank you deeply
for thinking of me, as always, at Chanukah.

Both the thought and the handsome
ties, which I shall enjoy wearing, are most
appreciated, believe me. It is good to have
real friends like you, whose friendship does
not depend on business.

Let me reciprocate from the bottom
of my heart all good wishes, not only for
Chanukah, but always. I would have written
sooner, except that I have been laid up with
a really severe cold and am just now getting
back on my feet.

Again, Mal, my thanks and my warmest
regards *also to your dear parents,*

Sincerely,

Louis Maier

LM/rf

sense to guarantee the reservation and they had given the room away. After begging and pleading that we were on our honeymoon, they finally found a room for us in the servants' quarters.

The highlight of our New York trip was fourth row centre tickets to *My Fair Lady*, the premier show at the time. One of my suppliers, Manny Eagle, had given us the tickets. It had just opened that season and it was a delight.

I mixed a little business with pleasure. I had lunch with my friend Louis Maier, a former supplier of mine when I was in the men's sportswear department. Louis was a stylish, elderly gentleman with roots in Germany who had became the largest sport coat manufacturer in the States. When Miriam and walked into the elegant dining room in the men's clothing building, all eyes turned to Miriam with her blonde hair and tall, hourglass figure.

Then it was on to Atlantic City for the remaining few days of our honeymoon week. Unfortunately, I had given my car to the doorman at the Waldorf Astoria but hadn't taken the wedding presents out of the trunk. I had assumed they were safe. I was wrong. The trunk was empty.

10

THINGS CHANGED

THE early years of our marriage were a trying time in my life – not because of our relationship but because so many things were happening in such a short time. I loved my work for the most part but had a full plate. Besides my new position as a buyer, I was "setting up shop" with my new wife and studying for my Masonic test. All of these things weighed heavily on me and from time to time depressed me. But I persevered.

I considered buying a home in Framingham as Russ and Sheila had done, a three-bedroom bungalow for $15,000 on half an acre of land. In the end I decided not to because of all my new responsibilities.

Instead, I rented an apartment in a new building in Mattapan on Morton Street very close to where my parents lived. Close, but still a short driving distance away. It was not a good move. Although the apartment was fine, the other tenants were elderly ladies, who, as Miriam put it, spent all of their time playing poker. Miriam didn't have her driver's licence so she was stuck there until I came home from work.

After a few months I succeeded in getting out of the lease and did buy that home in Framingham, on 26 Edith Road. It was a good decision. The houses in the area were unique for their time because they did not have a basement. Like the other houses in our area, our three-bedroom ranch (bungalow) was heated with pipes under the floor. The fridge was attached to the wall, which saved a lot of space and kept it out of harm's way of children.

Our daughter Robin was born during this time, in 1958. We were now a normal suburban family. I commuted to Filene's by car pool or by train and Miriam got her driver's licence and got around quite easily in our family station wagon. She had friends on the street but was not one to sit around having coffee with the neighbours. She spent her time with Robin and preparing our meals. She was a balabusta of the first order.

All of the money I had saved, $9,000, was put into the down-payment on the house to reduce our mortgage payments. Principal and interest each month were $125 and deductible from our income tax.

Believe it or not, in those years married women rarely worked unless they were very poor and had to make ends meet. It would have been an affront to most husbands with a reasonably good position if their wife went to work. I was one of those husbands.

My Sundays were spent mowing the lawn on our half-acre "estate." Then came the sweeping – what a drudgery. On many Sundays my parents came out with a care package, which we ate with them on our cement patio.

I would be remiss if I didn't tell you about Robin's birth. When the time came, I drove Miriam to Framingham Union Hospital, about 15 minutes away. After examining her a short time, the doctor came out to tell me it would be some time before Miriam would deliver our baby. He even told me to go home and that he would call me well before the birth. I went home and watched a Boston College football game on TV.

A couple of hours later I got a call to tell me to come to the hospital, but Miriam had given birth well before I arrived. She reminded me often over the years of the fact that while I was watching football she was doing hard labour. I didn't make the same mistake when our son David was born.

⁓

Soon after settling into Framingham we joined a Conservative synagogue there. It was a fledgling synagogue and needed a fundraiser.

Russ Jacobson and I were rabid Boston Celtics fans, as was almost everyone else in the area. We decided to bring several people from the team to speak at a fund-raising dinner.

The Framingham High School football team had had a particularly bad year, losing every game except the final one of the year, against their archival, Natick High School (Doug Flutie's school). Natick was undefeated coming into that game. Russ and I decided to initiate an award honouring the Framingham team for this extraordinary win with a trophy for comeback team of the year and make that the centrepiece of a fundraising dinner.

We invited Mike Holovak, the coach of the New England Patriots, as well as Red Auerbach, the famous coach of the Celtics, and star players Bill Sharman and Bob Cousy. Their fees were very expensive and left little money for dinner and the trophy. We knew it was a good investment because the room would fill to capacity, which it did. But we had no choice but to go on the cheap for everything else. We served hot dogs and beans and bought a very inexpensive trophy.

The night of the dinner Russ and I stood in the wings looking at the head table guests with much satisfaction.

After the Framingham coach and the captain of the team spoke, it was Red Auerbach's turn. We were appalled at the words that came out of his mouth.

"Whoever heard of giving a team a trophy to a team that won one game all year?" he said with a smirk.

That was bad enough, but then he said, "And the design of this trophy is so chintzy, I'm ashamed to present it."

Then he concluded with, "And the dinner – I've never been to one with just hot dogs and beans."

I guess this was his idea of a joke, but we didn't think it was very funny.

Bill Sharman spoke next and apologized for him.

We felt much better after counting the receipts, knowing we had achieved our goal for the synagogue.

~

With my income at Filene's and austerity at home we kept our heads just above water. All of my assets were tied up in the house.

In the late 1950s Russ Jacobson and I were both buying boys' wear for Filene's.

Russ was doing the buying for Filene's Basement, world-renowned for its automatic markdown policy and its great bargains. I was buying for boys' wear and for the Varsity Shop in the upstairs department store. We were both successful in our work and had good reputations in the store and with our suppliers.

At one point Russ and I got it into our heads to be entrepreneurs and start a store on our own. We both lived in Framingham. Not far from where we lived a strip mall called Sherwood Plaza was starting up. I hit on the idea of opening a discount store there selling boys' and girls' things under the name Robin Hood of Sherwood Plaza, a play on the famous Robin Hood of Sherwood Forest.

Now for the hard part. We went to see my cousin Danny Coven, who was experienced not only in accounting but also in business. He knew the developer and said he would approach him for us. We thought we would need 10,000 feet and drew up a budget on that basis. It called for an investment of $100,000, of which we could contribute nothing. We were depending on our reputation and skills as merchants to help raise the money from some of the manufacturers with whom we both did business. Cousin Danny said he would contribute $10,000 to help us out. He would also negotiate the rent for us.

Russ and I discovered that saying they could invest in a store we might open was a great ploy for manufacturers get on the right side of buyers. Then we discovered it was only a ploy, because very few came through with a promise to invest with us. The few who did wanted to own the major share of the business, something we could not accept. We did not want to trade Filene's for another employer.

Some time later in a conversation with Danny he told me we really did not need $100,000. However, as he put it, if it rained for a few days and things were not going well, he did not want us to get in trouble.

Because we were supporting families, had mortgages on our houses, and would be giving up good jobs with a respected firm, Russ and I realized that we needed to be very conservative. We aborted our business plan.

Lesson learned: Make sure you are reasonably well financed before you change direction in your career.

Shortly thereafter, in 1961, there was a change in management at Filene's. Harold Krensky of Bloomingdale's, one of Filene's sister companies and owned by Federated Department Stores, was appointed CEO of Filene's. He was a brilliant merchant who was responsible for much of the success of Bloomingdale's. Years later he became CEO of Federated Department Stores, which at the time owned many major department store chains in the U.S.

Mr. Krensky came to Filene's to change its image from a promotional department store with ongoing sales to something more like Bloomingdale's, with very little promotion and geared to sell goods at regular prices. I'm sure he knew it would cost us volume but was banking on profiting by increasing our markup. The theory was that the store would be better off in the long term.

For many years in that era the pendulum swung back and forth in some department stores from promotional to non-promotional. Under Mr. Krensky's campaign to change the image of Filene's, buyers were told to spiff up the look of their departments. We converted the tables in the boys' furnishing department to glass counters. My department now had a very classy Bloomingdale's look. However, as I expected, the volume suffered.

One day Mr. Krensky came through my department. I led him over to the display case with our hottest item: boys' sport shirts in vibrant colours. The shirts were displayed in vertical rows of solid colours, orange, lemon, lime, black, and purple. I told him we had sold 25 dozen the previous week and had a difficult time even keeping them in stock.

"Who do you sell them to, gangsters?" he asked with a laugh.

"But sir, in sizes 8, 10, or 12?" I asked.

His thinking was that the boys' uniform should be button-down Oxfords and tartan plaids. We did have this as a basic but the fashion of the day was to wear colourful clothes. He thought in terms of Cambridge and Harvard, but our customers for the most part came from the ranks of working-class Bostonians from Dorchester, Mattapan, and South Boston.

As brilliant a merchant as he was at that time, he was so Bloomingdale's-oriented that he didn't understand that reality.

Although I went with the flow, my demise as a boys' buyer would come soon thereafter. I was offered a lesser buying job, which I was not anxious to take.

Then I really got lucky.

I received a call from Abe Fish, my brother-in-law in Toronto, inviting me to move to Toronto and join him in a retail venture he had just started. Two of my heroes at Filene's were linen buyers, Star and Greenberg. They left Filene's to open a discount store. Now I had the same opportunity.

I flew to Toronto to see if there was a future there for me and my family. I came back to Framingham and told Miriam I wanted to move and be a partner with Abe. She was happy with that. Not only would the move give me what would prove to be the opportunity of a lifetime but it also meant she could be close to part of her family.

PART THREE

THE BIWAY STORY

11

A NEW PARTNERSHIP

I arrived in Toronto in the fall of 1961 as a landed immigrant, anxious to start my new venture. Miriam and Robin went to stay in Montreal with Miriam's mother Zlata while I searched for accommodations and waited for our belongings to arrive from Framingham. I rented the top floor of a six-plex at 44 Meadowbrook in the Lawrence Avenue and Bathurst Street area, where we would stay for two years.

Miriam and Robin joined me a few months later. Having equity of $9,000 in our home in Framingham and a small mortgage was a blessing. It was good to start our new life in Toronto with some money in the bank.

At the beginning of the 1960s, Abe had been partners with three pharmacists in the original Biway store at Islington Avenue and Albion Road in the Toronto suburb of Etobicoke but had sold his share and opened a store called Westport in Port Credit, on the western edge of the Toronto area. Just before I arrived he opened another Westport store, in Waterloo, over an hour's drive farther to the west.

The equity arrangement before I arrived had Abe owning 50% of Westport and Dundas Jobbers owning the other 50%. Abe tried to convince Dundas Jobbers to an arrangement whereby he, they, and I would own one-third each. Dundas would not agree, so Abe, true to his word, shared his 50% with my family.

In the long run, Dundas' refusal was very costly to them because Abe and I were free to divide equity in subsequent stores as we saw fit. Abe's and my equity was always equal, right through our time at Biway, from 1962 to 1990, 28 years of a wonderful retail adventure.

When I started working with him, he was doing well in the Westport store in Port Credit but not so well in Waterloo. The responsibility of the two stores was weighing heavily on him. Abe was a successful salesman selling merchandise but lacked retail experience. He did, however, have a simple idea to open a discount store at very low markup built around limited price lines so as not to confuse the customer.

"There is something special about a person who starts something," Rabbi Aronoff once said to me. That is certainly one of the ways in which Abe is very special.

Abe asked me to take charge of the Westport store in Waterloo. When I drove there for the first time, I was horrified to see merchandise askew on wooden tables that looked like orange crates. Some of the merchandise I was familiar with, some I was not. Green work pants, green work shirts, and those smelly doeskin shirts, staples in Toronto, were not the kind of thing you saw in Boston, even in basement stores. I remember saying to myself, "This is where you are – roll up your sleeves and get to work."

Abe had rented half of an IGA store and from what I saw, it was no surprise that he wasn't doing much business there.

At the outset, I was working long hours, travelling back and forth to Waterloo. Fortunately, Miriam quickly made new friends. More importantly, she was now living in a large city with her brother and his family close by. We knew we would be able to buy a house soon because of our $9,000 in the bank, a lot of money at the time, enough for a down payment. I was drawing a salary from Westport of $125 a week. Our rent on Meadowbrook was $125 a month, so financially we were in reasonable shape.

There was one girl on the selling floor of the Waterloo store who was both cashier and manager, and one stock boy to receive, sort, and mark the merchandise. It seemed we had enough winter hats with ear flaps to outfit the Chinese army, if not all of them then close to it. The hats reminded me of what I saw Mao's gang wearing on the TV news. We did own them very cheaply.

I went to work sorting the merchandise: I combined each category in price lines, and prepared an advertisement for the local newspaper: six items with big black prices. We owned something akin to snowsuits and placed them as one of the items in the ad. Snowsuits $8 – Shirts $2 – Jackets $5 – Hats 2 for $1 and a couple of other items I can't remember.

At the time we were averaging $150 per day in normal business. When I came to the store the morning the ad broke, lo and behold, there was a lineup waiting for the store to open.

"Wow," I said to myself. "This is no different than Filene's in Boston."

Well, it was not. After that initial morning we went back to our $150 a day.

We did try one more thing. IGA wanted out of the grocery part of the store. Abe thought it was a good idea to take over the food from them and so for a short time we were also in the grocery business.

The only thing that has stayed with me about this adventure over the years has to do with turkeys and hamburgers. We inherited 25 of the former and put them on sale for Thanksgiving at a very good price. The good news was that they sold right away. The bad news was that they turned green when defrosted and were returned by unhappy customers.

I spent time – and I had plenty of it because the store was not busy – watching the food manager prepare hamburger meat to go on sale. After seeing what he put in the grinder, I didn't darken the door of a fast food restaurant for over two years.

Having tried everything I could, we decided to close the store. I packed up the remaining merchandise in a truck and retreated to the store in Port Credit. The only solace I had was that there would be no more driving to Waterloo and no more sleeping in motels as a result of the snowstorms that were so frequent in the area.

—

Abe and I shared buying responsibilities in the Port Credit store as well as opening and closing the store. We were open until 10 p.m. every evening except Saturdays. We each did our own thing. Abe for the most part handled the non-clothing items and I handled the clothing.

One of the things that Abe managed to get into the store was Brach's candy. We sold the candies to our customers by the pound, which they picked for themselves from an assortment on a Brach's fixture. This was a coup on Abe's part because Brach's was a well-known brand selling in Eaton's and Simpson's at the regular retail price and we were discounting.

About this time Pierre Berton wrote a piece for his column in the *Toronto Star* that Towers, a large discounter, was cutting the price on Brach's candy and Eaton's was complaining about it because they were selling them at regular retail. Not surprisingly, Eaton's was trying to cut them off. Not too long afterwards Towers tried to cut us off from Brach's candy because we were underselling them. Abe informed Pierre Berton and he wrote a column calling Towers to task for being two-faced. We continued to carry Brach's candy.

Our overall buying arrangement was good, but only on paper. Abe and I had a somewhat different philosophy. Mine came from my department store training, his from his own market experience. We each had our merchandising responsibilities, but at times I overstepped my responsibilities. For example, when I saw something that obviously needed to be done and Abe wasn't there to do it, I took care of it.

A case in point was when I was on the selling floor and the pantyhose salesman came in for an order. The table of pantyhose was depleted. Even though this was Abe's responsibility, I placed an order to fill the table. Abe resented this sort of thing, which caused some friction between us.

I tried to discuss these problems with Miriam but got no sympathy from her. The Fish siblings always stood together. Any outside criticism was not acceptable. That bond could never be broken. I knew if I came home and told Miriam Abe said black was white, she would say Abe must have had a reason for saying it. The way she always took his side frustrated me.

It was obvious that we needed another store. About that time we learned that the original Biway store at Islington and Albion was up for sale. I asked Abe to go after it. Although it was only 1,600 square feet compared with the 4,000 square feet in Port Credit, I thought it had great potential.

I suggested to Abe that he manage that store because people in the area knew him and would be glad he was back. He refused, thinking it was a backward step for him to go to a smaller store. He said he would pursue purchasing the store only if I agreed to go there. I said I would.

Abe approached the owner, Herbie Title, who also owned drugstores. Herb had been an important partner of Abe's in this original Biway store because through his drugstores Abe was able to purchase many of the items that other discounters were not allowed to buy.

A few days later Abe came back to tell me that Herb was about to sell the store to Marvin Elkind. I was very upset because I had a good idea of the kind of volume they were doing and was confident I could do much better.

After getting that disappointing news, Miriam and I drove to Montreal to visit her family. As we sped along Highway 401 Miriam could tell I was down in the dumps and asked me why.

Her brothers had always said that she was the brightest of the three and she proved it that day.

When I told her what was bothering me she said, "How can it be sold so quickly? Don't give up so fast."

I pulled into a rest stop on the highway and called Herb, the majority owner, from a phone booth.

Herb told me that it was not sold yet and that he was having trouble with Marvin Elkind, the prospective buyer.

In the end we did buy the store. Furthermore, not only did we get that prime location but we also got the Biway name back.

I was very excited, and rightly so.

Dundas Jobbers, our partners, were a major supplier. Earlier they had tried to keep their partnership with us a secret for fear it would affect their business with other retailers. I went to the bank and received a line of credit for $10,000, which in the end we never used.

I retailed the stock we inherited with the store by using a method I learned from Russ at Filene's Basement: I paid the owners a percentage of the retail, which basically came out close to their cost.

I marked down their inventory at prices to sell quickly. I put a sign in the window and within two days we had sold enough of the merchandise that I had to make a trip daily to the jobbing district in my station wagon, sometimes even twice a day, to keep the store stocked.

Sid Mandel, a partner in Dundas Jobbers, was especially helpful. He worked with me to move the old tables out and arrange the new ones in a layout that I had prepared.

With the new merchandise, we hit the magic $1 million figure within 18 months, which was four times what the store had done previously. We used only a few hundred basement feet in addition to the selling floor. On busy days we had lineups at the register that stretched the length of the basement. Customers obviously loved the merchandise and the low overhead prices.

We were working on a 25% markup on retail – unheard of except at the Honest Ed's store in the Annex area of Toronto – and we were making a good profit. We were doing a good thing not only for ourselves but also for our customers.

My unspoken motto was, "Never buy anything you would be ashamed to bring home to your family." I operated on that motto for as long as I was a part of Biway.

~

For a long time my routine was to go to the Spadina jobbers three or four times a week. True to my reputation, I lunched at Switzer's one day, Shopsy's the next, and gave my stomach a rest with dairy at United Bakers on the third day.

Many times on the way back to the store I went to the steam bath in the basement of Lawrence Plaza. I would have my favourite sandwich, roast beef on an onion bun, and then go back to the store to close it. Most times I didn't get home until close to midnight because the cash had to be balanced and I had to re-merchandise the tables for the next day.

A very busy time was Victoria Day week when we sold many hundreds of boxes of fireworks. Norman Reisman worked one of those weekends dragging boxes of fireworks from the basement stock room to the selling floor. I have no doubt that that weekend convinced him not to go into the retail business. Instead, he became one of the prime developers in Ontario under the name Great Gulf.

Complaints about our merchandise were few and far between. On one occasion a recent immigrant confused a product called Neet for one called Heat. He had rubbed

Neet on his chest to relieve congestion and got a handful of hair instead. Luckily he did not use it for a headache. I gladly refunded his money and gave him three free bottles of Heat for his trouble.

Both stores were doing well. We were so busy we needed to get responsible, hardworking, and dedicated people to help manage them. To get the best people, we committed ourselves to opening another store where they would be our partners and have equity.

True to our promise, the first new store was with Sam Crystal on Brimorton Street in Scarborough. Subsequent managers and partners were Maury Halberstadt, Tom Inksetter, and Lenny Arnold. Each had equity in the store they managed.

~

After we had been living on Meadowbrook for close to two years, our neighbours were buying homes in Greenwin Gardens, an area just off Keele Street between Sheppard and Finch. The area was being developed by Al Latner and Al and Harold Green, so their siblings all bought homes there. These included Pauline Wolfman, her sister Zil, and an assortment of other members of the family.

Our son David was born in 1963. I drove Miriam to the hospital in the fog and stayed there for the birth, having learned my lesson when Robin was born.

I have fond memories of Zlata staying over and making her famous latkes, something that my neighbour Bernie Bedder still reminds me of. She must have made them for the whole neighbourhood. We all loved having her visit us. She was such a joy to be with and I can still picture her making those latkes in the kitchen. As fast as she made them, my kids gobbled them up. I loved her and the feeling was mutual. (It didn't hurt that she seemed to take my side in any arguments I had with Miriam.)

In the end we did not buy a Greenwin home but bought one from another builder two houses away from Pauline and Morrie Wolfman. Every home that Miriam and I lived in Toronto was always two houses away from the Wolfman family. The price of our home on Brantley Crescent in Greenwin Gardens was $24,000. I had enough money to buy it without a mortgage, having received some bonus money from the Westport stores.

We liked the house that was already built. However, Miriam liked the lot next to it because it had trees in the backyard, so we duplicated the same house on that treed lot. We paid a premium to get those trees. Within two years the trees died and it cost us $3,000 to remove them.

Although I was down at times because of the stress of the business, these were good times. I was making progress at work with the potential for a lot of added income. We spent some time with Abe and his family and made friends with a lot of the neighbours and joined them in a bowling league. My income was good and we lived up to it.

12

EXPANDING BIWAY

EVER since moving to Toronto I had kept in contact with Russ Jacobson, my classmate, friend, and associate at Filene's. After literally hundreds of lunches with him during my days at Filene's, I probably knew more about the work of the famous Filene's Automatic Basement better than anyone outside the basement merchandising people.

Within a few years of my departure from Filene's, Russ finally fell prey to the narrow-minded thinking of Harold Krensky that you had to have the look and dress of an Ivy leaguer to work for him.

Russ had had a successful career at Filene's Basement buying everything from boys' wear to furs and had been promoted many times. His final promotion was to the upstairs store as buyer of men's furnishings, one of the largest menswear departments. He replaced my first boss, Sam Maletz, when he left the store to become a merchandise manager in a Philadelphia department store.

Russ took a job as a New England sales representative for London Fog, a premiere raincoat maker. After a short time, he was asked to be national sales manager, which meant moving to Baltimore. He took the job reluctantly, knowing full well it would last only a few years: No sales manager had lasted much longer than that working with the owner, Izzy Myers.

Russ phoned me in 1968 and said he was going back to retailing, probably in Boston. Knowing his capabilities, I invited him to come up and take a look at our operation. He did and he liked what he saw. Abe and I decided to give him the same once-in-a-lifetime opportunity that Abe had given me. Russ became an equal partner in every store from then on with no dollar investment by him.

We opened a fifth store with him managing it at the outset and participating in the buying. Russ and I came from the same Filene's school. He was well organized, knew about the classifications of merchandise and how to expand them, and was

GOLD RUSH ALL OVER AGAIN

A recurrence of the historic gold rush days in the Klondike. Well, not exactly, although it might be fairly difficult to convince these frenetic shoppers. The grand opening of the Bi-way warehouse on McMurchy Street South attracted swarms of people in a mad dash to latch on to anything that sold for cut-rate prices. The store, which sells mainly men's, women's and children's wares, is the fourth in the chain that dots the Toronto rea. The stores are owned y the triumvirate of Abe ish, Mel Koven, and Russ icobson. Mr. Jacobson, who in charge of the new Bramp- operation, indicated that was extremely gratified n the response the store re- ed yesterday. "We have al- s felt that Brampton was ideal area and it was only a ter of time before we were compelled to satisfy our customers," he said. The reason behind the chain's success is quite simple, he indicated. "We operate with a low overhead, low fixturing, and we have no expensive executive or stockholders to answer to. This savings in markup can be passed on directly to the customer."

Coverage of our Brampton opening.

experienced in keeping in business on basic stocks 24/7. I can honestly say that without him we would never have reached the amazing count of 249 stores.

Our largest store when Russ arrived was the one in Port Credit. We wanted a larger store to fit Russ' talents. Abe found a 6,000-square-foot location near the Brampton fairgrounds on McMurchy Street. The property had just been bought from the Lewis family of Lewiscraft. There was an old tannery on the back end of the property and a building right on McMurchy, which was the building we were renting. As Russ soon discovered, the property had a full-time employee whose job was to stoke the furnace daily to provide heat for the building.

We went about buying merchandise, but a week before we were ready to open, the recent buyer of the property was overwhelmed with debt and was forced to give it back to the Lewis family. That left us without a valid lease. We could buy the property ourselves or not open the store. Doing the former was a problem because we didn't have the money. Doing the latter was not viable because the store was stocked with merchandise.

Furthermore, we had no guarantee that this store would be successful – it was, after all, in an oddball location across from a fairgrounds.

Abe negotiated an option to buy the property. If the store was successful we could afford to buy it. And was it ever! People lined up for the opening and we never looked back. I got so excited that I got a headache and had to leave the cash register. We did $12,000 that opening day, a princely sum then.

In later years, we would do well over $100,000 on a typical store-opening day. I never could understand why people would line up for hours to buy three boxes of Kleenex at 10¢ each.

Ben Mintz of Transcontinental (Trans) always gave me exceptional merchandise for the opening of a new store. He knew that if we were a customer for 500 dozen of an item at a normal price, the 50 dozen that he gave me at any price was not important to him but was very important to us. To say we could name our own price would be only a slight exaggeration.

The year we opened the store in Aurora, north of Toronto, Ben gave me 50 dozen little girls' two-piece knitted-wool dresses that were imported from China. They were gorgeous. We sold them for $1.99. They were originally made to retail at $6.99. You couldn't buy them today for less than $20. I am told that on the day school opened, almost every little girl in Aurora was wearing the same dress.

~

As the chain grew so did our power in the marketplace. In the beginning I was buying most of our clothing through jobbers. Typically I was on Spadina Avenue two or three times a week buying goods from Dundas Jobbers, Henry Wagman's, Chocky Silverstein, Rose Textile, York Jobbers, and Irving Matlow.

At that time we were paying the jobbers on 60- to 90-day terms and turning the stock every two weeks. This was a huge financial advantage for us. In fact, it was not unusual for us to have certificates of deposit gaining interest most of the fall season.

Even when I started to buy directly from importers, I still used the jobbers in particular situations. There was a very fine importer from Winnipeg, Diamond Importers, that made exceptionally fine man-tailored ladies' blouses imported from an excellent factory in Korea.

I placed a substantial order to be shipped directly to our stores and usually got preference on delivery. The exact same merchandise was sold to several jobbers. When the blouses started to sell well, I called the three jobbers and put what they had in stock on hold. I paid them a little more and absorbed the difference. That way we were able to repeat goods that wouldn't be available from the original importer.

I met an Eaton's buyer in the Trans showroom once and asked her what category she bought. She told me 7-14 girls' and asked me the same question.

"Infants, toddlers, 4-6x boys' and girls', 7-14 girls', 8-16 boys', menswear, ladies' wear, shoes, and linen and bedding," I replied as her jaw dropped.

I did much of that with Russ when we worked the major importers' clothing lines together twice a year. That was one of the reasons our prices and overhead were so low. Others also did multiple jobs. At one time Tom Inksetter was not only the manager of the store but also the toy buyer and personnel manager, and he oversaw our warehouse, too.

Maury Halberstadt not only managed his store in Oakville but also supervised six other stores in the area and was in charge of purchasing our fixtures for all of the stores.

We found out that a supervisor was not much of a supervisor if he did not manage a store at the same time. Abe devised a system in which each supervisor was the manager of one store and supervised several others.

Later we did hire several buyers but they always worked in close contact with Russ, Abe, and me. Outstanding examples of these buyers were Mike Rose and Maureen Mason, who worked with me much of the time on men's and ladies' wear respectively, Les Klein, who worked closely with Russ, and Steve Barnes, who worked closely with Abe. Other important buyers were Sheila Grew, Janice Licman, and Ann Roberts. They were hard-working, dedicated people. Some went on to successful merchandising careers at Sears, Winners, and Wal-Mart after Biway disbanded.

⁓

As for life on the homefront during this time, I became wary of the area surrounding Greenwin Gardens about five years after we moved onto Brantley Crescent. I didn't like what I saw when I drove past the high school, with so many students hanging out there.

I took a walk one day with my neighbour Morrie Wolfman and told him I wanted to move. I didn't want a larger house, I said, but would prefer a house with a larger lot. He told me he was building on Old English Lane in Thornhill. The lots there were 20,000 square feet (half an acre) compared with my present lot of 5,000 square feet. The lots were selling for $30,000.

I wasn't ready to move, but thinking of the future I decided to buy one. By that time our business was going well and I had enough money to pay for the lot. I picked out one with a For Sale sign on it and called Wycliffe Homes, the builder on the street.

Not long after that my phone was ringing off the hook. It was Morrie Wolfman, who said the lot I was interested in was the one he was buying. Obviously I had not been aware of this. I switched to a lot across the street.

We went to an architect to plan our home. It got very complicated and we decided to buy a Wycliffe home that was already built instead and receive credit for the lot that I owned. It was a beautiful corner lot with a 5,000-square-foot two-storey home.

This was in 1970. We paid $111,000 for the home. I sold our house on Brantley Crescent for $44,000, got a credit for $30,000 for the lot, and paid the rest with a bonus that I got from Biway. To get the proper financial picture, consider that anything over $100,000 was considered a mansion. I am sure that house today would be worth well over a million dollars.

The Bi-Way formula: Simplicity counts

By Frances Phillips

PHOTO BY PETER REDMAN

"If you can't write your idea on the back of my calling card, you don't have a clear idea."

THESE WORDS, written by the great American theatrical producer David Belasco, hang in President Mal Coven's tiny, jumbled office at Bi-Way Stores Ltd., Toronto.

These few words, more than anything else, echo Bi-Way management's "Keep it Simple" philosophy.

A clear, pragmatic approach to business has made the family-wear chain one of the most successful discount stores in Canada, and a major contributor to the bottom line of parent Dylex Ltd.

With sales per square foot in the $250 range (sales per square foot for junior department stores average $100), Bi-Way will account for about 35% of Dylex's total profit this year. As Bi-Way expands its operations outside of Ontario, this percentage is expected to rise.

Under the management of Abe Fish, Mal Coven and Russ Jacobson, the Bi-Way chain has consolidated its presence in Ontario, and now operates 104 stores in the province, with another opening in Toronto's Eaton Centre next week.

But armed with the breadth of experience the Dylex team has acquired from operating 11 apparel chains coast-to-coast, Bi-Way has long-term plans to go national. Mal Coven says the company will test the waters in Atlantic Canada later next year, or early 1985.

Although Dylex recently increased its 50% interest in Bi-Way to 100%, in return for more than 800,000 nonvoting Dylex A shares and an

Stocked floor to ceiling

undetermined amount of cash, the discount store's original owners are committed to carrying on business as usual. About the only change in the schedule is the regular meetings with Dylex management — not, Coven says, to nitpick at the numbers, but to exchange ideas.

Fish, Coven and Jacobson work out of a clutch of offices tacked onto the back of its Thornhill, Ont., store. The cramped headquarters overflow with manufacturers' samples, and it's obvious the thumbprint of Bi-Way's management team is indelibly imprinted on every facet of the operation.

Bi-Way stores average about 9,200 square feet and are stocked floor to ceiling with apparel, linens, miscellaneous household items and an assortment of health and beauty aids. Discount prices and commitment to quality have won over a loyal clientele. The average customer visits a Bi-Way

store every 8½ weeks; and makes purchases of about $12 each shopping trip, Coven says.

Sale items are advertised at even-dollar prices, because management assumes its customers are "intelligent people." The desire to bring quality goods into the store is such that Coven insists, "I wouldn't stock anything in the store I'd be ashamed to take home to my family."

But what has made this discounter so successful, faced as it is with much larger competitors such as K Mart, Towers, Woolco and Zellers?

Coven obligingly scribbled out a list that would have fitted on the back of a business card, with room to spare.

First, he says, "Keep it simple." By this, Coven means keeping the product mix, administration and goals within well defined limits. Next, Coven adds, "People: innovative; not afraid to take chances." And, finally, "Resources" [relationships with suppliers].

"We don't want to make anything more difficult than it has to be," Coven says.

The firm's six buyers are trained to mirror the company's "Keep it Simple" philosophy. For instance, rather than carry a high-, medium- and low-price range of jeans, Bi-Way puts all its buying power behind an established, medium-price brand and as a result, is among the top five accounts for Levi and Lee jeans in the country.

Paperwork is kept to a minimum, and store sales are processed once a week. Unlike many of the other companies in the Dylex stable, the discounter isn't into the high-fashion business, and doesn't watch fashion or sales trends on a daily basis.

Bi-Way doesn't believe in line supervisors. "Promote a store manager to supervisor, and within six months you'll have a lousy supervisor and a lousy store manager," Coven says. Instead, some store managers supervise other stores in their area, or take on alternative responsibilities, and one of its buyers is also manager of personnel for the whole company.

The advantages of deploying ground-floor experience into management decisions are obvious, and although this puts additional strain on his managers, an employee profit-sharing plan ensures they are reimbursed for their input.

Management isn't afraid to take chances. If a supplier has a good idea or product they'll go for it, even if there isn't room in the budget. Many of the suppliers that worked with Bi-Way in its neophyte years are still with the company today.

The store prefers to buy brand-name goods so customers can comparison shop. But to maintain continuity of lines, the chain has almost 20% of its merchandise made under its own

Briefs

They want service

AS CONSUMERS invade the department stores, there's a very real concern among retail analysts that store operators may blow their chance to regain some of the ground lost to independents. Margins have been shaved to the point where department stores are price competitive with the independents, but there are still great strides to be made on the service front. All the major stores cut back on sales staff last year, and although many part-timers have been rehired, shoppers complain sales clerks can keep up with this new boom in consumer spending, and service is slow.

Newspapers Act

ADVERTISERS HAVE expressed their concern over the proposed Daily Newspapers Act in a letter to Multiculturalism Minister James Fleming. While the Association of Canadian Advertisers

strategy behind the proposed legislation, it is worried about the execution of that strategy. The association believes the government's plans can be achieved by alternate means, without opening doors for further restrictive actions by governments and regulators of the future. The ACA has requested a meeting to discuss its views at the "earliest opportunity."

Not for caffeine-lovers

UNFAZED by the fact that soft drinks outstripped the coffee market in 1974, and the gap yawns wider each year, Shaklee Canada Inc. has developed a noncaffeine coffee substitute. The instant hot beverage is made from organically grown dahlia tubers grown by Shaklee in northern California and Oregon. The direct marketing company, which made its name selling vitamins and skin-care products in the U.S. and Canada, says the coffee substitute needs no sweetening and is particularly suitable for people wishing to reduce coffee consumption or those on sugar-

My only interview, ever.

13

HOW WE DID IT

To give you a better idea of our markup structure at Biway I'd like you to consider some examples of what a 25% markup on retail meant.

Typically, if we paid $2.25 for an item, we sold it for $2.99. If we paid 75¢, we sold it for $1. If we paid $15 for a garment, we sold it for $20. We did buy some classifications such as outerwear from both manufacturers and importers. At a 25% markup, as long as we did not overpay, we could undersell anyone. We never overpaid.

A principal owner of a company buying goods in the marketplace has a huge advantage over a buyer from a department or chain store. The supplier soon found out that we would be faithful to them year in and year out in marked contrast to department store or chain store buyers. Loyalty to our suppliers was very important to us. Sometimes we even paid a little more to stay with a supplier because we never knew what the next year would bring.

For example, one of our key suppliers of men's and ladies' knit shirts and blouses had made a good piece-goods buy by placing fabric orders early. These items came from a top manufacturer and this supplier's prices were excellent.

That season we committed in total to buy 30,000 dozen, half of them knits and the other half ladies' man-tailored blouses, as well as 4,000 dozen men's collar model knit shirts. They were mostly under the Van Heusen name but some were under the Wimbledon name – the licence for both was held by our supplier Triton.

A secondary supplier, Lady Manhattan, was 10% higher on similar goods. By all rights I could have cut that supplier out entirely but I did not. We gave him an order for 200 dozen to keep him on the books. The following year things might be different.

I remember seeing a Van Heusen ad in a trade paper in the U.S. in which that company bragged that they had a customer that used 1,500 pieces of a particular style of men's knit shirts sold only at men's fine stores and they refused to sell to discounters. Obviously they knew very little about what we were doing in Canada.

Flashing forward, after I left Biway, the Van Heusen license held by Triton had reached the end of its 20-year agreement and Van Heusen was looking around for a potential new licensee. The obvious thing to do was to go to Oscar Reisky of Mylord Shirt, the largest manufacturer and importer of men's shirts in Canada. I was not there but I am sure the Oscar reaction would have been, "Who wants Van Heusen? The only one who carries it is Biway and they are a discounter."

The Van Heusen people were shocked because of their policy in the U.S. As a result of that conversation, Van Heusen took the label away from Triton. A year or so later Oscar Reisky took the label and manufactured the goods in Canada. The Van Heusen business went from the $13 million that we were doing to not much more than $100,000.

We were able to command better prices in many cases than any other department stores or chains because some of our suppliers, in particular Trans, could ask for and receive a commitment from us before they went overseas. We would make that commitment whenever they asked for it.

Department stores and chain buyers had to wait for the "open to buy" signal from management. With us there were no such barriers. With our orders in hand our importers could make additional commitments and place larger orders at a much lower risk.

Another advantage we had was buying merchandise when an importer or manufacturer was clearing its goods. For the most part they would come to us first because we could commit to a large quantity, usually taking the whole lot. Even more important to them was the fact that they would get a quick yes or no answer instead of having their samples sit in some chain store office waiting for the buyer to get approval.

In many cases we could even offer more than a department store. For example, if we knew we wanted to retail an item for $10, we could pay as much as $7.50 with our 25% markup structure. If a department store wanted to sell it for $10, they couldn't pay much more than $5.

Another advantage we had with some of our key suppliers was that they could hold a portion of our order with delivery spread over part of the season so we didn't have to warehouse the goods. In later years we did have a small back-up in our warehouse to refill the stores, but always in cases not individual pieces.

You can see that we always worked closely with our key suppliers because we knew they were one of the reasons for our success. Typically, if some of the merchandise the chains or department stores ordered from overseas came in not exactly as ordered, they would refuse to take the goods in or asked for some exorbitant discount. Not Biway. In these situations we took the merchandise in and looked the other way at small things, not asking for a discount.

My style was if I could not make a reasonable offer on off-priced goods I would pass rather than insult the supplier by making a low-ball offer.

I was always on the lookout in my travels to Europe and the U.S. for styles and items to bring to our suppliers.

One day in New York I saw some sweatshirts and T-shirts with a Bloomingdale's bear on them. At the time, Bloomies was a nickname for Bloomingdale's. We registered the name in Canada not because our customers knew Bloomingdale's but because the name had great cachet for ladies' and girls' panties and undergarments.

Russ took the label, expanded it, and sold many thousands of dozens of merchandise items using that label. In addition, we copied the Bloomies bear on hundreds of dozens of ladies' and girls' sweatshirts.

Only recently a lady came up to me and asked where she could get the Bloomies ladies' panties she used to buy at Biway. Obviously they were not available anywhere else.

To expand on something I said earlier, one of the reasons for our success was our major suppliers.

With Trans Sales from Montreal we worked for the most part with Danny

Freedman and his brother-in-law Ben Mintz; with Diamond from Winnipeg we worked with Mel Leonoff; with Pacific Pants from Montreal, it was Sheldon Liebman, after his father Moe died; with Triton of Montreal (Van Heusen), it was Morty Cape and Morris Clapoff; with Mylord Shirt from Toronto, it was Oscar Reisky, Tommy Sandel, and Claudia Meier; and with Encore Sales of Toronto, it was Irving Bloomberg.

~

Brand labels were always important to me and one of the reasons for our success. Levi Strauss in the U.S. would not sell to chain stores like J.C. Penney and Sears – only to department stores and specialty shops. Canada was different. When they came here one of the first stops they made was to sell to Sears. They sold to Eaton's and the Bay, too.

We received a trickle of their goods through secondary sources but I decided to go right to the CEO of Levi Strauss in Canada. Normally he would not have met with a discounter, but we were well known in the marketplace. I offered him a huge commitment to buy men's and boys' jeans and some ladies' jeans. He said he would think about it and get back to me. He did and accepted my offer and we became a customer of Levi's. At one point we were their third-largest user of men's denims and the largest users of boys' denims in Canada.

Shortly after that we went after the Lee label. Russ had a personal relationship with Bob Landau, Lee's key representative, and they sold to us not long after. We became a large user of Lee's men's jeans and the largest user of their boys' denim and corduroy jeans in Canada. Strangely, Lee boys' wear outsold Levi's only because the leather patch on the waistband of their jeans was much more attractive than the Levi paper patch.

Our buying patterns were unique: limited variety and lots of depth in a classification. On some occasions in buying canvas footwear, I could afford to make the samples shown to us even better. We could afford to pay more to retail it at a desired price because of our low markup structure.

A case in point was a basic children's canvas shoe we were buying from the import division of Bata. Sears, the Bay, and Eaton's carried the same shoe with their own label. They were paying $7 and selling them for $15. We actually added 50¢ to our cost to give the shoe more heft. Our low markup structure allowed us to pay extra. We sold them every day for $12 and promoted them for $10. In true Biway style, we were giving our customers a better product at a lower price.

I had the opportunity once to buy high-profile branded children's footwear that had been carried only by department stores and specialty shoe stores because one of the brands was leaving Canada. I went to every other brand of children's shoes to see if I could complement the assortment with their merchandise. Normally they wouldn't sell to me but here they had an excuse. We ended up being able to sell Keds, Buster Brown, Wildcats, and OshKosh, among others.

The original retails would have totalled $5 million. We sold them anywhere from 50% to 75% off the original retail prices. It was extremely successful. I saved a copy of the ad that we ran and framed it for my kitchen wall.

⁓

About this time I bumped into Ed Mirvish in Forest Hill Village. He asked me if I still enjoyed buying for Biway. I opened the trunk of my car and showed him some of the samples.

"How can you not like this business when you can buy kids shoes like this and sell them for $10 or $12?" I said.

He was impressed with what he saw. I offered to send him a pair for one of his grandchildren as soon as they arrived in our warehouse. I saved the letter he sent me thanking me for making him a hero when he gave a pair to a granddaughter.

One of the better men's athletic shoe brands was Reebok. I met the fellow who controlled distribution in Canada at a shoe show. We talked, and after our conversation I felt there was a chance he would sell us Reebok athletic shoes.

In my entire career at Biway I probably wrote no more than three letters. One of them was to him. In the letter – three pages long – I offered him a commitment to purchase 3,000 pairs of men's athletic shoes and 1,000 pairs of ladies' athletic shoes either from his regular line or a special make-up. I said he had my commitment that

Honest Ed's Limited
E. Mirvish, president

Bloor & Bathurst Streets, Toronto M6G 1N3

Malcolm Coven
17 Old Forest Hill Rd.
Toronto, Ontario
M5P 2P6

Dear Mal:

    Thank you for the Osh Kosh shoes.

    You are a man of your word.

    I will give them to our grandaughter and become
a hero.

    If you have a few thousand pair to sell at a
good price Domenic our shoe buyer would be interested.

    Thanks again, good health and best wishes.

                              Sincerely,

                              Ed

I would not advertise the shoes. If he had a problem with his other retailers he could stop selling to me the following season.

I was furious because he never gave me the courtesy of a reply.

I knew that my cousin Danny Coven was very close to Paul Fireman, the CEO and principal owner of Reebok. I called Paul at his office in Canton, Massachusetts. He took the call only because I was Danny's first cousin. I told him that I wanted to meet with him and I did the following week.

At the meeting I said I was very upset that his man in Canada never gave me the courtesy of responding to my three-page letter. Paul told me the reason: He had been fired in the interim. Then I gave Paul my argument for selling Reebok shoes to Biway.

"You sell to Woolco, a discount store, you sell to Kmart, a discount store – why not to Biway?" was my first line.

He started to pick up the telephone to check on what I had said.

"Paul, you don't have to call," I said. "If I say it, it is so."

He was shocked because he knew nothing of this. He said he would think about my request and let me know his answer. I received a letter a few days later saying that he had decided not to sell to Biway. I had gone right to the top and done everything possible to get the brand but to no avail. In later years when my son David wanted Reebok off-price merchandise for his store, I wrote Paul again. Shortly after that, the local salesman called David and said it was okay to sell him. The salesman told David that the letter to him from Paul said, "It is okay to sell him. It is family."

I was also buying leather athletic shoes from Bata under the name North Star. The shoe was white with two blue stripes, much like the most wanted brand, Adidas, which had three black stripes. If we were not the largest user in Canada we must have been close to it. I'm sure any person in their 30s would remember their mother taking them to Biway for these shoes. We sold tens of thousands of them at $12 every day and promoted them at $10. At the very same time the department stores and specialty stores were selling them at $18.

We bought Sparx, a canvas shoe that came in both high and low cuts, to complement our athletic shoe line. It was a copy of the then popular Converse canvas shoe.

We were the largest user of Sparx athletic shoes from Bata and eventually we licensed the label from them.

The mainstay of our men's shoe department was suede shoes from Howmark, imported from Poland. We carried them in desert boot and wallabee styles. Their quality was exceptional in spite of the retail price of $5.99. (Abe himself wore them at times.)

Later, when Biway was part of Dylex, Ruby Austin, who was the CEO of a shoe chain also owned by Dylex, came up to me after one of the quarterly meetings and complained that he had too many SKUs (stock keeping units). He asked me how I ran my shoe department.

"In men's we sell 15,000 pair of desert boots and 12,000 pair of wallabees and that is my men's shoe department."

My famous branded children's shoe sale.

He looked amazed.

Claudia Meier was new, working in a division of Mylord Shirt, whose principal owner was Oscar Reisky. We were probably one of her first calls.

She approached me with samples of track suits from China. Chinese goods in many cases were of much higher quality than comparable merchandise from other Asian countries and usually cheaper to boot. When I saw the samples of track suits made with sweatshirt fabrics I got very excited about their potential. I placed an order in every gender size – 4-6x boys', 4-6x girls', 7-14 girls', 8-16 boys', men's and ladies' sizes. We put our Sparx label on them, which we owned exclusively from the licensing agreement with Bata.

I normally did not add up the dollars in buying merchandise. I always thought in terms of cases, usually three or four dozen to the case. Then I made a decision based on how many cases each store could take depending on whether it was an A, B, C, or D store. Only after placing this order for all gender sizes did I add it up. In the case of Claudia's call, the order cost over a million dollars. I'm sure she had never taken an order like that and perhaps never did so afterwards either.

We put these items on the front page of our circular and within a week we had sold every piece. Our custom was to keep much of the circular merchandise off the floor until the ad broke so the customer would see something new and different in our circulars and be assured that the quantity would be available at the proper time.

～

In the early years of Biway I was buying almost everything. One of my favourite classifications was toys. Even though I was in toys for only a very short time, I continued to follow the merchandise.

Our major source was Encore Sales. Irving Bloomberg was the principal owner. He not only was a great merchant but also was a fine husband and father. As a key resource he was certainly one of the reasons for Biway's success. When we met Irving we had two stores and he had just formed Encore Sales. He started as a toy salesman and decided to start a business of his own. Buying toys was particularly fun if you had young children. In later years toys were bought by Tom Inksetter.

I loved to seek out new items and had many successes in doing so. I found something for Irving in New York's lower East Side, an item called Clackers. There were two balls at the end of a string that clacked together as you swung around them over your head. I showed it to Irving and he ended up manufacturing it for himself. Unfortunately, I took one home to my children Robin and David and soon after discovered that our chandelier with five arms had become a chandelier with four arms. To this day I don't know which of them was responsible.

Years later, although I had no responsibility for toys, I was browsing a toy store in Richmond Hill. I noticed these small plastic figures called Smurfs at the checkout counter selling at $1.99. My usual style was to test the clerk by being negative.

"You can't be selling many of these because they are so ugly," I said.

In fact, they were really cute.

"We can't keep them in stock because they're selling so well," the cashier said.

I went to our buyer at the time asking whether we had purchased any. He said

there was a test order coming but not until the following month. I went back to the store in Richmond Hill and purchased 36 of the Smurfs at $1.99. I put them in our Islington store and displayed them at a retail price of $1.49. We sold them out in an hour. That test cost us $18 but prompted us to make a very large commitment through Irving at Encore Sales. By season's end we had sold over a quarter of a million Smurf figures.

Probably the most exciting and profitable purchase I ever made was from National Football League (NFL) Properties. I had gone with my son David to a Super Bowl game in California. We were staying at the Century Plaza Hotel, which at the time was the headquarters of the NFL. Every VIP who had anything to do with football was on hand for this premier event. Most of them, including both sport and TV personalities, hung around the lobby.

David and I saw Howard Cosell walking through the lobby. Two young boys tried to get his autograph and he rudely ignored them. That evening there was a dinner in the hotel sponsored by the Southern California Jewish Sports Hall of Fame. The dinner was to honour Dolph Schayes, a famous Jewish professional basketball player. David refused to go because Howard Cosell was the emcee.

I met someone in the lobby who was in charge of NFL licensed merchandise. I asked him if there might be any clearances he could sell us in Canada. At that point we were very large users and had around 150 stores, a number that would eventually grow to 249. No quantity was large enough to scare me, particularly if the merchandise had the NFL team logos on it.

He invited me to New York to see what he could offer. I was shown a sample of sizes 8-20 boys' jackets bearing an assortment of NFL teams' logos and colours. There were 10,000 of them. They looked great, with a light quilted lining that was wearable nine months of the year. As mentioned, I always worked in dozens or cases because it was easier for me. There were 850 dozen. Then I thought in terms of cases – two or three dozen in a case. In my mind I assigned an appropriate number of cases to each type of store in our chain.

When I went to see the garments I couldn't believe my eyes. They were all on hangers, representing every team. To this buyer's eyes they looked beautiful. What shocked me was that the price was so low. In fact, low enough to make me suspicious. The U.S. price was $5, which at the time meant it would land in Canada as $7.50. That would normally allow me, in our markup structure, to sell them for $10. In this case we took the unusual step of marking them at $15 because they could not be duplicated in Canada for less than $30. We sold most of them at $15 and promoted them at $12.

I remember the last two dozen jackets were all Philadelphia Eagles green. I could have thrown them away and still made a huge profit. We sold the last few for $10. This was typically me: always chasing something new and exciting and always aware of any opportunity to buy something no matter where I was.

When I started buying merchandise for Biway, one of the things I thought about was my experience at Filene's in Boston selling children's snowsuits in July. I was told nobody sold children's snowsuits in July in Canada. The chain store deliveries were usually the middle or end of August with a peak selling period of October and November. How could it be that I could sell snowsuits in Boston in July and not be able to sell them in Canada? I certainly was going to challenge that assumption. It took a few years but we finally built up a following for a July winter outerwear sale of which children's snowsuits were the mainstay. At one point we sold over $250,000 worth of winter outerwear in July. Some of our customers even called me at the office and asked when our July snowsuit sale was going to take place so they could plan their holidays accordingly.

~

As we grew larger we branched out into smaller Ontario communities. We caused a disruption there. Our presence hurt the Mom and Pop stores, many of which were owned by Jewish merchants. Those stores usually bought from jobbers, so our negative effect on these retailers eventually trickled down to the jobbers, too.

At that time we were buying most of our goods directly from importers. Consider this case in point. The small storekeepers were paying the jobbers $24 a dozen flannel shirts and selling them for $2.99 each. In this instance we could negotiate a better

price than even the jobbers who were paying around $19 a dozen. I had a $1.99 retail price in mind and wouldn't pay more than $18 a dozen. It was possible to get this price from our supplier only because we were huge users of merchandise and this was only one of 30 or 40 items we were buying from them.

In reality we were selling the merchandise cheaper in our stores than the storekeepers were buying it from the jobbers. In other cases, when merchandise was offered to us at $27 a dozen and that fit our retail price of $2.99, we accepted the price even though we knew the jobbing trade was probably paying 50¢ a dozen less.

The size of our orders was not the only factor that helped us get very low initial prices. It also helped that we were known to the importers or manufacturers for retailing at a very close markup and therefore needing the low prices we pushed for. Quite often the manufacturers' and importers' prices for department stores and chain stores were higher than the prices they offered us. A department store buyer would typically ask for a price that would allow them their necessary markup at the time, probably close to 50%. Quite often the department stores and chain stores, after negotiating for a price to retail at $6.99, ended up retailing them at a higher price. I think that is why we were always given the edge. If we said we were going to retail an item at $6.99, we could be counted on to do so.

There were a few other competitors that had one or two stores but they were meaningless in the marketplace. The exception was Bargain Harold's. I give them much credit because they took note of what we were doing so well when we had around 25 stores and copied us exactly, fixture for fixture, layout for layout. The only way we distinguished ourselves from them was by our private label merchandise and our assortment of brand names such as Levi's, Van Heusen, Bloomies, and North Star. Bargain Harold's was very successful, staying mostly in Ontario. They ended up selling their chain to Kmart.

In some ways Harold Kamin of Bargain Harold's was a lot smarter than we were. We were paying our bills taking 2% in ten days and paying net 30 days in most cases. He was paying in 60 to 90 days and using the money to buy much of the real estate his stores occupied.

~

Our advertising budget was devoted exclusively to tabloid circulars of either four or eight pages.

Typically, on a four-page circular Russ and I shared the clothing pages and Abe was responsible for the page with health and beauty aids and sundries. The front page was saved for something new and exciting in clothing items plus several come-on health and beauty items from Abe. These flyers were homemade but very effective. Initially they were mailed or hand delivered and eventually they were all mailed. We knew exactly the results that were produced by these circulars.

For example, if we were doing $15,000 per week per store without a circular, and then, following a circular, the volume jumped to $25,000 in a store, then obviously the circular brought in $10,000 extra per store. We knew exactly the gross profit we received from the additional volume, subtracted the cost of the circular, and could figure out the net profit that the circular brought in because our overhead did not change. Our markup on the advertised merchandise could have been 2% or 3% less than our average markup but the good net profit was still there.

Biway was not computerized and each store reported the week's selling of each item advertised in the circular to the head office so we would know pretty much how many of each item sold. Initially we had circulars only four times a year because we had a good everyday business and did not want to hurt it by over-promoting. Eventually, as we became hungry for more volume, we put out nine or ten circulars a year. We made sure that the specials in the circulars lasted for only a week. If you condition the public to come in only when there are sales, they won't come back to buy on a regular basis.

—

My mother died in 1973, during the week of the Yom Kippur. My sister Bea took on the responsibility of preparing Dad's meals. It was very difficult for her to work all day and come home to cook for Dad and her own family. Dad wasn't shy about telling her she "couldn't cook like Eva." The situation went on for some time before Bea called me to tell of the difficult time she was having coping with the situation. I discussed her problem with Miriam and without giving it a second thought, she said, "Let's bring him to Toronto."

I wanted to do this but would never have suggested it myself. I am indebted to her for making that suggestion.

Dad lived with us for a while and enjoyed being in Toronto. I took him with me as I made the rounds buying merchandise for Biway. I introduced him to some of my suppliers and could see that he was very proud to be with me. Sometimes Dad waited in the car while I made calls to suppliers, exactly as I had done as a kid many years before when I accompanied him on his runs to collect from his customers.

After a time it became difficult for him to remain in our home. Fortunately there was an Extendicare just a minute or two away. We approached Dad with the idea of staying there. I told him he would still be able to come with me any day that I was working and spend time with all of us on weekends. I showed Dad around the facility, which was very modern and well managed. He said a lot of positive things as we toured the premises. He liked it very much.

However, his final words after the tour were, "Very nice, now let's go home."

I took him back there a few days later and he met his roommate, Mr. Finkelstein, who had also been a peddler and they struck up a nice conversation. I left, pleased. When I came back the next morning, things had changed. Dad had had an argument with Mr. Finkelstein – I learned from the nurse that they almost came to blows. We moved Dad to a private room.

On another occasion a man approached me as I stepped off the elevator on Dad's floor.

"Tell your father to keep his hands off my wife," he said.

I tried to conceal a smile, realizing that there was still a lot of life left in Dad even though by now he was a very old man.

He passed away peacefully of natural causes in 1980 at the age of 89. I know that his years in Toronto were some of the happiest of his life. There is no doubt in my mind that bringing Dad to Toronto for his last few years was not only best for him but also for my family, particularly Robin and David, who were able to spend time with a kind and gentle man … their Zaida.

14

A NEIGHBOURHOOD STORE

WE were a neighbourhood store and even in our mall stores we were much smaller than the giant discounters we were competing against. Small can be a great advantage. On average our customers came back every two weeks, and they usually walked through the entire store. They visited our shoe department twice a month. You better believe my friend Leonard Simpson of The Shoe Company would like to get all his customers to come back every two weeks.

One time I wanted to see what an advertising agency could do to supplement our circulars with more sophisticated advertising in the newspapers. I went to Saffer Cravit, the retail advertising agency of note. I told David Cravit that I was doing this on my own and wanted to see what he could come up with that was different and exciting. I would pay him only his hard costs. I'm sure he agreed because of the prospect of much advertising work for us in the future.

After a few weeks he produced a series of advertisements featuring snowsuits and other key items that were selling in the stores, under the headline, "The Ugly Store with the Beautiful Prices." I don't remember if I ever showed Russ and Abe those ads but I did take them home for Miriam, Robin, and David to see. I got such a backlash from them that I dropped the whole idea.

"What do you mean by calling Biway an ugly store? They're beautiful," was the gist of what they said.

Neither to me nor to them nor to our customers were the Biway stores ugly.

The customers were concerned with quality and price and we gave them the best of both. I never veered from my motto, "Never buy anything you would be ashamed to bring home to your family."

I always tried to have a good relationship with our suppliers, large, small, and even fringe. I gave them all the courtesy of looking but was always very selective. It was not unusual to find a good item from a fringe supplier.

Sometimes a salesman who called on us went into business for himself. On his first visit as an importer, the first thing I would say to him was, "The first order is on me – after that you are on your own."

I knew how difficult startups are. I also knew the salesman would always remember me for that gesture. I'm happy to say that I did make one shidduch (matchmaking). Tom Sandel was a salesman for Mylord Shirts. He was an orthodox Jew from Detroit. Metropolitan Jobbers in Montreal was a fringe supplier. Mel Lehman, its principal, approached me one day to say he needed a partner, a good outside man who was aggressive, knew the business, and might want to be a partner in an importing business. I thought of Tom. He fit Mel's criteria, and, like Mel, was an orthodox Jew.

It was a good match. They started an importing business and were successful for many years under the name of Seaboard. The only complaint Mel made a year or so later was that they were doing so well and had expanded so rapidly that he had to invest more money in the business.

Twenty-five years later, Tom is still a friend. He resides in New York, and, luckily for my grandchildren, has the licence to produce NFL, NHL, and NBA merchandise in children's wear.

Sometimes we had to think globally to be a good neighbourhood store. We always kept our overhead low, but Russ and I did spend on an exploratory trip to the Orient. We were successful with what we bought but made the decision not to go again as we would have to devote too many weeks away from our families. When necessary, we bought with back-to-back Letters of Credit and paid a bit more.

When we had approximately six or seven stores we opened a head office on Doncaster Street in Thornhill. After having managed the store at Islington and Albion

Road, it was traumatic for me to move into an office and potentially lose touch with what was going on in the store. For that reason, among others, we always felt we needed a store next to our office.

That was the case on Doncaster. We had a 5,000-foot store there that was later expanded to 10,000 square feet in the back of our office. Including the office, the rent was never more than $1\frac{1}{2}$% of our volume. It eventually fell to 1%, including our salaries. Most retailers would probably find this unbelievable.

It was also the case when we moved to Commander Boulevard in Scarborough. Not only could you be in touch with the merchandise as it was being received but you could also hear complaints from customers.

My directive to all managers was this: "If a customer has a complaint, keep them happy, because if the matter comes to me I am going to give them whatever they think is right. So save yourself the embarrassment and do it yourself."

It does not pay to antagonize a customer for a few dollars even if they are dead wrong.

Once a lady returned a blouse to our store that she had not actually bought in a Biway store. I knew it was bought at a competitor but she insisted that she had bought it at our store. I gave her the credit for $5. If I hadn't, I would have lost a customer. I would gladly pay $5 for any customer if I knew she would come and shop in my store every two weeks, which was the usual pattern. Why would I want to lose a customer for $5?

⸺

Our suppliers were most important to our success whether or not they were key suppliers like Trans or Triton (Van Heusen).

A word about Trans. They were by far our largest soft goods supplier. In the early 1950s, Americans were not allowed to buy in China. Danny Freedman was one of the first in Canada to realize the potential of China as a resource for clothing. I am told that even many years later, after he was no longer doing most of the purchasing for Trans, he was treated like royalty at the Canton Fair. His word was his bond. That was his reputation, not only in China but in all of Asia.

M.I. Greisman Company at one time was the largest importer of gloves and headwear in Canada. When Joel Greisman took over the business from his father, he branched out into importing ladies' wear. For many seasons I gave him substantial orders because his merchandise sold very well. To say Joel was enthusiastic about his merchandise would be an understatement. His sales manager sat down with me to review the line twice a year and Joel came in repeatedly to give me an extra sales pitch.

I always felt more comfortable buying goods one-on-one. I felt that two-on-one put additional pressure on me. I had to be careful because my commitments were very large. I remember at one point asking Joel to leave the room because I was uncomfortable with the situation. I hope he didn't take it personally.

Sheldon Liebman inherited Pacific Pants from his dad, Moe. Sheldon grew the business over the years and prospered. He was important to us because, unlike most of the other importers, he always carried huge inventories.

Sheldon was a great basketball fan. He bought season's tickets for the Raptors and flew into Toronto for many of their games. He had a fantasy of sitting on the Raptors bench with a clipboard as if he were running the team. He told me if I could make that fantasy come true he would double the pledge he had made for a particular charity in which I was involved.

I've never been accused of being shy in those years. I called Richard Peddie, president of the Raptors who had previously volunteered to help me find and negotiate a home for my Toronto Terminators basketball team. I approached him with the idea of letting someone sit on the bench in return for a large donation to the Raptors' charity.

"During the game?" he asked.

"No, no, during practice," I replied.

He said he had no control over that and would speak to the powers that be. They turned him down. Sheldon gave me the donation anyway for good effort.

Another supplier was Albert Saragossi, a Montreal importer who called on me twice a year. He was a low-end importer. I kept seeing him as a courtesy but never bought anything from him. One day I gave him some advice.

"Albert, why do you carry this low-end garbage?" I said. "People are looking for quality, not just price. Would you bring this stuff home to your family?"

Albert took what I said seriously and traded up. Today he has several good labels and has gone on to great success. I would never have remembered this advice that I gave him 30 years ago except that he always reminds me of it when we see each other, once or twice a year.

One of Albert's claims to fame was that he was a baseball fan and knew all about the finer points of baseball even though he was born in Egypt. Obviously he was a rabid Expos fan. When the Expos left Montreal, in 2004, he went into mourning. He had a cap from every major league team in his office and always kept them in the order of their standing of that day. I doubt there is any other baseball fan in the world who would do that.

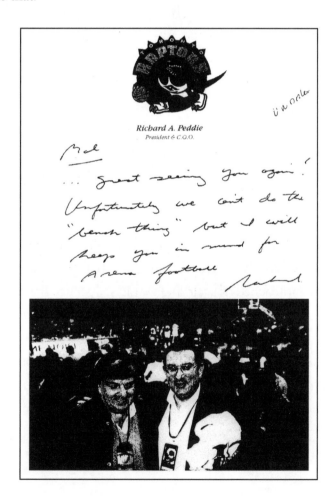

15

A NEW ASSOCIATION

W HEN we had approximately six Biway stores, the principals of Dylex, Jimmy Kay and Wilfred Posluns, approached Abe with the idea of owning half of our company. We turned them down because Abe thought we could grow faster on our own than with Dylex, which was a public company.

I saw Abe's point a little while later when we had about a dozen stores and I was fishing for a connection to another retailer. I called one of the Cohen brothers in Montreal who owned Metropolitan Stores. They were a public company and at the time were producing something like $75 a foot in their stores. I told him who I was and that we were doing over $400 a foot with a 10% profit before taxes. He said that was impossible and hung up the phone.

They were not very good retailers but they were very smart people. After World War II they owned the Sony brand for Canada until well into this century.

In 1978 Dylex approached us again and we did sell 50% to them. By then we had grown to 15 stores. We contemplated going public but the market turned bad and we changed course.

Other chains under the Dylex umbrella were mostly 50% owned. They were Town and Country, Thrifty's, Harry Rosen, Braemar, Suzy Shier, Big Steel, and Ruby Shoes. Dylex owned Family Fair, Fairweather, and Tip Top Tailors outright. The latter two formed the basis of the original Dylex.

However, by 1983 our profits were so strong that Wilfred made another offer and we did sell the other 50%.

This was not their usual practice. Wilfred once said to me, "When I own 100% of a company I have 100% of the headaches. When I own 50% of a company I only have 2% of the headaches."

With Biway he had zero headaches.

My partners and I decided to go ahead with the sale with the stipulation that we continue to run Biway as before with the same salary and bonus arrangements. By 1989 we had amassed a total of 249 stores, all profitable. Abe retired in 1987 and I followed him in 1990; Russ followed me the year after that.

⌒

Our plan at the start of our association with Dylex was to open one new store for every five we were operating, a pace that we were comfortable with.

Russ, Abe, and I met monthly with Jimmy Kay and Wilfred Posluns for an hour in the morning and kept them informed of our progress. Frankly, we discussed Biway for probably no more than 15 minutes of that hour. The rest of the time we talked – gossiped, you might say – about other things.

They had nothing to complain about because our chain was growing and our profits were good and constant. We were by far the largest of the ten chains that Dylex had in their portfolio. Newspaper articles rarely, if ever, mentioned Biway as part of Dylex's "fashion stores," which protected Dylex's image. This even though we grew to contribute as much as 40% of Dylex's profit.

We three partners continued to do our thing.

Abe was the president, but, as before, he bought and supervised the health and beauty aids, negotiated the new leases, and, I would say, was the father figure for our many employees.

Russ and I were responsible for the buying and merchandising of the soft goods and shared the preparation of advertising for the stores. This included preparing the monthly circulars, with each of us doing the pages of the merchandise we were responsible for.

Even though some of my merchandise responsibility shifted over the years, for much of the time I was responsible for shoes and ladies' wear, men's wear, and children's wear. The exception was buying shoes, which was always my responsibility.

At the beginning of our first Dylex quarterly meeting, all of the stores were represented except for Thrifty's. At the time Thrifty's was flying high as they were the jean store of note in Canada. Well into the meeting the principals of that chain arrived, bedecked in Hawaiian shirts and leis. I assumed they were just in town from a board meeting in Hawaii.

I sat with Russ, and Abe sat next to Wilfred and Jimmy. I pored over the results from the other divisions with Russ. I'm not sure if it was he or I who said, "In Boston, at Filene's, you would be fired for some of these performances." At any rate we both agreed.

At each of these quarterly meetings one representative from each of the divisions stood up and summarized their results from the previous period. Then they took questions.

"Harry, how much time do you spend in your ladies' wear division?" Irv Levine, one of the principals at Fairweather, once asked Harry Rosen.

Even though Harry Rosen unquestionably was the finest men's store in Canada, Harry had ventured into ladies' wear with several stores.

"About 25% of my time," Harry replied.

"Some of us in the ladies' wear business think ladies' wear is a full-time job," was Irving's response.

Everyone chuckled. Not long after that Harry closed his ladies' wear stores.

Notably successful was the Town and Country chain. These stores were by far the best profit maker in the ladies' wear division. The chain was 50% owned by Nathan Gold, who had retired at the age of 65 from his ladies' wear manufacturing business. He had decided to come out of retirement and had bought a small chain of three stores long before we arrived at Dylex.

During our time with Dylex, Town and Country grew to 165 stores and pioneered in petite sizing. Nathan invariably had a profit before taxes of close to 10% or more. He invited me to visit his warehouse. It was so clean and orderly that you could literally eat off the floor.

On that occasion I saw some of our $1.99 ladies' tee shirts that we were selling at

Biway in packages on tables. Nathan had put them on hangers, steamed them out, and retailed them at $6.99. Any merchant reading this will appreciate that. After Nathan retired the whole chain became defunct and was closed by Dylex.

Family Fair was a discount chain that Dylex initiated. At one point it was run by Al Sandler, a fine retail merchant who had a successful retail operation in Peterborough. He was there in conjunction with George Fine, who owned a successful cleaning chain, Parkers. George was also a real estate developer.

Family Fair's operation was different from ours because they operated with 25,000-square-foot stores in major malls. We later found out that even though their operation was struggling, George Fine had negotiated some extraordinarily favourable leases – some as low as $2 a foot and long-term to boot.

Dylex wanted to turn Family Fair over to Biway and have us convert the stores to Biway stores. We were hesitant because our expertise was in stores up to 8,000 or 9,000 square feet and we were not sure how we would fill 25,000 square feet with our merchandise mix. We did finally decide to take over the 35 Family Fair stores when Wilfred offered us a deal we couldn't refuse. No cost to Biway.

Of course we changed the name from Family Fair to Biway, with one exception. Our best Biway store was in the Brampton Mall. It was approximately 9,000 square feet and did well over $4 million. Family Fair had a 25,000-square-foot store just across from our store, doing something under $1 million. That lease was very favourable: It was long-term and cost around $2 a foot. That was George Fine's handiwork.

After much pondering we decided to keep the Family Fair name on this store but fill it with a slightly expanded mix of Biway merchandise.

After the first year our Biway store in that mall dropped a half a million dollars to just under $4 million, but the Family Fair store increased from $1 million to $4 million. A few years later we purchased a small chain of six stores, one of which was in the Brampton Mall. We ended up having three profitable stores in the same mall.

We had a similar situation in Pickering. We owned a store in the Pickering Mall and inherited a Family Fair store as well. In this instance we changed the name of Family Fair to Biway and operated two Biway stores in the mall, both very successfully.

The purchase of Family Fair gave Biway the impetus to expand more quickly than we would have done otherwise. That move was a coup for our bottom line.

One of the factors in our success from the very beginning was our low overhead. As mentioned, our head office expenses, including the salaries of the three principals, was an unheard of 1% of our volume. The other Dylex chains' head office expenses were at 10% or more.

The first head office at Doncaster was very cramped. There was a lot of activity between salesmen and other Biway staff. Russ, Abe, and I decided that we needed some quiet space, so we rented a large room across the street. It was very simple. It had new carpet and little else and we bought some chairs and a large table to serve as our boardroom. The whole cost of this secondary office was approximately $20,000.

We later found out that one of the other Dylex chains, the name of which I will not mention, paid $75,000 for a rug in their office. That was just not our style.

～

When Abe retired in 1987, after having been president since Biway's inception, the title fell on my shoulders. Most of my merchandise responsibilities continued as before except now I had the added burden of being responsible for expansion. By this time we had grown to over 150 stores in Ontario and had just started to open in Winnipeg. Wilfred suggested, and rightly so, that we expand to the Maritimes.

As a former American I knew nothing about the Atlantic provinces. Halifax was the major city and I decided to make our first start there. I had seen in the newspapers that Kmart had decided to compete with us in our strip mall locations under the name Big Top Store and had signed some leases in the Maritimes. The stores were to be about the same size that we intended to lease. What I read was that they were going to sign the leases first and then worry about the merchandise mix afterwards. As it turned out for them this was not a very smart idea.

You could be sure that when Kmart came to town the price of rents tended to go way up. That was what I was facing in my first foray into the Maritimes. I asked Abe and Russ to fly with me to Halifax in January to look for locations in the city, which was unfamiliar to me. They were reluctant to go because January was a downtime in the retail business and too close to the holidays. As president, the task was mine alone.

It was snowing quite heavily in Halifax and the plane took two passes before we finally landed. The malls were empty and the strip malls were covered with snow. There were no customers to speak of. Nothing looked good. I was searching for up to three stores in locations that I deemed safe but was hampered by being so unfamiliar with the retail landscape.

Finally I came across a mall with Sears as one anchor and the Bay as the other. About 7,000 feet were available for me to lease. That was safe. That was the competition we liked to have.

I negotiated a potential lease with a fellow who knew Abe from Montreal. The price was $7.25 per foot, which fit our budget. I negotiated that and one other lease and returned to Toronto feeling that I had made a successful foray into the Maritimes.

When I sat down with Abe to tell him what had transpired in Halifax, particularly about the lease with his friend, he said, "Let me call Murray Frum, who has some plazas and strip malls in the Maritimes. Let's see if $7.25 is a good price."

Abe told me that Murray had said, "He paid too much money. It shouldn't be more than $4 a foot."

"Are you crazy?" I said to Abe. "Kmart had just been there and was paying well over $7 a foot. And this was in a mall. This is a huge bargain."

To this day I don't know whether they were pulling my leg. I went back and saved another few cents, something I never would have done under any other circumstances.

Not too many months later I was looking for locations in Fredericton, New Brunswick. I came across a strip mall that belonged to Murray. I called him and asked him how much the rent was.

He said, "$9.50 a foot."

I said, "What happened to $4?"

He answered, "Things have changed."

~

We had a very good store on Yonge Street in Toronto in the original Tip Top Tailor building right across from the Eaton Centre. I decided to go after space inside Eaton Centre. It was very difficult to find locations in prestige enclosed malls because landlords and developers were reluctant to let discounters in. I thought getting a store in the centre would legitimize us in the eyes of the landlords of major malls.

I approached Jim Bullock, who was CEO of Cadillac Fairview at the time. Even though we were discounters, he offered me some oddball space on the lower level close to Eaton's. It was not more than 1,200 square feet. While that wasn't usually appropriate for us, I felt it would do the trick for my purposes.

Eaton's had to approve anyone taking the space because it was close to its store. I met with Fred Eaton and must have convinced him that the store I was proposing would draw Biway customers into the mall away from our Yonge Street location. He gave his approval.

We continued to expand in all of the Atlantic provinces including Newfoundland. It was an excellent territory for us. Kmart both opened and closed their big top stores in the interim, which made it easier for us to find locations. The next thrust of expansion was Ottawa, where we were very successful.

~

My involvement with Magic Mirror, which allowed you to see yourself in different clothes without trying them on, started when I decided to go to Paris to visit my son David who was in school there for a year with his girlfriend, Michelle Barkley.

Barbara (more about her in the next chapter) had told me about this invention by a Paris couple. It was being used at one of the largest department stores in Paris, Galleries Lafayette. I told Barbara I would look into it when I was there.

I arranged to meet the inventors for breakfast at the Meurice hotel the morning I was to leave Paris for home. I was doing this only as a courtesy to Barbara. However, I was impressed by what the inventors told me, particularly when they said they had also placed Magic Mirror in L.S. Ayres, a U.S. department store.

I decided to look into it further and checked back into my hotel room. I went to the local department store where it was located after making an appointment with the merchandise manager, Mr. Goldstein. I had Michelle accompany me because she was fluent in French and Mr. Goldstein spoke only French and Yiddish. When I saw how it worked, I was even more impressed.

Our law firm, Stitt, Baker, had an office in Paris and I worked with them to negotiate a 60-day option for Barbara. Little did I realize just how magical this mirror would be: It would prompt Biway to open in Edmonton.

When Barbara was in the process of trying to place Magic Mirror in one of the major Toronto department stores, we came across the youngest of the Ghermezian brothers and the president of Five Star Realty, Ruby Stahl. Ruby was responsible for leasing at the Edmonton Mall, which was the largest mall in North America and was owned by the three Ghermezian brothers.

The Ghermezian families were immigrants from Iran and originally arrived in Montreal where they were selling imported rugs from Iran. When the youngest Ghermezian brother heard about Magic Mirror he got very excited about the possibility of using it in the Edmonton Mall. He said he might want to buy six or eight of them.

It was the middle of June. Barbara and I arranged to fly out to Edmonton where we met the inventors of Magic Mirror. Barbara paid their fare from Chicago to Edmonton. I assumed it was not more than an hour's flight, not realizing, as a former American, that coast to coast in Canada is 4,500 miles, not 3,000 miles as in the States, and that the distance between Chicago and Edmonton was 1,600 miles.

During that week the Ghermezians were flying in a group from Minnesota that included that state's governor and one of its senators. They were there to work with the Ghermezians in opening a similar mall in their state. Barbara and I were wined and dined along with the group from Minnesota.

When I saw the mall for the first time I was amazed.

It was huge, unlike anything I had ever seen before. It had everything, including pirate ships, submarines, hockey rinks, a car dealership, some unique stores from California, and even a Montreal delicatessen, which the Ghermezians' father frequented daily.

There was even a miniature copy of a street in Paris, and, incidentally, several department stores. Planeloads of tourists from Japan stopped in Edmonton just to visit the Edmonton Mall.

Store opening, Edmonton Mall.

Ruby Stahl, the president of Five Star, gave me a personal tour of the mall. We came across a spot that was not leased for the opening of the second phase of the mall the following September, just a few months away.

"I want you to open a Biway store here," Ruby said.

I thought he was kidding. Edmonton was over 2,000 miles away from Toronto. We had just barely opened stores in Winnipeg, which were much farther east.

"Let's move on," I told Ruby, refusing to even discuss the possibility, but he kept pressing me.

I gave him all the reasons why I wouldn't even consider opening a store there, which included the fact that we paid only gross rents and had never paid over $100,000 gross to lease a store. I knew full well that other Dylex stores were paying $35 a foot plus common area, which probably came to not much under $50 a foot. Using that calculation, our rent would have been $350,000 a year.

The more he pressed me, the more firmly I said no. When you don't want something you become a very good negotiator.

Finally he said, "I'll give it to you for $100,000 gross but you have to open the Biway store in September in conjunction with our second phase."

I was tempted. I had fallen in love with the mall and knew we could do very well there.

Ruby took me up to meet Raphael Ghermezian, who started negotiating the price with me all over again, to no avail. I stood firm on the price and said I would have to go back to Toronto and get my partners and Dylex on board with the idea of moving to Edmonton. Before I left I negotiated the price for two other locations in malls that the Ghermezians owned in Edmonton to be opened the following spring to make sure they didn't overcharge me.

To say my partners were reluctant would be a vast understatement. They thought I was crazy. Maybe so. However, I loved that mall so much that I kept pressing and the final decision was left to Wilfred Posluns. He gave me the green light. Now I had to make good on the deal. I had stuck my neck way out. Time was very short. It was now only seven weeks until the opening.

The quiet before the storm: The shoe department just before the Edmonton store went live.

I got lucky. One of our managers was from Edmonton so I had a good man to manage the store and he was happy to move back home. The merchandise to be bought for the opening was to be loaded onto tractor trailers and then dropped to be priced and marked at space I had rented. I had to make sure the store opening was a success.

Even though I had not been buying some of the classifications for some time, I had always kept in touch with many of the suppliers and they were eager to help me out. I went to six or more that were our soft goods suppliers and obtained merchandise that we were able to retail at a third less than our normal cost.

Barbara and I flew out for the opening. As I expected, the store was mobbed. Barbara was busy behind one of the cashiers packing the merchandise. No doubt that was the first time she had ever done that. We did well over $100,000 in sales that opening day in a store that had not more than 7,500 square feet.

I remember one item in particular: comforters that we were selling for $10, well under what our normal wholesale cost would have been. They just fit into our

Health and beauty aids at the Edmonton store.

large Biway bag. For a few hours, hundreds of our customers were advertising for us, walking around the mall with a Biway logo full face on that bag. It reminded me of the fellows who used to walk around in sandwich boards.

We were located at exit 53 of the mall – the mall was so big there were over 60 exits. The store turned out to be an A store for us. It was not our best, but with the other two stores we opened in Edmonton the following spring, I felt that my efforts were worthwhile.

~

After 1991, when all of the Biway principals had retired, Biway's along with Dylex's fortune took a turn for the worse. Dylex got into financial difficulties and eventually filed for bankruptcy. Some of the chains continued under new ownership but Biway did not survive. It was sold to a U.S. company that wanted to turn the locations into dollar stores. The deal never materialized and Biway was liquidated.

After we left Biway, Federated Department Stores, the owner of Bloomingdale's, sued Dylex to stop them from using the name Bloomies, claiming that they sent mail-order advertising to Canadians. Dylex did not want to fight them so they caved in. I am sure if I were still at Biway we never would have lost that name.

Biway was a unique institution – one of the forerunners of the discount business in Canada and still remembered to this day. We reached a volume of close to a half a billion dollars. For 28 years we served millions of customers who took advantage of our low prices and quality. I am proud to say that all of our goods were bought under my motto to never buy anything that I would be ashamed to bring home to my own family.

Biway was a success, not because of Abe Fish, Russ Jacobson, or Mal Coven. It was a success because of the scores of people – from store managers to cashiers to supervisors and people serving on the selling floor to dedicated buyers – who together were part of delivering quality merchandise to working-class people at the lowest everyday prices in Canada.

It was also a success because our suppliers, large and small, were able to deliver the kind of quality merchandise we demanded at their lowest possible price.

BIWAY STORES LIMITED

EXECUTIVE SUMMARY

BiWay Stores Limited ("BW" or the "Company") is wholly owned subsidiary of Dylex Limited, Canada's largest retailer with sales in excess of $1.8 billion. BW is a national chain of convenience discount stores selling the following categories of merchandise:

- Food and drug, including health and beauty aids.

- Clothing, mostly of a basic needs nature but also include some fashion items.

- Miscellaneous general merchandise, including household products, toys, school supplies, housewares and electronic products.

Province	Stores
British Columbia	7
Alberta	18
Saskatchewan	5
Manitoba	14
Ontario	202
Nova Scotia	16
New Brunswick	15
Newfoundland	12
Prince Edward Is.	1
Total	290

The BW concept is to offer customers quality merchandise that provides excellent value for the money at competitive prices in conveniently located stores that are easy to get in and out of.

There are currently 290 stores located in all provinces of Canada except Quebec, of which 202 are located in Ontario. The majority of the outlets are located in neighbourhood strip malls. Store size varies from 4,000 to 25,000 square feet, with the majority (189 or 64%) falls between 6,000 to 10,000 square feet. Included in the total of 290 are 9 stores in the BiWay/Drug World combined format, all in Southern Ontario. The Division plans to concentrate on its new 10,000 square foot store concept, for which there are 9 prototype stores. Exhibit 1 provides a detailed listing of the store locations as well as a summary of stores by square footage.

All store premises are leased from third party landlords, except for 4 locations which are leased from Dylex Limited. The majority of the leases have renewal terms at various rate options. A summary of leases by maturity is provided in Exhibit 2.

Part of a report by Bill Eisenberg.

BIWAY STORES LIMITED

Approximately 15% of the merchandise is purchased by the local store managers, of which about two-third are shipped directly from the suppliers to the stores. The remaining 85% of the purchasing is handled centrally by 4 merchandising teams, each comprised of a merchandising manager, a merchandising co-ordinator, a merchandiser and 2 to 3 buyers. In addition, the 2 top executives of BW are also closely involved in the purchasing function of the Company.

Store merchandise is shipped from two central warehouses. Hard goods are delivered once a week to the stores by an independent warehouse agent out of central facilities. Soft goods are distributed twice weekly through the 618,000 square foot distribution centre of Dylex. As a result BW does not have a need for its own fleet. Total distribution cost approximates 2.2% of sales, which, after deducting an average 0.6% rebate, is a very respectable 1.6% rate.

After many years of consistent profitability, BW has suffered considerable losses in the last two fiscal years. The financial performance of BW is summarized below:

	for the year ended January 31						
	1993	1992	1991	1990	1989	1988	1987
# of stores	290	270	263	256	228	215	199
Sales	646.6	675.2	606.3	497.0	456.7	432.5	395.6
Gross profit	115.3	125.1	130.0	110.5	112.0	110.1	98.9
Store contribution	(17.7)	0.6	17.0	17.9	29.7	37.7	31.2
EBIT	(31.9)	(12.5)	5.8	11.4	22.9	31.0	20.6
Total assets	145.5	186.7	154.2	121.2	115.3	105.5	80.5
Divisional equity	56.9	75.7	74.9	72.5	67.4	55.2	39.3

NEW MANAGEMENT COVEN, FISH, JACOBSON

The Division's performance problem can be traced back to 1991, when it embarked on a plan to expand the business using a "Drag Thru" approach: stock up the stores to draw more customers, which would increase sales and hence gross margin and profit. While the number of stores and inventory increased during this expansion, sales per store remained basically flat, resulting in lower inventory turns, declined gross profit and higher selling expenses. The problem was exacerbated by the installation of a new Point of Sales system, the implementation of which was not executed properly, resulting in a total lack of reliable information and data. Consequently, the management of BW was slow in appreciating the effect of the change in operating style and philosophy.

Out-of-towners at David's Bar Mitzvah, in a tent set up in our backyard.
Standing: Miriam (left), me, Aunt Esther, Edith Levy, Cousin Marilyn and husband,
Aunt Rose, and Uncle Joey. Seated: Dad (left), Uncle Fritzy, Aunt Sally,
sister Bea, and her husband Harry Richman.

16

MEANWHILE ... LIFE

MUCH happened on the home front throughout Biway's association with Dylex from the mid-1970s to my retirement from Biway in 1990, some of it happy, some of it sad.

During this time Miriam went to university as a mature student. By 1981 she had received excellent grades and had 14.5 credits toward her 15-point degree. She was not to graduate, however.

It happened so suddenly. It was a Saturday that year. We were getting ready to go to our son David's graduation at Thornton Hall. We were all looking forward to seeing him in a play. Miriam suddenly got a severe headache. I rushed her to North York General Hospital and she was then taken by ambulance to St. Michael's for a CT scan. She had an aneurism, regaining consciousness for a short time but succumbing six days later.

We were all devastated. My children could not believe that they had lost their mother and I my wife of over two decades. Miriam was a special lady. When she walked into a room it lit up with her personality and beauty. Her brothers, Morris and Abe, always said she was the smartest of the three. She had great common sense and could analyze a problem and usually come up with a solution. Our home would never be the same without her.

~

After Miriam died I knew I would eventually be leaving our home on Old English Lane in Thornhill. Robin was off to law school in Ottawa, and David was starting his studies at the University of Toronto. I decided I would be better off living in Toronto proper.

At the time Miriam passed away she had a new Mercedes convertible that she loved but we had also kept her previous car, which was the first Mercedes we had in the family. I paid $12,000 for it in 1970. The car was on its last legs with rust spots and paint peeling.

Robin told me she would need a small car for getting around in Ottawa. The car she wanted, a little Volkswagen, looked unsafe to me. I decided to invest some money in Miriam's old sedan. I spent $1,500 to have all the rust spots welded off, the dents fixed, and the whole thing painted to its original colour, chocolate brown. When I picked the car up it looked gorgeous.

I proudly presented it to Robin as her Ottawa car.

"I can't take that car to Ottawa," she said. "It looks too good. They will think I am very rich!"

I convinced her that safety was my primary concern particularly during the Ottawa winters. She relented and drove it for close to four years in Ottawa. When she graduated I sold it for $5,000.

~

I spent a lot of my time looking for a new place to live in the city. I bought a town-house at 73 Hazelton Avenue because it was close to Yorkville, an area I had always liked. I paid $329,000 during a bad recession. That was very cheap at the time. I had it inspected and was told that the previous owners had spent about $125,000 to renovate it. I couldn't have done that for less than double that amount.

I rented it out for $2,000 a month and it carried itself; I knew it would be a good investment until I was ready to move.

Then I had a change of heart. I also liked the St. Clair and Yonge area. I was returning from a Blue Jays game on the way to The Brown Derby, a Montreal delicatessen that had opened on Yonge Street at Delisle, for one of their smoked meat sandwiches. On the northeast corner of Delisle and Deer Park were two townhouses for sale. It was 5 p.m. and a representative was taking down an Open House sign. I had to talk him into showing me one of the townhouses.

I bought it the next day. My thinking was I would rather live in that neighbourhood and visit Yorkville. I rented it out for $2,500 a month. It carried itself. I was still in no rush to move.

Nine or ten months after Miriam died I had my first date. My friend Jerry Levinson in Montreal called me and convinced me it was time to start dating. He knew a lady who had worked for him in Montreal and had moved to Toronto. Having visited Jerry in his office in Montreal, I knew that one of his criteria for his own staff was that they had to be attractive. I said okay.

There was one drawback. She was not Jewish. We went to the theatre together. She was very nice but since I didn't want to be seen with a non-Jewish woman, I decided to take her to the coffee shop in the Prince Hotel on York Mills Road. It was midweek and I was sure I was safe.

We had just sat down and ordered coffee when who walks in but Rabbi Erwin Schild, my rabbi from Adath Israel, and his wife. I was flabbergasted. If a rabbi couldn't tell a non-Jewish girl from a Jewish girl, then who could?

I decided that my best defence was a good offence. I couldn't count on his not seeing me so I went right up to his table to say hello. That was the end of the encounter, or so I thought.

The next morning I received a call in my office from the rabbi.

"I'm glad to see you're going out, Mal," he said. "There's a lady I would like you to call."

She was a member of his congregation and had moved to Texas with her husband who was a doctor. He had died and she was back in Toronto for a visit. Rabbi Schild always had a good eye for the ladies and this one was lovely. She had been single for quite a while and was looking to get married. I was not.

In the summer of 1983 I was in my office at Biway and received a call from Donna Pearl of Cooper Communications. She told me she had an advertising vehicle called

Media Cube that she was showing to retailers and asked if I could come by to see it. I always liked to keep abreast of anything new and different and said I was going to be in the Spadina area that afternoon and would drop by.

Donna was very nice and even though I was impressed with Media Cube, I quickly realized that it would not be useful to Biway.

A few days later I received a call from Aubrey Golden, the husband of Judy Golden. They were both friends of Miriam and me for many years. Aubrey said there was a young lady he would like me to meet. I never made the connection that it was the Barbara Cooper of Cooper Communications.

I called her for a date and arrived at her home on Wembley Road dressed in my uniform at the time – a navy double breasted blazer and tie (I always wore a tie in those years).

I rang the bell and peered through a small window in the door and saw a beautiful blonde wearing a white blouse that just suited her. I'm not sure why, but I got the feeling that this lady was destined to be something special in my life.

She was 37 years old, 17 years my junior, and recently separated. She introduced me to her sons, Stephen Spencer, 14, and Adam Charles, 11, and their dog, Tyson.

Barbara has reminded me that we went to the Courtyard Cafe at the Windsor Arms Hotel on that first date. After dinner she couldn't decide if she wanted the mile high ice cream pie or the chocolate mousse. She went to the ladies room and when she returned she found both desserts in front of her. She was really impressed by my generosity.

We dated a few times and along the way I spent time with her two boys. I was impressed with all three of them: Barbara with her beauty and charm and business acumen, Stephen with his sensitivity and intelligence, and Adam with his athletic prowess.

I played ball in the side yard with Adam. Stephen was interested in business. He was fascinated with banks and wanted to be a bank executive one day. He had at least three personal accounts in different banks and trust companies in order to follow the different systems and their interest rates. I am sure his balance in each was in no more than three digits.

"How do you start a chain of stores like Biway?" he asked me once.

"You open one store and if you are doing well you open another and another," I said.

Adam was at Bialik School at the outset. His teacher at the time told him he would never be a doctor or a lawyer but that he was creative. He then transferred to public school. That teacher was right on. In later years Adam created a business of getting exclusive franchises for products in North America from Europe and as far away as Australia.

I was very comfortable with the family – except for Tyson, after he greeted us after a formal evening with a load on the kitchen floor. Cleaning up the mess while still in my tuxedo was not a good start for us.

Bacon was in the fridge at their house. Having come from a kosher home this bothered me no end. I am told that knowing this, Stephen suggested to Barbara that bacon be eliminated from their diet at home. Barbara took his advice.

Barbara and I continued to go out. I knew I loved her but could not decide if I wanted to be a father all over again. I was still living on Old English Lane but staying with Barbara on the weekends. I always left her home by 5 a.m. on Monday to go back to Thornhill because I didn't want my kids to know that I had slept there.

The first time I introduced Barbara to the Dylex crowd was at Jack Posluns' 50th birthday party. I don't remember what Barbara was wearing but it was probably something I had bought with her in New York on one of our trips. Frankly, I was not too happy with some of her clothes and I made it my business to upgrade them.

Wilfred Posluns took me aside and asked me where I had found this beautiful young lady. My stock sure climbed with him and the fashion-conscious Dylex people.

The day after the party I received a call from Wilfred. He asked me who this Cooper lady was from Cooper Communications whom I had told to call him. Of course I never did. Barbara used my name thinking the connection could get her some business.

The fact that Barbara was a smoker did bother me. I tried to bribe her to quit and promised her a new rug to spruce up her house for Adam's upcoming Bar Mitzvah party. She did quit for a while but then went back. I didn't take back the rug.

At one point Barbara had to go to the hospital for a serious operation. I spent a lot of time with her helping her. After those sessions in the hospital I made up my mind to ask her to marry me. She happily accepted. I inherited a whole new family: Barbara, Stephen, and Adam. (My nemesis Tyson had died in the interim.)

I had known that Barbara had gone out a few times with George Hartman, a retail analyst. I didn't know him personally but he had been bugging me for an interview for some time. I finally caved in and met him for lunch at the Four Seasons. I'll never forget the surprised look on his face when I told him that Barbara and I were engaged to be married.

All during this time Barbara was involved in the process of divorcing her husband, Marvin Cooper. I remember going to one court session with her to lend her moral support. I knew she was very fragile and felt bad that she had to go through this messy situation.

I decided to take the bull by the horns and meet with Marvin personally to negotiate the last remaining issue. I believe it was $2,500, a paltry sum. When I met with Marvin he agreed to put the money involved aside for the children's education.

Barbara and I planned a small wedding at the Four Seasons Hotel just for family and a few close friends. Barbara made a beautiful bride. Some 30 years later she looks just as beautiful, maybe more so, in my eyes. I was very romantic and original in those days and still am. Before this we were sitting at dinner in Toronto when the waiter delivered an envelope to Barbara.

It was an invitation, handwritten in calligraphy, saying, "You are invited to Paris, transportation Air Canada, accommodations Le Meurice – the purpose is to buy a wedding gown." Was she ever thrilled!

We went to Paris, walked the fine shops, and ended up at Louis Féraud's atelier. Barbara picked a magnificent wedding dress. It was oyster coloured in the style of the 1920s. The top was all lace with a round neck and long sleeves. It fell to below her hips and tied at the bottom with a self sash. The skirt was the same oyster colour, silk with soft pleats that fell to her ankles.

She was determined to have a veil in the mode of Ophelia so Mr. Féraud sent us to a nearby milliner. It didn't look very nice but she was afraid to say anything because she didn't want to hurt my feelings. We went to buy a white silk camisole at Le Printemps. When we went back to pick up the dress after several fittings, all of the ladies who had worked on the dress lined up on the stairs and applauded as Barbara walked down.

We were married on January 5, 1986. It was a small wedding at Windows in the Four Seasons Hotel with close family and friends. Our good friend Rabbi Aronoff agreed to marry us even though he hadn't performed a ceremony in many years. Barbara made a beautiful bride in her Louis Féraud gown.

During our last days at her house before moving into our new home I insisted that she throw out all her non-kosher dishes and start anew. The only thing I allowed her to salvage was a bread knife that belonged to her grandmother.

I knew that the two townhouses I owned would not be appropriate for me now that I had a new family. I sold them both and bought a home for us at 17 Old Forest Hill Road. We did not want a large, pretentious home. The house we chose was a three-storey Georgian in the heart of Forest Hill. I had always kidded Barbara that she had never travelled north of Eglinton in her entire life. An exaggeration but there was some truth to it. She had grown up in the Forest Hill area.

We did a number on the house. We renovated the first and second floors and finished the third floor for an apartment for Adam.

I remember Stephen remarking how wonderful his new room was with the built-in drawers and desk, ideal for someone who loved clothes and studying. Unfortunately, he never got to use it. He died on May 4, 1986, just before we were to move in. It was an immense tragedy for all of us, particularly Barbara. She has not recovered from it to this day. The two of them were close.

Stephen was an unusual son. He was caring and supportive of his mother, particularly during the trying times of her separation. He was a very sensitive young man who had great potential that was not to be fulfilled.

Adam loved his apartment on the third floor. He had his privacy and the whole floor to himself including an extra bedroom for friends who occasionally stayed over.

At Adam's Bar Mitzvah: Barbara with sons Stephen (left), and Adam.

He did complain that I was too strict with him. He once said I was a lot easier on my son David. He was right. I got smarter after so many years. Although I am sure he liked me, Adam was his father's boy. At one point he threatened to move out and live with his father, who lived a few blocks away. I invited him to try it. He did, but returned after two days.

The only thing that bothered me about Adam was that he was not as nice as he could have been to his mother. He respected her for her business accomplishments but always favoured his dad. I am very happy to say that he has changed over recent years and has become a kind and considerate son to his mother.

It seems to me his generation is better than mine at being a father. He has two beautiful daughters, Erin and Lesley. My son David of the same generation is a great father to his boys, Isaac and Samuel, and to his twin daughters Ruby and Pearl.

During the time Adam was living at home with us I did all of the things with him that only an affluent parent could do. Trips to the Super Bowl and to the Olympics in Atlanta in 1996 come to mind. I had always had season's tickets to the Blue Jays and Raptors games and on many occasions took Adam with me.

～

For a few winters Barbara and I rented a place in Key Biscayne and enjoyed the time spent there. The only downside was that Barbara could not drive on the highway and it was difficult for her to get around without me.

One of those years I bought season's tickets to the Dolphins. They were moving into a new stadium and Russ and I both got season's tickets. It was quite inexpensive as there were only eight games involved. For the years I had the tickets I had never been able to use them. I never realized that the season was practically over when we would go to Florida in December.

With Barbara at Joso's on New Year's Eve, 2011.

One year we did go in November and my team, the New England Patriots, was playing the Dolphins. The game was on November 15, which happened to be Barbara's birthday. I told Barbara that we were going to that game even though it was her birthday.

"Fine, I'll bring a book," she said.

I said that would embarrass me in front of the many people I knew, who would be sitting near us. She was a good sport and left the book at home.

The people around us during the game were very friendly. They were mostly Russ's friends from Revere. They offered to bring us drinks. Barbara was very impressed with their hospitality, remarking how nice they were to us.

"They should be," I said. "They've had my tickets free of charge for three years."

We decided to buy a place in Palm Beach. It was a beautiful apartment on the fourth floor overlooking the water. It was just south of the Lake Worth pier, which lit up the water at night. When we got up in the morning we could see the surfers riding the waves. We made friends in Palm Beach and went to some of the charity affairs. It was easy to get invited. All you had to do was make a donation to the charity.

We met some people from Minneapolis through John and Myrna Daniels. One gentleman was in a wheelchair and we became friends. He and I had one thing in common: We didn't play golf or tennis. I invited him to go to the racetrack with me. He declined but invited me to a poker game that he played in weekly with a group of his friends.

After I accepted I thought that, this being Palm Beach, they could be playing for very high stakes. I comforted myself, however, with the thought that they could only get me once: If I wasn't comfortable, it would be my last evening with them.

There were six gentlemen at the game. One in particular was one of the original founders of Weight Watchers, a tall, lean man who was wearing plaid pants. I knew the fabric from my days at Filene's. It was woven material from Galey and Lord, very popular in the 1950s when I worked at Filene's.

George Mann was usually at the game but was absent this evening. I had not played poker for many years and knew only the standard five- and seven-card games.

Barbara (64), Bella (4), and Sophie (6).

They were playing games I had never heard of, such as Fiery Cross. They were playing for quarters and the pots weren't particularly big. One was only $12.

An argument ensued because even though I had the winning hand, I didn't declare it. On this subject there were two schools of thought: either the cards won or you had to declare. The gentleman with the plaid pants insisted that he was the winner. So he received the grand amount that was in the pot: $12.

Later on George Mann told me that if he had been there I wouldn't have lost that pot. He believed, as many others did, that the cards alone showed who won. I didn't think that gentleman in the plaid pants was very nice to give a hard time to a guest for such a paltry amount. In fact, I thought of him as a cheap, wealthy bastard.

Not too long after that, Barbara and I went to New York to view the estate of Jacqueline Kennedy. Some of her things were being auctioned off and we went there more to see what was available than to bid. We did put in a bid for a couple of items but as I suspected, most items sold for two or three times the estimate. One diamond ring was eventually sold for $400,000.

With Barbara at Luminato in Toronto.

That evening we were watching *Larry King Live* and who should appear as one of the guests but the gentleman in the plaid pants. He was the purchaser of that diamond ring.

"That cheap bastard, there's no way that he would spend $400,000 for a diamond ring," I said to Barbara.

Larry King asked him if he was nervous when he was bidding and he answered, "No, I was buying it for someone else."

"See?" I yelled. "I told you he was a cheap bastard."

He was bidding for John Kerry's wife, whose late husband was from the wealthy Heinz family.

Some of our Palm Beach neighbours were definitely not Biway customers. One day I introduced John Daniels to a discount store, a place he'd never been in his life. I ended up taking him to Syms and convinced him to buy a denim jacket, which I doubt he ever wore.

~

The investment in our Palm Beach apartment was too large for the amount of time we spent there. We sold it and decided to go back to Key Biscayne and rent.

During the following years we rented a lovely apartment in Key Biscayne large enough to accommodate some of my children and their children on at least one occasion. Later we moved to Sunny Isles Beach and rented there. Barbara was particularly happy because of how close it was to many of our friends and to Bal Harbor and Aventura. We met Joyce and Gord Strauss and through them Ruth and Harry Greenspan, who are good friends to this day.

I always thought that Barbara and I had a good marriage and so did she. Nothing in this world is perfect, however. Barbara had what I call a midlife crisis and asked for a divorce. To this day I am not sure exactly why. To find out you will have to ask her.

Even though we were divorced we never really parted company. I wanted to make sure she would be able to live reasonably well. In my mind, if she did not it would be a bad reflection on me. Unusual, I guess, but that is me.

I remember tellling my divorce lawyer, Phil Epstein, what I wanted to do for

Barbara, that it was not negotiable, and that he was to tell Barbara's lawyer the same. Phil thought I was being too generous and I probably was. He turned to the young lady who was taking notes and said, "If you ever have to get a divorce, make sure you get one from a guy like Coven."

Barbara was entitled to half the proceeds of the house and had made a deposit on a luxury rental. I talked her out of it and told her that with the proceeds of the house I wanted to buy two apartments at The Prince Arthur and she could choose which one she wanted. She agreed.

It was not a good move, but a great one. Not too long ago she downsized from 2,600 feet to 1,600 feet and walked away with close to a million dollars for the difference. Ironically, to this day she likes her present apartment better than that first one.

We both continue to live at The Prince Arthur, and, even though we are no longer married, we love each other and continue to have a great relationship. We have decorated our own places to suit ourselves. Most of the little things that get in the way of a marriage relationship do not exist now.

My restored Coke machine from the 1950s now sits in my kitchen. My original Las Vegas slot machine is in my office. Both had lived in the basement of our home on Old Forest Hill Road. I was able to develop a hobby taking pictures of family and friends that cover the walls of my apartment. I also have a sports memorabilia room with appropriate pictures. Anyone who has been to my apartment #514 at 38 Avenue Road will know that I've done my own thing.

When I decorated my own apartment I chose the interior decorator Joanne Chesler. I saw her in the lobby of our condo and hired her on the spot. That is not something you can do when you are married.

As I look back on my 27-year relationship with Barbara, they have been some of the happiest years of my life. I am very proud of what she has accomplished as a mother, a business person, and a volunteer, the last particularly when she was Chair of the Toronto Jewish Film Society. I have always loved her from the first right through to today. She has always supported me in all my endeavours, whether or not she approved of them.

In Robin's backyard, 2008 ...

*With my grandchildren Daniel (left), Nomi (holding Pearl), Isaac,
Sam (sitting in front of me), and Miriam (holding Ruby).*

*With Daniel, Miriam, Sam (in front), Isaac, David and
Victoria (holding Ruby and Pearl), Nomi, Tim, and Robin.*

From: saps@rogers.com (saps@rogers.com)
To: feedback@biwaybook.com;
Date: Sat, August 6, 2011 11:49:40 AM
Cc:
Subject: Why I miss shopping at The BiWay- Steve Aps

Hi There,

BiWay was a special store for me as a child and teen. I remember whenever a special occasion would arrise, whether it was my mother's birthday, Fathers Day, Christmas, I could always count on the BiWay to find a a gift that was worth giving yet it didn't break my piggy bank.
I miss walking through the doors and seeing the sales bunkers with great deals. Even if I didn't buy anything, my friend and I would often spend time just browsing for items, making mental lists that we'd later shyly convey to our parents as a birthday would appraoch.
As a teenager, my friend and I would stop into BiWay for our teenage neccessities. While yes we'd purchase our deodorant, chips, and hair gel at a reasonable cost, we had other reasons for shopping there. We found the most colourful floopy disks that would serve our needs in our computer class, or we'd buy our multi pack of recordable cassettes to make our own summer play mixes. Sometimes we'd stock up on BiWay brand cashews, nuts, and other treats just before leaving on a camping trip.
When we found out our local BiWay was closing shop, we felt disheartened. Afterall, BiWay was in my community, a place I met some of my now long time friends. A place we can meet up and spend our allowance and still walk out with some left over. Till this day, my friend and I stroll to the same plaza that were the store was located. We often reminisce and often say "remember when BiWay" was there. Funny, as a kid you don't take much notice of the stores you'd browse and become loyal to. Sometimes they were video games store, toy stores, your favourite mall food court chain, and in our case that included BiWay. Today, my friend still has an old Biway nuts tin that he keeps his pens and pencils in. Everytime I see it on his desk I chuckle as I remember the good old times we had as kids, and BiWay was part of that memory.

Steve Aps
4-11 Fairglen Ave
Brampton On
L6X 5E8
Shopped at BiWay in the plaza on the corners of Ray Lawson Blvd and McLaughlin Rd

17

WHAT CUSTOMERS REMEMBER

THE following is just a sampling of the hundreds of emails and letters I have received from customers and employee customers. It is remarkable to me that Biway is remembered so fondly even so long after its closing.

From: Eileen Bellan (sebellan@hotmail.com)
To: feedback@biwaybook.com;
Date: Tue, July 5, 2011 8:34:25 AM
Cc:
Subject: miss shopping at the Biway

Hello, Mr. Coven
   The Biway has significant importance in my life since 1967. I started working part time, during the school year and summers/ holidays as a 15 year old student, at your Biway store, at Keele and Finch with Tom Inksetter and Mr. Crystal. I hope they are well.
   They were extremely kind to me and I worked hard, achieving the position of cashier in a short time. That job enabled me to save for college. I stayed at that location until I started College. I became an Xray Technologist and worked many years at a Hospital.
   I recently shopped at Party City on Doncaster Rd and saw the little card about your contest. Seeing the Biway logo, it brought back such wonderful memories and felt that I had to email you. I would love to see you bring back the Biway. The merchandise was excellent quality and you always found what you were looking for in the store. I was very proud to work there.
   If I am fortunate enough to win a gift, I would love the Canadian Tire certificate.
       best Regards, Eileen Bellan (Eileen Natanson)

My Biway Adventure

My father died when I was five years old and was raised by my mother who was of Italian descent. She may not have had a lot of formal education but she gained practical skills that she learned over the years and applied in different jobs, to support the two of us.

I turned 14 in 1968 and the time had come for me to contribute to the household expenses. I started my first part time job at a Dairy Queen located at Lawrence and Culford (the establishment is no longer there). It was run by two brothers of Greek descent. My first work experience was not the most satisfying. Let's just say that as employers they had a lot to learn about how to deal with employees. I quit at the end of the summer.

The next summer, I started searching for summer work very early in the season. I went to several retail stores near my home as well as far away as Scarborough with no luck. I read in the paper about a job posting at Biway. I thought I had nothing to lose so I immediately went to the Islington and Albion store to submit my application. I received a call back that very day and started working the next day. I was thrilled to have a summer job and this was the start of my adventure at Biway.

The Store

The store was the first one established in Toronto (Biway was started by three co-owners in Kitchener). It was located at the south west corner of Islington and Albion, a good location to get to for people living in the area as well as for those living further away. They could easily arrive from different points by car, bus or by foot to purchase items at discounted prices.

The store was on two levels. It could be described as being compact, which is a nice way of saying that it was narrow and jam packed full of merchandise. There were no fancy displays or interior designs, it was just a simple and practical store.

The first floor (or main floor) had numerous tables to display clothing for men, women and children. Along the west walls there were personal hygiene products and useful kitchen items. The front had seasonal items on display that needed to move quickly and there were bins everywhere for small items. The cash registers were also at the front and the office and staff coat room was at the back.

The lower floor, which one reached by going down a set of steep, wooden stairs, had less merchandise space than the first floor because there was a stockroom. The lower floor contained mainly men's work clothes and boots along with other items such as shoes, kitchen equipment, throw rugs etc; items that were more specialized.

Along the west side of the lower floor there was a section for the person who priced the clothing goods with something that looked like an old fashioned press machine. I believe her name was Ella and she had been with the store since its opening. She would be standing, in a tight space, with boxes of merchandise on a table or on the floor next to her, pressing down the handle to attach the price tag and pins into the clothes. She moved quickly and efficiently. There were at least 50 to 80 boxes of different sizes stored in the area and around her work station, at any one time. She would find the box of merchandise that she needed to work on and either move it herself or ask the manager or stock boy to move it for her. Once she completed the pricing, the manager or one of the male staff would take the boxes to the appropriate level so that the merchandise could be taken out of the boxes and displayed.

On the same side but in the opposite direction of the pricing station there was a long, narrow corridor that staff would walk through to go for lunch or break. The lunch area was a small space with a table and several chairs. There were always one or two other staff members to sit and chat with when one went down for a break or lunch.

The store was a diamond in the rough where people came to find good deals. Lack of décor was certainly not a factor in peoples buying habits at Biway. As a matter of fact, the customers seemed more comfortable with that kind of setting as I would opine it would remind them of a similar place from their home country. And they probably felt that they were actually getting a deal at a place like Biway rather than a fancier store.

<u>The Owners</u>

There were three co-owners; Mr. Coven, Mr. Jacobsen and Mr. Fish. The one that we saw the most especially in the first year that I worked at Biway was Mr. Coven.

I'll start off first with the other two as they are minor players in my recollections. Mr. Jacobsen was a true gentleman; softer spoken than the other two, attentive and courteous to all. He was rarely in the store but when he was there he was a gentler energy than the others. The story that comes to mind about Mr. Jacobsen's character was the one that was recounted to me several times over the period of my employment. Mr. Jacobsen had served in the Second World War and was stationed in Italy. He was so passionate about opera that he would exchange his cigarette rations for the opportunity to attend an opera performance. Now that speaks volumes about his values and priorities. Towards the end of my tenure at Biway, when I had completed university and was ready to find a permanent job, it was Mr. Jacobsen who offered me a full time job at Biway's head office. Alas I turned it down for a government job. Who knows if I did the right thing??!!

Mr. Fish was also rarely seen but when he did come into the store I would describe him as "intense". He tended to be everywhere and find fault with everything. All we could do is try to keep up with him.

And then there was Mr. Coven. He was a serious type. We knew when he was in the store as he was everywhere, at one time, checking the displays, asking about the stock and generally making sure that everything was according to his standards. The store may have been a discount store but he had pride in ensuring that people got value for their money. Mr. Coven liked order in the store, productive staff and efficient processing of merchandise. He was demanding but respectful to staff especially if he knew that the person was a good worker however, if he wasn't pleased with someone's performance he would let you know. He would especially go after the manager, Mr. Sussman who wasn't always on top of the game. By the time, Mr. Coven left the store we were all tired and had enough work to keep us busy for three days.

As I indicated, he was proud of the staff at the store and he would make it known to his colleagues. I found out about this at one of the new store openings in Hamilton. Staff from the different stores was recruited for the week to work on the cash registers and generally help out with getting the store ready for the big opening.   Mr. Coven had advised one of the managers that I was quick on the cash register but the other manager made it known that his staff member was the fastest in the whole chain.   Well on the day of the opening there were line-ups around the block and we had to work quickly to move people in and out of the store. I was concentrating on working the keys on the cash register and my hands were literally flying that day to keep up with the number of people.   At the end of the day I found out that I was the fastest cashier and Mr. Coven gave the other manager a gloating smile when the manager conceded defeat.

Mr. Coven was quite a character but no one ever underestimated him as he was a shrewd businessman.

The Merchandise

Biway sold a myriad of goods ranging from clothing to kitchen gadgets to shoes to tools. The merchandise was sourced from both Canada as well as foreign countries such as Pakistan. The Chinese invasion of imports had not taken hold at that time.

Although the clothing may not have been name brands they were good solid quality and lasted a long time.   I remember buying a pair of men's sweat pants and a lady's sweat top and I just disposed of them two years ago because they had paint and other stains on them. The clothing was good value for the price unlike today's merchandise that falls apart after one wash.

The kitchen basics such as wax paper, aluminum foil etc. were at prices below the supermarkets and people tended to stock up on them especially during sales. The personal hygiene products like toothpaste, shampoos etc were also lower than the drug stores and customers always came back for more.   There were always special "buys" that arrived every so often and they were quickly snapped up by customers.

The baby section was especially frequented by young families. At that time, people had more than one child; actually one family that were regulars had 7 children at the time I left and they were expecting more.

The owners knew their customer base and stocked a variety of useful, fair priced merchandise that they confidently knew fit the needs of their customers.

The Customers

The customers were mostly from around the area but many came from a distance to shop at Biway because there really wasn't another store like it around. Honest Ed's was a similar store but it was downtown and the customer base didn't have the time to travel downtown to shop especially after long days at the factories.

The customers represented the immigrants that had settled in the area or nearby and with every new wave of immigration we would see them find their way to Biway. They were Italians, South Asians, East and West Europeans and Pakistanis. The people may not have been very sophisticated and many did not have a good command of the English language but they had survival skills and came to buy what they needed to run their households.

If I were to profile those who came to the store, I would describe them as hard working men and women from different parts of the world, of varying ages but mostly young to middle age couples, who were looking for reasonably priced merchandise for them and their children that fit their pocketbooks. Many were not high paid workers nevertheless, the husband and wife would both be working in factories so that they could buy a home and save enough money to send something back to their relatives in whatever country they came from. I remember hearing from many customers that they bought extra stuff so that they could send it back home. Biway made it affordable for them to do so.

I recall some of the families that shopped at the store. They would arrive with their children, as I mentioned before there was one family in particular that impressed me as they had 7 children and counting and they were always happy. The husband and wife were tall and good looking wholesome individuals and the children were well behaved. Others were looking for a better deal to an already good deal they had picked up! They would find fault with an item or haggle over the price until they wore down the manager. Still others would know exactly what they came to buy and would come in and out quickly. The men who worked in construction especially liked the hard toed safety boots that were sold at the store and the work clothes. The older people would come into the store on an almost daily basis scouring for that special "deal" and left satisfied with something to take back home to their family.

As the families established themselves in a house or apartment, they would come to buy kitchen gadgets, rugs and everyday items that were part of the necessities of life for them and their children.

The store was always busy and especially so on weekends. During seasonal peak periods such as the start of the school year or Christmas the line ups would continue for weeks. It was a store for the working class and it did a great job of providing value and dignity.

The Staff

The first thing I found at Biway was that everyone was one big family. There were few men in the store and for this reason they were memorable. They were either the manager or assistant manager or the stock boys. One of the main reasons, I think, that management was composed of men was because they had to pull double duty to lift and move merchandise as well as carry out the management duties. The women worked on the cash register, stocking the tables with new merchandise and keeping the tables neat and tidy. We were all responsible for keeping the store clean.

The supervisor, at the time, was an older woman (I guess everyone looks old when one is 15) with white hair and a stocky build. She ran a tight ship with a no-nonsense attitude but she trained well and looked after the interest of the company while still being fair with the employees.

She left shortly after I arrived and a tall, overweight, loud American arrived named Mr. Sussman. Mr. Sussman was a good talker and was always telling us tall tales. He was a smoker and would take frequent breaks. When he had to do some work it was painful to watch him as he would lumber around and sweat profusely when he lifted more than two boxes. Every time Mr. Coven visited the store he was sure to harangue him about something that he wasn't pleased about. Mr. Sussman was inconsistent in the way he expected things to be done and how he treated staff; one day he wanted things done one way and another day he would change his mind, one time he would have one person as his favourite and waste hours talking to them about his exploits and then he would change his allegiance. Let's just say that he was tolerated by staff.

Then there was Barry, the Stud (or at least he thought so) and he was the stock boy and spy for the manager. He would tell the manager what the staff were doing or not doing and would strut around like he owned the place because he knew he was protected by Mr. Sussman.

There were two assistant managers that came through when I worked there. One was a short Jewish man who was very insecure but made up for his insecurity by driving a Corvette. We all thought this was a bit of a disconnect! He stayed for about two years, learned the ropes and was then transferred to another store. Shortly after him an Italian assistant manager arrived and he did not last very long perhaps he was moved to another store or left the company altogether. I do not recall.

The female staff was a true reflection of the customer base. There were Italians, Canadians, South Asians and Blacks. One didn't really pay attention to the mix, at the time, as it was just the way it was. Those responsible for hiring would select people who they thought would fit in and work hard. I do not recall anyone being fired for incompetence or other reasons such as theft. Staff was grateful to be working to augment their husband's wages or as in my case to help towards tuition costs. However, looking back, Biway was an equal opportunity employer with a diverse workforce even before that was fashionable or the law. The owners were not selecting according to backgrounds or ethnicity but rather capability.

The women were always sharing stories about their lives and sharing food that they brought from home. There was a bit of a Peyton Place atmosphere with the younger female staff as there were broken romances, upcoming weddings, some who were interested in Barry, the Stud and so on. There was always some intrigue which was left for lunch or break times when everyone would catch up on the latest instalment of the dramas. It kept things lively but it never interfered with the work that needed to be done.

Ella however, was a unique character. She was the person who priced the merchandise. She was one hard-nosed, no nonsense individual who was completely dedicated to her work with no unnecessary down time. She was petite, her eyes were always red and watery and she was a chain smoker. There was a permanent cigarette hanging from the side of her mouth, at all times. She had a steady routine when pricing clothing items and she did not like to be interrupted. I sometimes relieved her, if she there was a big shipment. One day I thought I would be of help as she had been off sick but I inserted the strip of pins incorrectly and jammed the machine. I thought she was going to kill me the following day when she returned as I had messed up her domain. You just do not find employees like her anymore with such a strong work ethic.

Thinking back I know that everyone that worked there had pride in their work and carried out their duties to the best of their abilities as they were interested in the success of the store (and ensuring they continued to have a job). Staff felt as if they owned a piece of the store because of their contribution.

Summary

Biway was many steps higher on the discount store chain than the Dollar stores that we have today. It served a similar customer base but it had more diversified products and of far better quality. In reality, other than Honest Ed, the Biway's and Bargain Harold's and other similar stores no longer exist. There are either lower priced merchandise being offered by Dollar store type establishments or higher prices at the Zeller's or Walmart's. Merchandising has changed over the decades whereby products are more geared to specific customer groups, price points are very competitive, quality is no longer important and big stores are considered to be better.

Oh well, the retail era I knew has passed but I enjoyed working at Biway for the six years I was there! Moreover, it prepared me for the clients that I eventually dealt with as injured workers at the Workplace Safety and Insurance Board.

Luisa Giacometti

August 2011

From: stephanie giordano (stefygee@hotmail.com)
To: feedback@biwaybook.com;
Date: Mon, August 8, 2011 11:44:51 AM
Cc:
Subject: book contest attn: Mal Coven

Dear Mal Coven,

 Shopping at Biway brings back special memories for me because it was the place where my mother would alway's take me for" back to school"shopping. We did not have a lot of extra money growing up, however my mom always tried her best to see to it that I was up on the latest trend's and not feel left out, I remember looking through the flyer with giddy anticipation as I would mix and match the clothes, schoolbags and other essential's . We would embark on our " **BiWay Back to School** " shopping expedition together and were alway's greeted by first name by the friendly cashier's and floor staff . BiWay was a place where you never had to compromise ,you could always find brand names & great quality for the best price.
 Inthe era of -BIGGER IS BETTER- as a shopper I feel bombarded by the flashy displays,overwhelming advertising and mass production I find in the present day discount stores I miss the days of talking to the store staff and having them greet you by your first name, of knowing where everything is in the store and not getting lost, of feeling like a customer and not just a receipt number.
 Now as a mother myself I miss the simplicity of the back to school shopping experience I enjoyed with my mother. BiWay will always stay in my memory as the back to basics,simply savings,family feel discount store.

Sincerely,
Stephanie Giordano

From: familymartin@sympatico.ca (familymartin@sympatico.ca)
To: feedback@biwaybook.com;
Date: Tue, August 9, 2011 11:31:07 AM
Cc:
Subject: Why I miss shopping at Biway

I grew up in the Jane and Finch area. In the Jane and Finch Mall, there was a Biway store. Back then, going to Biway was like going to Toys R Us now. It was exciting. It was one of very few stores (in those days) that sold EVERYTHING - toys, clothing, candy,bedding, household items, etc. The quality of merchandise and low prices could not be matched anywhere else. There was a competitor's store called Bargain Harolds (I think that is what it was called) but their merchandise was inferior to what was sold at Biway, so we always shopped there. In August, we used to go in to buy our Back to School clothes, shoes and school supplies. In December, we used to pick out things we wanted for Christmas. We used to pick out our birthday presents from Biway too. I still think about Biway from time to time. It was a very good store that is sadly missed!

Arlene Martin
74 Mainard Cres
Brampton Ont
L6R2T8

(905) 654-1218

From: Patty George (pattygeorge@hotmail.com)
To: feedback@biwaybook.com;
Date: Mon, August 8, 2011 7:01:33 PM
Cc:
Subject: biway book contest reward

I remember taking a saturday afternoon shoppign trip with Mom and Dad, to the next big town that had a Biway, it was such a large store compared to anything in my small hometown. The variety was amazing, Mom and Dad thought the prices were great too, what did I know at that point? But I soon learned, when I got married and Money was tight, thats where i headed for supplies of all kinds, staples for the kicthen, linens for the bedroom and bathroom,. It was such a shame that it closed its doors , but i still remember those black and white bags, and they didnt cost us 5 cents each like the stores charge today!!

pat george

Why I miss the Biway

In my earlier years I remember walking to the Biway by myself or with friends. It was so convenient to walk to because it was right around the corner from my house. They sold virtually everything you needed or wanted (of course, at the time I would love to scope out the toys.)

It is a big childhood memory of mine and from time to time I tend to bring it up "hey, remember when Biway was open just around the corder there?"

Now the Biway is no longer. What use to be the home of the Biway which was later turned into a Montessori School now lies garbage, weeds and dirt due to a fire. Not only making my neighbourhood look like crap but making a huge waste of good space.

Another good reason why I miss Biway is when I was about 8 or 9 I used to walk over to the Biway during Christmas and buy all my family members gifts from there with my allowance money. It was the only place I could afford and walk to without my parents knowing what I had bought them for Christmas. Mother's Day and Father' gifts were bought from there and occasionally a few birthday presents.

Until this day My mother and I would say....its too bad that its not around anymore.

Stephanie Avila

① Dear Co-Founder, Mal Coven   Aug. 6 2011.

Why I miss shopping at The BiWay?...

Well for me it starts back in the 70's.
It's back to school time, grade 9 for me
My mom and I take a trip to the
BiWay store in Etobicoke. Paper, Pen's,
Binder and some clothes. I'm ready for
high school (NEW SCHOOL) The fourth day of
school I bring my new supplies.
A girl in class said- Your Mom Shop's at BiWay.
I said nothing, I felt embarrassed as I
sat looking at the black and white BiWay
bag on the table. Latter I told my mom
what happen. I was told to never mind
what someone said and do my best
with what I have. Year after year my
school supplies still came from BiWay.
I got my grade 12 and school was over.
I soon needed a job for myself and I
made my way to Bramalea City Center,
shopping mall to try for a job at BiWay.
It was a easy bus ride and I like the
store. As I walked around in the store
I see the girl who made the comment

②

about Bi Way from grade 9. (4½ YEARS AGO)
We make eye contact, as she is putting
men's shirts on a rack. You Work at Bi Way
I said. She smiles and nodded her head
yes. I walked around the store found a
pair of sunglasses paid for them and left
I have NEVER been back to that Bi Way again
I did get a job at the same mall but at
Fizannes fabrics. Most of the 1980's I worked
and would spend my money on a littel something from the Bi Way store. 1991 I move to
an apartment with my "boyfriend" still in
Brampton, We both had Friday's off so
we would go to the bank then to Bi Way
the store at Shoppers World Brampton or the
one on McMurchy Ave Brampton. It was our
first apartment and we needed stuff. Our
first buy was a fan, then came towels,
comforter, sheets, Kitchen stuff. There was
always a birthday card or gift I had to
get for someone. Our first Christmas tree
(FAKE 4 FOOTER) came from Bi Way and gift's
wrap and bows too. 1995 We moved again
still in Brampton but, to our "OWN" home.
I would still look forward to my Bi Way

③

flyer each week and I always see something I would like or for family. Then the store's were going to close, Bye Bye BiWay oh I was upset to see them shut down, it's like I lost a "good friend." I know other stores are out there and "Giant Tiger" is kinda like BiWay but, I miss the clothes. I got and still have and put on from BiWay I liked the "Cabin Creek" collection so much that I got myself 4 hoody sweaters and a spring jacket with pants and because the store had a fitting room I didn't need to return thing's anymore. July 1 2011 I was down in my basement looking in some old boxes and I found so many other things I got from BiWay. I guess everything old is new again even the pair of sunglasses I got from BiWay in the 80's. My mom was right, do the best with what you have.. I did, I spent my money on good things from BiWay and I still have them and use them all the time. What do I miss from shopping at The BiWay? The store and the staff, small store, great place to shop. I always found something at a good price.

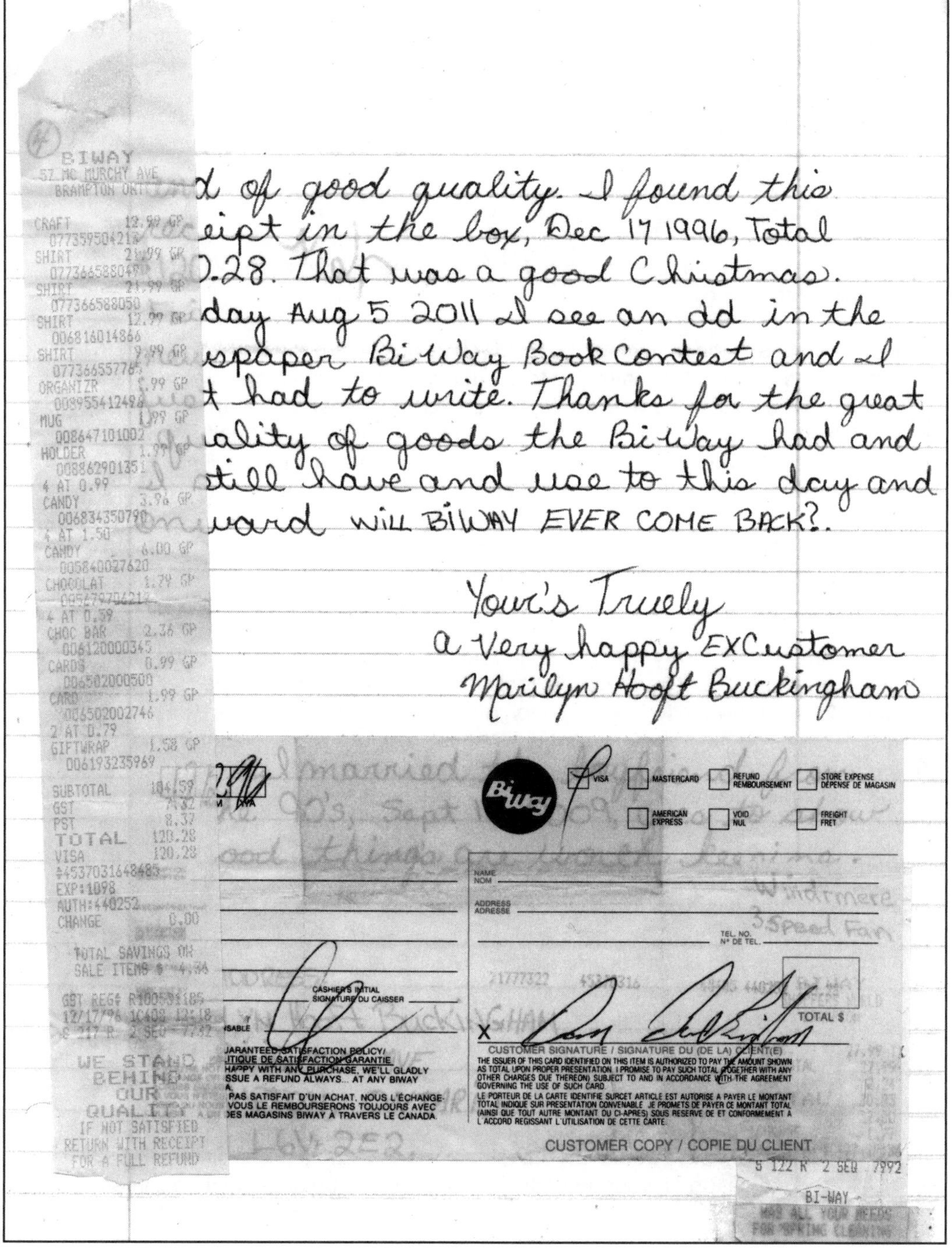

d of good quality. I found this
eipt in the box, Dec 17 1996, Total
0.28. That was a good Christmas.
day Aug 5 2011 I see an ad in the
spaper BiWay Book Contest and I
t had to write. Thanks for the great
uality of goods the BiWay had and
still have and use to this day and
ward WILL BIWAY EVER COME BACK?.

Your's Truely
a Very happy EXCustomer
Marilyn Hooft Buckingham

BIWAY
57 MC MURCHY AVE
BRAMPTON ONT

CRAFT	12.99 GP	
077359504218		
SHIRT	21.99 GP	
SHIRT	21.99 GP	
077366588050		
SHIRT	12.99 GP	
006816014866		
SHIRT	9.99 GP	
ORGANIZR	5.99 GP	
MUG	1.99 GP	
008647101002		
HOLDER	1.99 GP	
4 AT 0.99		
CANDY	3.96 GP	
4 AT 1.50		
CANDY	6.00 GP	
CHOCOLAT	1.79 GP	
4 AT 0.59		
CHOC BAR	2.36 GP	
006120000345		
CARDS	0.99 GP	
CARD	1.99 GP	
2 AT 0.79		
GIFTWRAP	1.58 GP	
006193235969		
SUBTOTAL	104.59	
GST	7.32	
PST	8.37	
TOTAL	120.28	
VISA	120.28	
EXP:1098		
AUTH:440252		
CHANGE	0.00	

TOTAL SAVINGS ON SALE ITEMS

WE STAND BEHIND OUR QUALITY
IF NOT SATISFIED RETURN WITH RECEIPT FOR A FULL REFUND

BiWay

VISA · MASTERCARD · REFUND / REMBOURSEMENT · STORE EXPENSE / DÉPENSE DE MAGASIN · AMERICAN EXPRESS · VOID / NUL · FREIGHT / FRET

NAME / NOM
ADDRESS / ADRESSE
TEL. NO. / Nº DE TEL.
CASHIER'S INITIAL / SIGNATURE DU CAISSIER
TOTAL $
X
CUSTOMER SIGNATURE / SIGNATURE DU (DE LA) CLIENT(E)

GUARANTEED SATISFACTION POLICY / POLITIQUE DE SATISFACTION GARANTIE

CUSTOMER COPY / COPIE DU CLIENT

BI-WAY

25Aug/2011

Co-Founder, Mal Coven
38 Avenue Rd. Ste. 514
Toronto, Ont. M5R 2G2

Dear Mal Coven:

In response to your request for input for the BiWay Book Contest, I would like to submit the following:

Recently at our cottage, my adult daughter was poking around under the kitchen cupboard, searching for something to scour out the sink, when she discovered this old can of Ajax under there, the top of which was quite rusted. "Oh my God, Mom," she hollered, "look how old this is! It came from BiWay!" True enough, we inherited this can of Ajax when we took over the cottage and surprisingly, it still has the BiWay price sticker on it, bright orange and marked .88 cents. (By the way, there is still some Ajax in it, and it still scours pretty good!)
I have attached photos taken of the can; unfortunately you can barely make out the price on the sticker in the photo, although it shows clearly on the original can.

A week or so later, coincidentally, your ad appeared in our local paper (Brampton Guardian) and our family was sitting around the kitchen table at the cottage and I was telling them about your request for BiWay stories. My son immediately said, "I remember BiWay clearly -- we used to go to the Bramalea City Centre all the time and it was down the stairs and through the turnstile, and you used to buy me Lee jeans there because they were cheaper, and everyone else was wearing Levi's, and the first time I bought myself a pair of Levi's they used to be too stiff at the back of my legs and Lees were always a lot more comfortable, so I went back to wearing Lees."

I remember the first time I had ever heard of BiWay. My friend Donna, who lived down by the Lakeshore, phoned me all excited to tell me about the new store that had just opened up down her way, called BiWay. She said the prices were terrific and they had so much variety and she was just delighted with it, so the next time we went down to see her for a visit, we joined her on a trip to BiWay, and I was hooked too. We didn't have anything like that at the time in Bramalea, but it was not long before our BiWay opened up in B.C.C. and I was thrilled.

My daughter told me that she could remember coming home from school around Baby Bonus time, and I would call out to her, in a sing-song voice, "I think there's something for you up on your bed," and she would race up and find a new treasure from BiWay, usually a new piece of clothing. "Oh yes," she said, "I used to love Baby Bonus time because you always bought me something from BiWay."

To this day, I still have three Cabin Creek blouses in my wardrobe, which I still wear and originally bought from BiWay. (But this is our little secret - right?)They were made in Korea, Permanent Press, have been washed many, many times over these past at least 30 or so years, and I defy anyone to find a ripped or frayed seam, button missing or anything wrong with them. They were certainly well made, well-priced and well worth the money. Too bad we can't purchase anything to compare to this type of quality, in this day and age, without costing an arm and a leg.

Christmas wasn't Christmas without a trip to BiWay for the stocking stuffers, chocolates and nuts, and usually several gifts within our price range without going into debt. And you know what? Everyone was happy and satisfied and we never had a disappointed long face from anyone.

Yes, we fondly remember BiWay and your ad certainly re-kindled some old memories and lively conversation. Thank you for taking us on a trip down Memory Lane.

Good luck in your book-writing venture!

Jackie Robinson
24 Peaceful Place
Bramalea, Ont. L6S 4E6

Encl.

AUGUST 7, 2011.

To MAL COVEN,
38 AVENUE RD, SUITE 514,
TORONTO, ON., CANADA. M5R 2G2

DEAR MR. COVAN: RE: ARTICLE IN THE BANNER
                         WHY I MISS SHOPPING AT THE
                              BIWAY

        I LITERALLY "LIT UP" WHEN I WAS READING
THE BANNER AND NOTICED THE "BIWAY BUTTON".!! THERE
ISN'T A DAY GOES BY THAT I TALK ABOUT AND MISS
YOUR STORE ON DONCASTER IN THORNHILL. I THINK I
SUPPORTED ALL OF YOUR LOCATIONS.

        I'M STILL USING ITEMS PURCHASED IN YOUR
STORE SO MANY YEARS LATER. I'M LOOKING FOR A
STORE THAT COMPARES TO BIWAY FOR QUALITY PRODUCTS,
PRICES, VARIETY, CUSTOMER SERVICE ETC. ETC.
I COULD GO ON AND ON.   ONE OF YOUR ORIGINAL
CASHIERS NOW HAS A SMALL STORE OF HER OWN
AND SHE REMEMBERS ME FROM "BIWAY".!!

        I THINK THIS TESTIMONIAL OF BIWAY IS
SUFFICIENT TO SINCERELY TELL YOU HOW SATISFIED
I WAS WITH EVERYTHING ABOUT YOUR COMPANY,
AND WOULD CERTAINLY SUPPORT YOU IN THE FUTURE
PLEASE G-D IF YOU SHOULD RETURN.

                      SINCERELY YOURS,
                      GERTRUDE ISAACS,
P.S. THERE IS NONE OTHER   18 HASKELL CRES.,
    LIKE YOURS.   AURORA, ON. L4G 5T2.
                            (905) 713-4430
                                (OVER). P.1

BIWAY

I WAS LOOKING FOR A DISCOUNT STORE
A VERY SPECIAL KIND,
ONE THAT WAS JUST LIKE "BIWAY"
WAS WHAT I HAD IN MIND,
I HUNTED HIGH
I HUNTED LOW
BUT THERE WERE NONE AROUND
AS THERE WAS JUST "ONE BIWAY"
AND NO OTHER COULD BE FOUND.

GERTRUDE ISAACS,
18 HASKELL CRES.,
AURORA, ON.
L4G 5T2
(905) 713 4430

P.2.

Mary Hasted
15 Gordon Drive
Brampton, Ont L6Y 2A8

I am writing this letter to let you know
how I and other people felt about shopping
at the Bi-Way.

I not only shopped there I also worked for
the company for over 25 years. When the
store closed I felt like I had lost a part
of my family. I had 3 kids and the
store had affordable clothes that I could
buy for them + the styles were pretty trendy.
The grocery and drug department had great
prices when they had there weekly sales.

We would see the same people come into
the store weekly for the specials.

Now that I am retired + I shop at other
stores and I run into one of the customers that
use to shop at the BiWay, they see me
+ say you look familiar where have I
seen you before and I will say the Bi-Way,
O ya I remember you. I miss shopping at the
Bi-Way they use to have some great deals.

The old Bi-Way warehouse on McMurchy
in Brampton

PART FOUR

AN ENTREPRENEUR'S MIND AT WORK

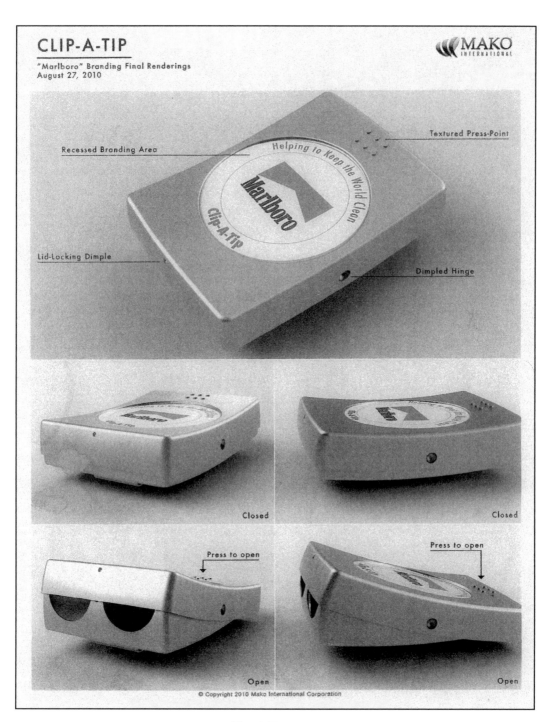

Clip-A-Tip prototype.

INTRODUCTION

IN this part of the book I tell the story of some of my original projects as well as others in which I was a participant and in which I had an important role in their development.

Some were started during my career at Biway but most were developed after my retirement. I have tried to put them in chronological order as best I can. The exceptions are the four I am currently working on at this writing – I'm starting with those first. They are *My First Car, Clip-A-Tip, Special Occasion Condoms,* and *The Biway's $5Max Store.* I have patents and trademarks for all these. I have not yet attempted to market them because this book has been my first priority for the last year.

Mockup for Neiman Marcus.

My actual first a car, 1953 Dodge.

18

CURRENT ORIGINAL PROJECTS

My First Car

From my own experience I know the joy of owning one's first car. I'm sure almost every man when he turns 16 dreams of buying a car that is his and his alone. No more going to Mom or Dad and pleading to use the family car.

I had been working for a few years and had managed to save $1,200. I was living at home with free room and board except for a few dollars that I gave Mom. Truthfully, they were very few. My income at Filene's was $38.50 per week. The only expenses I had were streetcar fare to get to work, lunch at work (many times I took my own), dates (which were mostly house dates in those years), a few movies, and that was it. My uncle Louis Coven volunteered to lend me the balance of the money I needed to buy my new 1953 Dodge convertible. He gave me $1,500 with the stipulation that I pay him back monthly – no interest, principal only.

In the beginning I left it at the subway station and then took the train to Filene's. I did drive it on dates. Typical dates were going to movie houses or drive-in theatres. In the case of the latter you drove your car into the theatre, which consisted of an open field with a huge screen, and pulled up next to a post that projected the sound through an earphone. You took a date there only if you knew you could snuggle up to her.

We also went to house parties and often on blind dates. The latter started by

DAROB LTD.

38 Avenue Road, Suite 514
Toronto, Ontario, Canada M5r 2g2
Tel: (416) 513-0101
Fax: (416) 934-1943
malcoven@rogers.com

June 21, 2011

PERSONAL & CONFIDENTIAL

Andrew Davies
Vice President, Automobile Merchandising
Canadian Tire Corp.
2180 Yonge Street, 3rd floor
Toronto, Ontario
M4P 2V8

Dear Andrew:

Enclosed is the original letter I sent to Reg McKay at the suggestion of my friend Wayne Sales. If you are old enough you would know of the company I founded, BiWay.

"My First Car" is a unique gift item selling nostalgia. Every guy remembers his first car.

In the US it will be sold in a department store at probably three times the price of the $25 I would suggest for you. This is Canada. I am enclosing an actual sample.

I would like to meet with you and tell you more.

Sincerely,

Mal Coven

Enclosure

DAROB LTD.

38 AVENUE ROAD, SUITE 514
TORONTO, ONTARIO, CANADA M5R 2G2
TEL: (416) 513-0101
FAX: (416) 934-1943

April 4, 2011

Canadian Tire
Reg McKay

"My First Car" is a registered trademark of Darob Ltd.

To every man, and some women, the purchase of their first car is a momentous occasion. "My First Car" documents the nostalgia of that occasion.

This beautifully framed memory makes an ideal gift for any member of the family to give a father, uncle or grandparent. A 5x7 silver frame contains a scanned photo below a caption reading "My First Car". Below the photo itself another caption indicates the recipient's name, along with the make, model and year of the car.

A photo of any car is available via the Internet at no cost or, in some cases, a nominal cost. Enclosed are sample pictures in both black and white as well as full colour. We feel them to be equally effective. The wording on the mat can be easily made by computer by either you or us.

We are offering Canadian Tire, on an exclusive basis, a licence for a fee and period of time in Canada to be arranged, to merchandise the framed version of the "My First Car" concept either online, catalogue, or in your store.

The retail price will vary obviously depending on the frame size and quality you choose. However, Darob Ltd. reserves the right to preapprove the retail selling price. On request, Darob will send to you the actual samples pictured in our email.

If you have an interest in pursuing an exclusive licensing agreement with Darob for the framed version of the "My First Car" concept, please contact me by April 30, 2011.

Mal Coven

telephoning a girl who was usually recommended by another friend, male or female. A typical opening line was, "You don't know me but I know you."

I also went to King Phillips in Wrenthem and danced under the stars at Norumbega Park, which had a large band. Dates were usually double dates. Some of my friends at that time were Joey Albert, usually referred to as House Date Joey because he could not afford to date any other way (he was saving his money for his college education and went on to medical school and became a dermatologist); Willy Gershlak, inaccurately nicknamed by my brother-in-law Harry as "Willy the Bad Influence"; as well as Jay Long, Benny Diamond, and Frank Weiner. Jay and Benny took turns going steady with my cousin Marilyn Furman.

As described earlier in this book, my beautiful 1953 black Dodge convertible with the red leather seats really changed my life. On a week's vacation I decided to take the car on a long drive from Boston into Canada and ended up meeting my future wife, Miriam Fish, near Montreal.

Some 55 years later, as I was reminiscing about this, I was sure that if my first car was that important to me, the same would be true for others. I mocked up three samples of 8" x 10" silver frames with a picture of a car. Above the photo, in calligraphy, were the words *My First Car*. Under the photo I put the words, *Mal Coven, 1953 Dodge Convertible*.

Because each sale would take time to assemble, I thought it best to approach a catalogue house. Neiman Marcus was first on my list because it is well known for its Christmas catalogue. I got through to the appropriate buyer in Texas, who tried to discourage me from coming to see her. I didn't want to tell her what I hoped to sell her because it is too easy for someone to say no on the telephone.

I persisted and she finally gave me an appointment. I showed her the three samples of silver-framed cars with the *My First Car* heading. The frames I had bought retailed for $25, $35, and $99. The highest-priced one was silver.

Later, after reviewing them with her merchandising manager, she said she wanted one of them for her fall catalogue.

I always assumed the pictures of the cars would be available from the manufacturers and they were. However, because they had not yet been converted to digital, their price was extraordinarily high. I couldn't deliver within budget so I put the project on hold for over a decade.

Now, in 2012, all of these pictures are available on the Internet at no or low cost. This is the year I will be approaching a major company in both the U.S. and Canada.

CLIP-A-TIP

Every city that has banned indoor smoking has a huge, ugly mess on its hands. The litter caused by cigarette filter tips takes three to five years to disintegrate and represents over 50% of the litter at beaches and parks. You see cigarette filters everywhere. In Forest Hill Village they are at the bus stop and in front of coffee shops and stuck in the cracks between bricks in sidewalks. Recently, Toronto councillor Josh Matlow told me he went to a park in his area with volunteers to clean up. He described the park as "one big ashtray."

My son David, who lives with his family close to Exeter, U.K., sent me a clipping from *The Echo*, a local newspaper, which said it is costing the city well over a million dollars a year to clean the streets and the main culprit is filter tips. Fines for littering cigarette butts have been ineffective.

I know I have found a way to solve the problem. Education and legislation are important. We know from surveys that people who smoke don't like disposing of their cigarette filters on streets and sidewalks. We also know that cities, provinces, and states have been mandating citizens to return beer bottles and pay for plastic bags.

Regarding cigarette filters, we eventually need legislation mandating that smokers must return their filters in order to purchase another pack and a simple and effective way for people to comply: a device that stores the filter tips. I am told by Mark Sarner that when it comes to changes like this, an initial 10% of the population complies immediately, another 25% or so follows their lead, and the rest need the motivation of legislation.

I worked with my friend Marcel Merolla, who put the original idea to cardboard. Thus was born the Clip-A-Tip device. I had a prototype made.

We provide space on the device for a cigarette company or any company to advertise, under the tagline "Helping to keep the world clean." In our plan each smoker would initially receive one free of charge, for the most part paid for by the advertisers.

You'd think that the major cigarette companies would jump at the chance to help clean up the mess their cigarettes cause. One cigarette company spokesperson, Jennifer Golisch, media affairs manager for Philip Morris, even went on the record in 2003 to say, "We believe we have a role to play in the reduction of litter."

The tobacco companies have stonewalled us. They just do not take any advice from outsiders. These are the same manufacturers such as Philip Morris, British American Tobacco, and Imperial Tobacco that for decades maintained that cigarette smoking was not a health hazard.

I'll be approaching people in the provincial government to make them aware of the breadth of the problem and show them my solution. I have no doubt that using Clip-A-Tip to solve the problem in Toronto and across Ontario will encourage other cities and jurisdictions to fall in line.

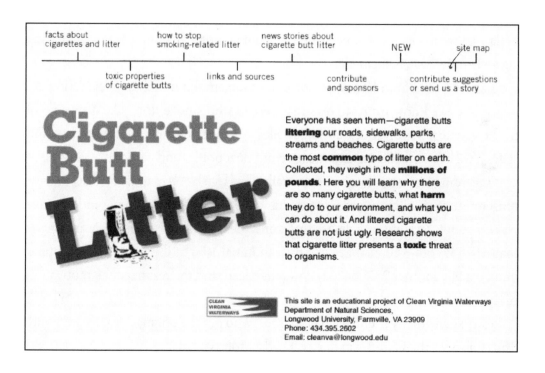

THIS IS LITTER TOO

This message brought to you by
Keep Palm Beach County Beautiful, Inc.

Keep Palm Beach County Beautiful, Inc.
1920 Palm Beach Lakes Blvd., Suite 210
West Palm Beach, FL 33409
Phone (561) 686-6646
Fax (561) 686-6642
keepPBC@bellsouth.net

30,000 cigarette butts litter ski slope ($$)
Source: Times Of London (UK), 2004-02-16

A French ski resort is selling portable ashtrays to tourists to try to reduce the millions of cigarette butts deposited on Alpine slopes every year. Officials at Val Thorens, which attracts thousands of British skiers, say that they find 30,000 butts under a single chairlift during the winter season. These pollute the water supply when the snow melts in the spring. . . . A French researcher, Jean-François Donzier, recently gave warning against such pollution of mountain streams. "Their flow is always slow and that means that the impact of pollution is much greater than in rivers," he said. "Mountain streams are the world's water tower. It is important to look after them."

Getting Tobacco Manufacturers Involved with Litter Prevention

"Earlier this year, we began carrying an anti-litter logo on several brands. We believe we have a role to play in the reduction of litter." —Jennifer Golisch, media affairs manager for Philip Morris 2003

DAROB LTD.

38 AVENUE ROAD, SUITE 514
TORONTO, ONTARIO, CANADA M5R 2G2
Tel: (416) 513-0101
Fax: (416) 934-1943
malcoven@rogers.com

MEMO

April 2011

Murray Kessler
Chairman and CEO
Lorillard Inc.

An idea on how to cut a growing problem down to size

Darob has come up with an idea and an invention designed to address the growing problem of cigarette butt litter. Properly executed, an increasingly damaging situation can be contained.

The Situation

Increasingly, public and media attention is turning to the problem of cigarette butt litter. Butts are everywhere – on sidewalks, in front of buildings, in parks and other public spaces - and on beaches where estimates are that they account for over 50% of litter.

There is growing pressure for government action. The chorus of concern is getting the attention of municipal, provincial and state governments everywhere.

Here in Ontario the media is trumpeting the need for legislative action.

Unaddressed, this thing can easily get out of hand. The usual suspects – smokers and the cigarette companies – will inevitably be fitted with black hats and the crusade against smoking will get another big boost.

The issues are simple and irrefutable. The cumulative effect of these butts is an unsightly mess. Then there are the environmental issues, slow biodegradability and toxicity. The move will soon be on to both pass the related costs onto the industry and to create and enforce legislation targeting smokers.

What To Do

One option: the industry can choose to hunker down and prepare to defend against a growing public outcry, increasing government rumblings leading to action, and the prospect of more stigmatization of smokers and increased demonization of manufacturers.

Not a good plan and certainly not a winning strategy. It could drag things out but that is about it. And at a cost.

Undoubtedly for these reasons, Jennifer Golisch, media affairs manager for Philip Morris, said back in 2003: "We believe we have a role to play in the reduction of litter." At that point Philip Morris was carrying an anti-litter logo on a number of brand packages.

Since then the problem has continued to grow - and along with it the demand for action.

We have a better idea.

It is proactive.

It engages smokers as partners in the solution.

It positions your company as a responsible environmental player and a responsible steward.

It provides your company a perfectly legal brand-promoting vehicle and the basis for a branded marketing campaign to address the issue.

It enables your company to provide valuable partnership support and traffic-building tools to tobacco retailers.

It opens up the opportunity to build a working partnership with government around effective legislative action that pre-empts more negativity towards the industry.

It creates a new product that has profit-making potential down the road.

The Way Forward: A Six-Step Plan

Here, in brief, is the plan of attack.

1. ***Embrace the problem***: Get out there and declare that this matter must be addressed and commit to leadership in doing so.

2. ***Introduce the solution***: A simple course of action that enables smokers to take responsibility for their butts.

3. ***Provide the means***: Clip-A-Tip (see attached picture of the prototype – patent pending). This simple-to-use, easy-to-carry tool enables smokers to solve the problem at the source and to easily dispose of butts appropriately. It is available where cigarettes are sold.

4. ***Promote the right smoker behaviour***. Through all media, online and POP. A branded campaign to foster voluntary compliance.

5. ***Build and promote a partnership***: With government to develop appropriate legislation to drive increased compliance.

6. ***Collaborate on policy implementation***: With government in the first 12-24 months.

The Benefits Are Compelling

Improve Image: As part of the solution, not simply drivers of the problem.

Increased Influence: With government, media and the like. And with retailers.

Income protection: By preventing further encroachment on smokers' opportunities to smoke and therefore their purchase of cigarettes.

Income Generation: Through the sale of Clip-A-Tip in various formats to consumers.

The Clip-A-Tip cost is estimated at somewhere in the range of $2-$3.

The final cost will be a function of volume. We expect that the initial production run would be in the hundreds of thousands. Manufacturing will be done in China.

So that's the idea. I look forward to hearing the response and welcome the opportunity to come in for a presentation and discussion with the appropriate people.

Mal Coven
President

MAL COVEN

July 27, 2011

Councillor Josh Matlow
City Hall, 2nd floor, Suite B26
100 Queen Street West
Toronto ON M5H 2N2

Dear Josh:

As per our original phone conversation and my email to you recently, I am enclosing some information about me and my passion for solving the cigarette litter problem in Toronto. I know it can be done with little or no cost to the city but it needs the support of aggressive councillors like yourself. I have no doubt that when we succeed every city in North America will follow.

Please take a few minutes to review what I am enclosing and after that I would like to spend a few minutes with you in person.

Sincerely,

Mal Coven

4 enclosures

38 AVENUE ROAD, SUITE 514
TORONTO, ONTARIO, CANADA M5R 2G2
TEL: (416) 513-0101
FAX: (416) 934-1943
malcoven@rogers.com

DAROB LTD.

38 Avenue Road, Suite 514
Toronto, Ontario, Canada M5R 2G2
Tel: (416) 513-0101
Fax: (416) 934-1943
malcoven@rogers.com

July 20, 2011

Tom Bevan
Express and Echo
Heron Road
Sowton, Exeter
EX27NF UK

Dear Tom:

My son David Coven forwarded to me your article of 23/04/11 *"Exeter's cleaning up after smokers cost the taxpayer more than £1 million a year in Exeter"*.

Sorry for the delay as I have been rushing to complete my autobiography. Separately, I am emailing you something about that which you might find interesting. I started a discount chain that we built to 249 stores. It also lists some ten original projects that I conceived in my retirement. One is Clip-A-Tip which, in part, this letter is about.

We have a similar litter problem in Ontario as does every other jurisdiction that bans indoor smoking. Cellulose filter tips are not only an ugly toxic mess in the cities, but represent 50% of the litter in beaches and parks. They take 3-5 years to disintegrate. Fines for littering are useless. My councillor, Josh Matlow, in cleaning up one particular park with volunteers, called it "one big ashtray". I have approached both the province and the City of Toronto with a plan that will once and for all solve the filter problem. The response has been very positive from both quarters. It is a cooperative plan which needs business, citizens and government cooperation. It is similar to what I am outlining for Exeter.

You state that the Exeter cost for clean-up is over £1 million. It is easier for me to talk in dollars so I will convert very conservatively. In fact, I will use the figure of $1 million which is way below the £1 million you quote.

Even though the Exeter population is 100,000, the trading area is 500,000 as your High Street is one of the focal centres of Greater Exeter. I have been there and have seen there every store imaginable from the highest end to the lowest end. Assuming North America figures, the smoking population is 100,000 (20%). We have developed an instrument the size of a small cell phone that clips off the butt end of paper and tobacco and stores the filter.

Eventually we need legislation that will mandate that the filters will have to be returned to the retailer in order to purchase a new pack of cigarettes. We intend that the instrument - preferably our Clip-A-Tip which was designed for this purpose - would initially be given out to all smokers free of charge. It would be paid for by local merchants and cigarette companies under the banner of "Helping to keep our world or city clean". The City could actually make money selling the replacement after the initial distribution. The saving for the city and taxpayer is tremendous.

The cost of Clip-A-Tip would be no more than $200,000 plus $25,000 for an advertising campaign to get it off the ground. We know from our survey in Toronto that citizens do not like the idea of dumping their butts on the street and will cooperate. Initially, some 10-15% will do it straight away. Then another 20-25% will be influenced. That is when the legislation making it mandatory will kick in. In our jurisdiction there are laws concerning disposition of beer cans, plastic bags and picking up dog feces, so this is the type of idea that has been accepted in the past.

The saving in the hundreds of thousands of dollars are obvious for a one-time investment. The savings would continue yearly.

The only fines needed would be to the retailer who would cooperate and not risk it for the few cents he makes on the sale.

Even <u>The Echo</u> would benefit as they would certainly be part of the promotion campaign.

Sincerely,

Mal Coven

Enclosure

Special Occasion Condoms

During the months of April and May 2011 you could not help but know that a royal wedding in the U.K. was in the offing.

One evening CNN was showing various items bearing the royal couple's picture. First came royal mugs with the royal couple and then a small colourful box that said *Royal Condoms*. At first I thought it was a joke. It was not.

I asked a friend, Sue Zamkow, who lives in London, to buy a box for me. Her response was, "They're sold out!" She did finally get one for me on eBay for approximately $48. The original price was $18.

If they can sell condoms for that special occasion, I thought, why not for others? I registered and trademarked *Wedding Night Condoms, Honeymoon Condoms,* and *Anniversary Condoms,* as well as other names. A prototype of them is in the works and I hope to license the names to a condom manufacturer.

THE BIWAY'S $5MAX STORE

Email to Larry Rossy, Dollarama, 4 a.m., January 19:

Good morning, Larry.

Thank you for the warm reception and the time with you and your associates. Before you decide on whether you will be adopting my proposal to start up the Biway's $5Max Store, I must tell you that I have had a change of heart. You might remember Victor Kiam's TV commercial when he bought Remington: "I liked the shaver so much, I bought the company." Well, I like my proposal for the Biway's $5Max Store so much I have decided to do it myself, to open in 2013. Please return the copy of the proposal I left with you along with the samples.

Separately, I might be looking for investors in the very near future. If you have any interest, let me know. I am sure that the thousands of former customers of Biway will appreciate that Biway will be reborn in a new format still delivering quality and value under the slogan, "I never sell anything in a Biway store that I would be ashamed to bring home to my family."

Good luck and good health,
Mal

19

EARLIER ORIGINAL PROJECTS

Heritage Plaques

The world-class city of Toronto was not just figuratively but literally built by immigrants and their children. Among them are the Green, Reisman, Daniels, Del Zotto, and Greenberg families. I live in The Prince Arthur condo in Toronto, built by the Greenbergs through their company Minto. In my opinion that trade name is certainly one of the best in Toronto.

Back when Mel Lastman was mayor of Toronto, he was looking for ways to raise money to help the city out of a deficit. My idea was twofold: to honour the families of immigrants who had helped to build the city (I was particularly familiar with the Green families, who were some of my first neighbours when I immigrated to the city from Boston) and to honour immigrant storekeepers.

I knew there were plaques honouring famous entertainers and politicians. Why not plaques to honour the people who actually built the city?

Also, I could picture small plaques embedded in the sidewalk outside a store with details of the establishment that had been founded there by an immigrant decades before, for example, *Rotstein Furniture – 1902-1946*.

I researched the project and found it would cost $500 to make and install each plaque. In addition, I would ask for a $1,000 contribution to the Toronto Heritage Grant Program from any family that wanted to participate. I approached Al Sandler,

Leo Goldhar, and Al Green, among others, some of whose families had retail stores in the city, and got a positive response. I made a sample plaque for the Green family and then approached the city. All of the six or seven officials I spoke to were positive, including some councillors and other well-placed people in city government.

Next I attended a subcommittee meeting chaired by Mike Feldman, the purpose of which was to solicit ideas for helping the city raise money. Around eight different groups were in attendance to propose projects. Each one was looking for the city to fund their project.

My proposal was different. I was not looking for funds. Quite the contrary – I was looking to help raise funds for the city through the $1,000 donations to the Heritage Grant Program. The other participants came over to congratulate me on my idea and everyone on the committee was positive about it, too.

In spite of this, my plan was rejected. I was told in writing that the plaques embedded in sidewalks would be "a danger to pedestrians walking the street."

Right. Watch out for those dangerous 5" x 7" plaques sunk into the cement! I walk the streets every day and see so many things that are a danger to pedestrians and they are not a problem. Why the plaques?

It's still a great idea. Anyone among my readers interested in pursuing this?

Sidewalk Heritage Project™

PROPOSED BY

MAL COVEN
THE PRINCE ARTHUR
38 AVENUE ROAD, SUITE 514
TORONTO, ONTARIO
M5R 2G2

TELEPHONE (416) 513 - 0101
FACSIMILE (416) 934 - 1943

October, 2001

Mal Coven

His Worship Mel Lastman   January 17, 2001
City Hall
100 Queen Street West, 2nd floor
Toronto, Ontario M5H 2N2

Dear Mel:

This letter is to formalize in writing a proposal given orally to Angelo Rossi today. He said he would speak with you about it in the next few days.

I am requesting permission of the City to affix small bronze plaques, 8" x 8", imbedded in the sidewalk at various addresses in the City. They would be bought by people or for people or families who lived there in earlier years.

Most people have great pride in the place they grew up, or where their parents or grandparents lived and taken their grandchildren to show them where they started out. You may have done the same with yours.

Here are some very rough examples:

52 Clinton Street Residence of Lastman family 1942-1967	Residence of Lastman Family	First Bad Boy Store Opened July 1957

I think this not only adds continuity to the City but could eventually, if promoted properly, become a tourist attraction with the many celebrities that would be included.

The City would have no involvement in the project. The majority of the profits would go to City and local charities. I think the potential is well into seven figures for the City. Ten minutes in person and I could give you more details.

Best regards,

Mal Coven

P.S. In case you don't recognize the name, I'm the BiWay guy.

THE PRINCE ARTHUR
38 AVENUE ROAD, SUITE 514
TORONTO, ONTARIO
M5R 2G2

TEL: (416) 513-0101
FAX: (416) 934-1943

TORONTO

Mel Lastman

Mayor
City Hall, 2nd Floor
100 Queen Street West
Toronto, Ontario M5H 2N2

Tel: (416) 395-6464
Fax: (416) 395-6440
mayor_lastman@city.toronto.on.ca

February 22, 2001

Mr. Mal Coven
The Prince Arthur
38 Avenue Road, Suite 514
Toronto ON   M5R 2G2

Dear Mr. Coven:

Thank you for your letter of January 17, 2001, advising me of a proposal to place plaques on City sidewalks to reflect the heritage of Canadian personalities and celebrities.

Toronto welcomes new and enterprising ideas that encourage tourism while supporting fundraising strategies for local charities. I appreciate that you would like to meet with me to discuss your intentions, however, my schedule does not permit me to do so at this time. I have forwarded a copy of your letter to Mr. Joe Halstead, Commissioner, Economic Development, Culture and Tourism, for his information and review.

Once again, Mr. Coven, thank you for writing and bringing your suggestion to my attention. Please accept my warmest personal regards and best wishes on your future endeavours.

Cordially,

Mel Lastman.

Mel Lastman
Mayor

copy: Mr. Joe Halstead, Commissioner, Economic Development, Culture & Tourism

(Coven/jsc)

⩗⩗ TORONTO

City Hall
100 Queen Street West
Toronto, Ontario
Canada M5H 2N2
www.city.toronto.on.ca
Tel: 416-392-9046
Fax: 416-395-0278

Culture Division
Economic Development, Culture and
Tourism

FAX TRANSMITTAL

DATE: April 27, 2001

TIME: 2:35 PM

NUMBER OF PAGES INCLUDING COVER: 1

TO:

Mr. Mal Coven

FROM:

Brad Eyre
Division Coordinator, Culture

FAX NO.   416-934-1943

TEL. NO.   392-9046

COMMENTS/SUBJECT

Mr. Coven,

A quick note in response to your voice mail message to Rita Davies yesterday. The name of the fund that would be used to receive revenue from your plaque initiative is the Public Art Reserve fund. Monies deposited would, however, be clearly identified as funds to go towards Historic Plaques and their maintenance (not into the general reserve fund). This would enable us to allocate funds to an appropriate project when necessary.

I am happy to hear that Ms. Antoniou has followed up with you so quickly after my call and that things are moving forward (albeit slowly). I expect that one of the most pressing concerns to the Works department is the issue of maintenance and responsibility. Some of the funds allocated to the Public Art Reserve fund (generated from this project) could, of course, go towards ongoing upkeep of the plaques – if necessary.

Please give me a call if you require further assistance. My direct number is 416-392-9046.

Best wishes for a speedy recovery from your cold,

Brad Eyre
Division Coordinator, Culture
beyre@city.toronto.on.ca

If you do not receive all the pages, or experience transmission problems, please call 392-8674

Mal Coven
38 Avenue Road, Suite 514
Toronto, Canada M5R 2G2
Tel: (416) 513-0101 Fax: (416) 934-1943

Ms. Rita Davies
Managing Director of Culture
City of Toronto
City Hall, 4th floor
100 Queen St. W.
Toronto ON
M5H 2N2

October 18, 2001

Dear Rita,

I am taking the liberty of sending you a first proof of my "Sidewalk Heritage Project", which I am told I will eventually be presenting to a Committee of Council.

I would like to have your comments and if you still show the same enthusiasm for it, I would appreciate a note to that effect. I would like to include your letter with my proposal to Council.

Many thanks,

Mal

November 2, 2001

Mal Coven
Ste 514 - 38 Avenue Road
TORONTO, On M5R 2G2

Dear Mal:

The "Sidewalk Heritage Project' is an excellent idea that would do much to enhance an awareness of the history that is around us.

It represents a way that people can mark the past and provide a sense of pride and history for citizens of Toronto.

Good luck with your proposal.

Yours truly,

HOWARD MOSCOE
City of Toronto Councillor
Ward 15/Eglinton-Lawrence
Ids/Letters General/Congrats and Support//Mal Coven Sidewalk Heritage Project

TORONTO Councillor Howard Moscoe, City of Toronto - North York Spadina

Toronto Office:
100 Queen St. West, Suite B30, Toronto, Ontario M5H 2N2
Telephone: (416) 392-4027   Fax: (416) 392-4191
E-mail: councillor_moscoe@city.toronto.on.ca

North York Office:
5100 Yonge Street, North York, Ontario M2N 5V7
Telephone: (416) 395-6410   Fax: (416) 395-6430

TORONTO

Urban Development Services
Paula M. Dill, Commissioner

City Planning
Toronto City Hall
100 Queen St. W.
19th Floor, East
Toronto, Ontario
M5H 2N2

Eric Pedersen
Program Manager, South District
Urban Design

Tel: 416 392-1130
Fax: 416 392-1744
Email: epederse@city.toronto.on.ca

November 12, 2001

Mr. Mal Coven
38 Avenue Road
Suite 514
Toronto, Ontario
M5R 2G2

Dear Mr. Coven:

Thank you for sending me a draft copy of your Sidewalk Heritage Project. You have taken your idea to a very polished implementation proposal.

I look forward to seeing plaques along the sidewalks of our city marking buildings where families and businesses "got their start".

Good luck.

Sincerely,

Eric Pedersen
Program Manager
South District, Urban Design

EP/ms

JOANNE FLINT
Councillor Ward 25

100 QUEEN STREET WEST, OFFICE 12, 2ND FLOOR
TORONTO, ONTARIO, CANADA M5H 2N2
TEL: 416•395-6408 FAX: 416•395-6439

January 16, 2002

Mal Coven
38 Avenue Road Suite 514
Toronto, Ontario
M5R 2G2

Dear Mr Coven:

Thank you for your letter of November 9th and enclosed draft copy of the Sidewalk Heritage Project. It is an interesting concept that deserves merit.

I look forward to receiving the final copy.

Best wishes for the New Year.

Your truly,

Joanne Flint
Councillor Ward 25

ti/ Coven.wpd

CBC ⬤ Radio-Canada

Canadian Broadcasting
Corporation
Société Radio-Canada

To: MAC COLIN

Fax Tel Nbr: (416) 934—1943

FROM: CBC Radio Toronto

- ------ Regional News
- ✓----- Metro Morning
- ------ Ontario Morning
- ------ Ontario Today
- ------ Here and Now
- ------ For Your Information

NUMBER OF PAGES INCLUDING COVER SHEET------- 1

NOTES: REMINDER OF OUR
CONVERSATION RE
SIDEWALK HERITAGE

Initials------------- Time------------ Date-----------------

CBC Radio
205 Wellington St.W.,
Toronto, ON
M5V 3G7
FAX--------(416) 205-2729

KEEP ME INFORMED.
THANKS.

JOE SOLWAY

(TEL)
(416) 205-570

Millionaire TV Monopoly with Chuck Weir

I got to know Chuck Weir through Barbara. He is one of the finest persons I have ever met. He was an exceptional athlete in high school and university. At one stage in his life he was a coach in American football in France. For many years he was a writer on the well-known Canadian TV program *Front Page Challenge* and co-wrote and produced the long-running musical *Toronto, Toronto*.

I had the idea of adapting the game of Monopoly for TV. Monopoly has been popular among the young and old for generations and my family was no exception. This was the age of television so I thought, "Why not a TV program built around that game?"

Chuck was the go-to guy for help because he had written for TV programs. He loved the concept and we sat for hours kicking around ideas for how the show could be put together. Chuck wrote the script for the proposal and it was my job to sell it.

The only person I knew with even a remote connection to TV was Sumner Redstone, chairman of Viacom, which owned CBS. I wrote a letter to Sumner, knowing that he was a proud fellow graduate of Boston Latin School (class of 1934). I had seen him interviewed on *Charlie Rose*. When Charlie asked him how he first got started, he said, "I went to Boston Latin School and on to Harvard Law School. Harvard was like kindergarten play compared to Boston Latin." I knew he would respond to my letter and he did, but unfortunately he wasn't able to help.

My daughter Robin was a neighbour of Monty Hall's brother, who was kind enough to give me Monty's home telephone number. Monty had been king of the game shows on television for a long time. He told me I had made a mistake. I should be going to Hasbro, which owned the rights to Monopoly. That was a break because at Biway we had sold a lot of Hasbro's goods through Encore Sales.

My Biway connection helped me get through to Hasbro's CEO. Lo and behold, she told me that they were planning to do a TV program built around Monopoly and that Donald Trump's daughter had the rights to it. She said the Creative Artists Agency was in the process of picking a format.

I called the appropriate person at Creative Artists, who told me to submit our format. She had several others and would be picking the winner in the next few weeks.

Two weeks later she called. She thanked me for my efforts but said she had picked another format.

To this day a Monopoly show has never appeared on television. I learned a lot through this effort and felt it was still a great experience, particularly because it gave me the opportunity to get to know Chuck Weir and appreciate what a wonderful and talented person he was.

MILLIONAIRE TV MONOPOLY
Game Show Proposal

Mal Coven
C.W. Weir

Mal Coven
38 Avenue Road, Suite 514
Toronto, On. M5R 2G2
Canada
416 513 0101

C.W. Weir
181 Madison Avenue
Toronto, On. M5R 2S6
Canada
416 413 1613

MILLIONAIRE TV MONOPOLY

CONCEPT

MILLIONAIRE TV MONOPOLY is a one hour television game show where each week four contestants playing a specially *adapted-for-television* version of the world famous and popular game, MONOPOLY, vie for the opportunity to win more than a million dollars.

CAST

On set there are four regular cast members. The **HOST** keeps things moving, applies the rules, conducts quick interviews, challenges the Players, and involves the audience. The **BANKER** receives and pays out monies, collects rents, and settles any financial disputes that arise. **TWO ARMED PINKERTON GUARDS** protect the Banker.

SETTING

The game is played before a live audience who, along with the viewers at home, follow the action on a huge classic MONOPLY BOARD projected on one wall of the set. Along with this MAIN BOARD, a digital CLOCK keeps a running time of the actual play, and four SCORECARDS keep a running total of each Player's assets and cash.

There is a platform on which the contestants stand looking at the board, and a special "gaming table" in front of them where they roll the dice during play. The Host controls the pace of the game and calls out the numbers on the dice. The Host handles the dice between throws, taking the moment to relate to the Players.

To one side, but in reach of the Players, is a secure steel cage with a door that can be locked, and an opening through which transactions can be conducted. This is the Banker's position.

Beside the cage there is a specially crafted MONOPOLY SLOT MACHINE.

CONTESTANTS

Each game pits four pre-selected Players against each other. They are planted in the audience until the Host calls them out onto the set, and they play all aspects of the game in the order in which they appear on set.

OPENING

To theme music and applause, the Host appears on stage, interacts with the audience and sets the scene for the game to come. He introduces the Banker who arrives hand-cuffed to a steel strongbox and accompanied by two armed Pinkerton guards. The guards open the steel cage, lock the Banker inside, and take up positions on either side of the cage. Once secure, the Banker opens the strongbox and reveals TWO MILLION DOLLARS IN REAL CASH to the audience and the viewers at home.

The Host calls the Players out of the audience one by one, and each Player approaches the cage and receives $15,000 in cash from the Banker. The money is in $100, $500, and $1000 bills. As each receives the money, the total flashes up on the Scorecards.

Now, armed with their cash, the Players take their place in front of the slot machine.

DIVISION OF PROPERTIES

There are twenty-eight properties on the MONOPOLY Board, including four Railroads and two Utilities. These six are held by the Bank. The other twenty-two properties, along with four Jokers, are configured on the wheels of the slot machine. (The Jokers' sole purpose is to influence the odds on the wheels. They have no value.) Each Player, in turn, spins the wheels, and buys the properties that show up from the Bank. They do this, in order, twice. If a Player draws three Jokers, they get an extra try at the machine. If a Player comes up with a property already claimed by another Player, they can buy the other two (or one, as the case may be, or, conceivably, none!). Any properties unclaimed or unselected after each player has had two chances at the machine belong to the Bank. Those properties are unavailable to the Players except under certain circumstances. In the meantime the Bank charges rents for Players that land on all Bank properties, Railroads and Utilities.

As the Players buy the properties that come up on the wheels, their properties (assets) are identified on the MAIN BOARD, and their Scorecards keeps track of the cash value of those assets and indicates remaining cash.

TRADES AND DEALS
After the Distribution of Properties, the Players are given a short period to assess the board and to trade and/or buy properties from each other, the object being to establish a monopoly block -- or to prevent one! The Players can appeal to the audience for advice on trades.

THE GAME
The Host invites the players to choose a TOKEN (a racehorse, sports car, power boat etc) to represent them on the MAIN BOARD, readies the Players and starts the clock.

The game will end when twenty minutes of playing time has elapsed, or one of the players goes bankrupt.

Each Player in turn throws the dice and pays rent to or collects rent from the owners of the properties on which they land, the game evolving much as the regular board game. If a Player throws a double, they get another throw (after settling up his debt, if any), but a third double in a row sends them to JAIL.

In this TV version of Monopoly no houses or hotels are built, but players who fall on the Community Chest and Chance Squares are rewarded and fined as in the original game. Salted among the cards are options to buy Bank owned properties (except for Railroads or Utilities), or prizes that force the Player to make choices: for example, to take a prize (such as an all expenses paid vacation) but pay for it by losing a turn with the dice.

If, during the course of the game, a Player does not have enough cash to pay rent, he may return one of his properties to the Bank for half its face value. BUT other Players, if they so desire, may offer more than the Bank, bidding for the property in a spontaneous AUCTION. Such an auction is clocked as playing time by the Host.

Players are encouraged to build monopolies because RENTS DOUBLE for those who land on properties that are part of a monopoly.

A Player is BANKRUPT when they do not have a combination of enough cash and assets to meet their obligations. A bankrupt Player turns in all cash and assets he has left to the bank before leaving with a consolation prize.

At any time during the course of the game, as long as he has the dice in his hand, the Host may interact with the Players, do short interviews, pose questions on strategy, and involve the audience.

TAKE IT OR LEAVE IT
Once one of the Players has passed GO, six of the squares on the board light up. These special MARKER squares, randomly scattered over the board, show six CASH PRIZES of $1000, $5000,

$10,000, $50,000 and $100,000 also in random order. Once a Player has passed GO and they land on one of these special squares, they may either pick up the MARKER or forego it in favor of a chance at one of the other more valuable MARKERS farther along the board. Take it or leave it! A Player may not pick up a MARKER (even if he lands on a marked square) until he has passed GO once. No Player may hold more than one MARKER. Once a Player has picked up a MARKER he may not trade it for another even if he lands on another marked square.

BUT, in order to cash in the MARKER, the Player has to WIN THE GAME.

THE FINALE

After one of the Players has gone bankrupt or after twenty minutes of playing time has elapsed, the Player who has accrued the most value in combined assets and cash is declared the WINNER. All the Players keep whatever cash they have left, and the value of their properties (assets) as indicated on their Scorecards is paid in cash on the spot by the Banker. Any MARKERS the three losers may have picked up are void.

The Winner is paid his accrued value. Family members and/or friends join the Winner on stage for a celebration.

THEN, if the WINNING PLAYER has a MARKER, he is invited to take either the value of the MARKER, or to wager it against the BANK on a throw of the dice. If he chooses the wager, he will be paid TEN TIMES THE VALUE OF THE MARKER, unless he throws a two or a twelve -- "Snake eyes" or "Boxcars" -- and the MARKER is valueless.

The Host holds out the dice.

After consulting with friends, family and the audience, the Winner declares his choice and either takes the value of the MARKER in cash, or he takes the dice from the Host. If he takes the dice, ten times the value of the MARKER rides on his throw!

RUNNING TIME

The running time of a Network television show is approximately 42 minutes. MILLIONAIRE TV MONOPOLY -- with three minutes of set-up, twenty minutes of actual game time and all the intros and extros -- can conceivably stretch to fill an hour, or, in the case of bankruptcy, end at any time within the hour.

If a game times out to the exact hour, next week's game starts out as outlined in the **OPENING** above. In the event of an early bankruptcy, a new game begins with the Banker and Guards retiring while four new Players are assembled. The entourage returns, is locked up, and the process begins -- the handing out of the cash, the slot machine distribution of property and the game until that episode's time runs out.

In the event of a hold-over game, the following week's show begins with the Players in place, the MAIN MONOPOLY BOARD reflecting their properties and the Scorecard their assets and cash to date. The Banker and Guards appear, the money secured, and the game proceeds from that point on.

THE GREEN MONSTER

Growing up in Boston as a fan of the Red Sox, I was familiar with the team's many stars from Lefty Grove and Jimmy Foxx in the late 1930s and early 1940s to Ted Williams and Dom DiMaggio in the late 1940s and early 1950s. They were my heroes.

Green Monster is the name that has been given to the left-field wall at Fenway Park, where they play. It is 250 feet high and difficult to hit over. If a batter hits the ball well enough to be a homer in another park, in Fenway it hits the wall, usually going for a double or a single depending on how quickly the left fielder gets the carom off the wall.

For most of his career in left field, Ted Williams was adept at playing the carom off the wall and many times threw out a batter who was trying to stretch a single into a double. Between batters Ted also carried on a conversation with the score keeper, who posted results of the plays manually. The scoreboard was at the base of the Green Monster.

Even in this modern era the scoreboard is still operated manually to keep intact some of the traditions of the oldest ball park in the major leagues. One change they did make was replacing the netting with additional seats, which were needed because Fenway Park was always filled to capacity.

Once when I was in the tourist section of Ottawa I saw several cartoonists drawing caricatures of passersby. That gave me the idea I needed. I would turn the Green Monster into a character. I approached one fellow and hired him to do a few renditions of a green monster. I received them within a few weeks. Two were really good. I picked one and armed myself with it and a list of items that I thought would be appropriate for the character.

To get to the right people is always difficult when they don't know you, which was the case this time with the Red Sox. I did know the marketing person for the Blue Jays and asked him to make a call to his counterpart with the Red Sox. He did and I went to see him.

This man said he liked the idea and would approach upper management with it. He did but the idea was rejected. At the time the owner was Jean Yawkey, widow of the late Tom Yawkey. She was well into her eighties and I assume she did not comprehend what a great marketing tool a Green Monster character would be. I was disappointed, of course, but as an entrepreneur you have to accept defeat and go on to another idea, determined to make it work.

Many years later the team was sold and the new management did just what I had proposed, and very successfully, too. I was happy to know that the idea was as sound as I thought it was.

The Green Monster at Fenway Park.

FREE
CATALOGS!

PLEASE PRESENT
AT CHECKOUT -
NO CHARGE

2 PER PERSON

BLOW-UP OF
CATALOG
COVER

Marketplace for Catalogues

I have always been a great fan of specialty catalogues. Poring over them, whether they are from L.L. Bean, Lands' End, or Hammacher Schlemmer, is always a pleasure.

I knew how expensive it is to mail these catalogues and I came up with the idea of distributing them through bookstores like Barnes & Noble, Borders, and, in Canada, Indigo. Books were their business but they did carry magazines, too.

My idea was to display various high-profile catalogues in the stores. I was sure the companies had a customer base similar to those who frequent bookstores. Here was a chance to expose potential customers to the catalogues. The catalogue houses would be happy to have them distributed through prestigious bookstores to customers who knew their names but more than likely had not bought from them.

I had some computerized drawings made showing how the catalogues could be displayed. We drew a typical hexagonal fixture that both Barnes & Noble and Indigo used, with the catalogues stacked on both the table and a step-up riser. My concept was that they would be given away free or sold for a nominal amount of 25¢, probably the latter to make sure they went through to the cashier.

I knew that each catalogue was numbered because when you call in to purchase merchandise, the operator always asks for the catalogue number.

The plan was for the bookstore to receive a commission of 7% from all sales emanating from the catalogues bought or obtained in their store. Our projections showed a net profit from the small hexagonal fixture of $30,000, a lot of money when multiplied, for example, by 600 stores, which was the number of stores in the Barnes & Noble chain. Included in my projection was the cost of rent and the people servicing the display.

So, with the proposed marketplace for catalogues in hand, I approached knowledgeable retailers for an opinion.

My first call was to Wayne Sales, CEO of Canadian Tire. I had dealt with Wayne previously and he was kind enough to spend over an hour with me making some suggestions. In general he thought the plan was sound.

I called Tom Stemberg, CEO of Staples. I knew him, having met with him several times about bringing Staples to Canada. In fact, I had done a survey of the Canadian market for him. However, the board of directors turned down any Canadian outlets to be opened at this stage of their expansion because they still had ample room to grow in the U.S. They did come to Canada quite a few years later and with great success. Now he gave me some suggestions for the catalogue project. He thought it was worthwhile.

I then decided to approach Heather Reisman, CEO of Indigo, a book chain similar to Barnes & Noble, not to sell it to her but for her opinion. In many ways Indigo did the same thing as Barnes & Noble, only better.

I wanted to introduce myself to Heather because she had rented a suite in my building at 38 Avenue Road while her home was being renovated. I had made a practice in retirement of meeting important people in the retail industry and she was certainly that. I asked a dear friend of mine at the time, Maxine Cooper, to bake something that I could leave with the concierge for Heather as a welcome. I knew Maxine not only as a first-class mother but also as a wonderful baker. She obliged by baking mandelbrot, which she packaged in an elegant basket to be left with the concierge.

I received a thank-you note from Heather a week later. On the following day two books were delivered to me. I thought that was very kind of her, although one book was on aging by Kirk Douglas. I didn't take this personally because she had never seen me before.

With that background I delivered a copy of my project with a note telling her it was for Barnes & Noble and asking her opinion as to its viability. Heather's people did not give me the positive response I was looking for.

Unfortunately, despite my determination I could not get in front of the proper person at Barnes & Noble. I put my proposal in the mail as they suggested but knew it probably would never be read. I did receive a letter from Borders with what I thought was a reasonable response. They thought it had merit but said they were not prepared to undertake it at that time. (They have since gone bankrupt.)

Later, during the recession of 2009, business was poor, particularly for book retailers, who faced an erosion of their store business and were looking for alternative merchandising avenues. I tried my idea again with no success. To this day I believe it is workable.

DAROB LTD.

MAL COVEN, PRESIDENT

38 AVENUE ROAD, SUITE 514
TORONTO, ONTARIO, CANADA M5R 2G2
TEL: (416) 513-0101
FAX: (416) 934-1943

AN ORIGINAL CONCEPT

CATALOGUE MARKETPLACE LTD.

A PROFIT CENTRE

Catalogue Marketplace is an original concept retailing high profile brand name catalogues in book superstores. It is the first time catalogues have been arranged in this way, creating a marketplace.

This proposal is designed particularly for Barnes & Noble but it will fit easily into any book super store. I believe my concept is sound. A few of the numbers I have taken an educated guess at but I don't think I can be off enough to scuttle the bottom line.

As you read further you will see:

A. The net income is very substantial
B. The ongoing expenses are small
C. The initial expenses are small
D. The total investment is small.

It should be tested in one store and my figures are based on that premise for a year.

It takes approximately 30 sq.ft. (one of your octagonal fixtures) only.

ALL ASSUMPTIONS ARE BASED ON THE PREMISE THAT CONSUMERS LIKE TO BROWSE NAME BRAND CATALOGUES AS THEY DO BOOKS AND OTHER PERIODICALS THAT PARALLEL THEIR INTEREST.

Page 1 of 6

MAL COVEN

<u>**PERSONAL & CONFIDENTIAL**</u>

Steven Riggio   April 26, 2005
Vice Chairman & CEO
Barnes & Noble Inc.
122 Fifth Avenue
New York, NY 10011 USA

Dear Steven:

I appreciate your quick response to my letter. I am enclosing my proposal for the "Marketplace For Catalogues" which you have agreed to treat in a confidential manner. It is an original concept. Please read the proposal in its entirety. It is the result of many hours of research and consultation with several retail CEOs whose work I admire.

I think my numbers are reasonable and in some cases very conservative. But as they say, "The proof is in the pudding." Only 30 square feet in a test store for a year will tell the story. If we can provide the catalogue sales I have projected, others will be standing in line to join in.

I am also enclosing six LL Bean catalogues (free, of course) in case you are not aware of the specialized explosion in the number of catalogues being mailed by my "Big Ten." Simultaneously, they have 25-30 alive and running. This trend towards specialization represents a big advantage to my proposal.

Brick and mortar still represent 75% of the business. The catalogues are a sophisticated representation to allure one to buy in the safety of one's home.

To clarify a few things: I will do all of the preliminary work before you have to make a final decision. That means basically getting an agreement with the "Big Ten" in writing as outlined in the proposal.

..2/

38 AVENUE ROAD, SUITE 514
TORONTO, ONTARIO, CANADA M5R 2G2
TEL: (416) 513-0101
FAX: (416) 934-1943

The only thing I would like from Barnes & Noble is a LETTER OF INTENT after the 4-6 months I estimate it will take me to get the Big Ten on board. Only then do you have to make your final decision on the 30 square feet in a typical 25,000 sq.ft. Barnes & Noble store. Until that time I am the only one investing time and money before we start the test store.

In conclusion, Stephen, "Catalogue Marketplace" is a pioneering work. The pioneering book supermart concept of your dad changed the book distribution industry. Pioneering "Catalogue Marketplace" has the potential to change distribution patterns.

The only difference is in this case you need not commit resources until you see how it works. Your father did not have this luxury.

In "Catalogue Marketplace" you have no downside but huge upside potential.

Sincerely,

Mal Coven

Borders Group, Inc.
100 Phoenix Drive
Ann Arbor
Michigan 48108-2202
t: 734 477 1100

BORDERS
GROUP

May 25, 2005

Mal Coven
Darob LTD.
38 Avenue Road, Suite 514
Toronto, Canada M5R 2G2

Subject: Catalogue Marketplace

Dear Mr. Coven:

Thank you for your interest in Borders Group. At the request of Borders senior
management I have reviewed and considered your proposal for the Catalogue
Marketplace concept in Borders Stores.

Although the concept is interesting and original, Borders is not interested at this time.
The proposal is not aligned with our new product and store initiatives that will reinforce
Borders as the preferred place to shop for book lovers. We will keep your proposal on
file and contact you again if we feel our interests are better aligned in the future.

Borders wishes you and your company the best.

Sincerely,

Jon Kinsey
Sr. Manager - Corporate Strategy & Business Development
Borders Group Inc.

Tilley

Tilley Hats and the finest travel clothing in the world™

Fax: (416) 934-1943

April 29, 2005

Mr. Mal Coven
DAROB LTD.
38 Avenue Road, Suite 514
Toronto, Ontario
M5R 2G2

Dear Mr. Coven:

Re: Marketplace For Catalogues

Tilley Endurables is interested in pursuing your proposed distribution channel for our catalogues.

As material is available please send me details on:
- Time period for initial test
- Cost for program – distribution and percentage of sales
- Name of book store(s) where test will be done and area of USA
- Number of catalogue companies participating
- Amount of shelf space each catalogue company secures
- Names of participating catalogue companies

Yours very truly,

MC Shanahan
President & CEO

Tilley Endurables, Inc., 900 Don Mills Road, Toronto, Ontario, M3C 1V6
Telephone (416) 441-6141 • Fax (416) 444-3860 • www.Tilley.com

L.L.Bean INC.
FREEPORT, MAINE 04033
Outdoor Sporting Specialties
TEL. (207) 865-4761

April 18, 2005

Mal Coven
DAROB LTD.
38 Avenue Rd, Suite 514
Toronto, Ontario
M5R 2G2 Canada

Dear Mal Coven:

I would like to "thank you" for contacting L.L.Bean regarding establishing a business relationship with *DAROB LTD*.

I have reviewed your letter forwarded to me from Chris McCormick and while your proposal is a viable marketing opportunity; we have decided not to pursue your offer at this time. I will retain your email on file; and if we should reconsider our decision at a later date, I will be sure to contact you.

Again thank you for contacting L.L.Bean Inc.

Sincerely,

Steve Fuller
Sr Vice President
Corporate Marketing

An Outdoor Tradition Since 1912

MAL COVEN

Wayne Sales
President & CEO
Canadian Tire Corporation
2180 Yonge Street
PO Box 770, Station K
Toronto, Ontario
M4P 2V8

April 1, 2005

Dear Wayne:

Thank you so much for giving me an hour of your time today and going through my proposal in the detailed manner that you did. You really made my day (plus) with your opinion and your encouragement.

You told me about your dreams, the one in particular in Canada. I think (1) it is a very good plan; (2) it's do-able; and (3) more importantly, you're the only one that could do it. No question in my mind.

At this point in your life it's not a matter of money whatever you decide to do. You met the Canadian Tire challenge and we see the results. The other is a new challenge. Your idea, as you outlined it to me, is very sound. One always considers the downside and the upside in matters like this. The downside is nil. If you don't succeed (and you will) nobody can think badly of you and you will go onto something else. What is the upside? It's taking the <u>oldest company in North America</u> currently on life support and turning it around. If there was a retail history book you would be in it with that accomplishment.

Either way, good luck and good health.

Sincerely,

ber, I'm old enough to be your father. Nike says 'Do it.' Me too.

38 AVENUE ROAD, SUITE 514
TORONTO, ONTARIO, M5R 2G2
TEL· (416) 513-0101
FAX. (416) 934-1943

MAL COVEN

November 22, 2010

PERSONAL & CONFIDENTIAL

Heather Reisman
CEO
Indigo/Chapters
468 King Street West
Toronto, Ontario M5B 1L8

Dear Heather:

To reintroduce myself, I am one of the founders of the BiWay stores. You were a neighbour of mine at 38 Avenue Road for about a year. You may not remember but I sent you a basket of homemade *mandelbrot* as a welcome. You were kind enough to send me in return two books, one of which was by Kirk Douglas on growing old. I did not take that personally as you had never met me in person.

My reputation at BiWay and in part one of the reasons for its success was thinking out of the box, something I have continued to do in my numerous projects since retiring from BiWay. It is one such suggestion I am giving to you free of charge, no strings attached.

It's quite obvious to anyone who follows retailing as I have continued to do that book retailers like yourself need to add a new dimension to your bricks and mortar stores. Your expansion of box games and gifts does that, I know, with great success.

I really want to tell you about my original concept that can add much to your bottom line without inventory and minimal floor space (one hexagonal fixture).

I want to put you in the clothing business in a unique way without inventory. You or I would solicit six or eight high-profile catalogues, mostly American, the likes of LL Bean and J. Crew, to name two. Their catalogues would be stacked on the 35 sq. ft. hexagonal table and step-up to be sold at nominal cost, 25 cents. These US catalogue houses are dying to make major in-roads to Canada. They are making special offers to Canadians you see by the enclosed catalogues.

..2/

38 Avenue Road, Suite 514
Toronto, Ontario, Canada M5R 2G2
Tel: (416) 513-0101
Fax: (416) 934-1943
malcoven@rogers.com

As you may know, every catalogue is numbered. When you call to buy something the first question they ask for is the number assigned to the catalogue. When your customer brings a catalogue to your check-out for payment, that catalogue number would have to be captured by you. From then on you would be entitled to a commission of around 8% on any merchandise sold out of that catalogue. Whatever the percentage agreed upon, it would be small compared to introducing the catalogue house to a new customer. In addition, you could charge them a nominal amount for distribution (25 cents). This compared to one dollar or more through the mail. I think they would recognize your customer profile and theirs are very similar.

I did a run-through on some of the numbers a few years ago which I am updating in this letter. You could do the same knowing your customer count. In my original assumption one of every five customers would pick up at least one catalogue (only two per person) and something like 10% would actually buy.

Advantages to you:

1. Income from distribution.
2. Income from commission.
3. Income from sale.

Advantage to catalogue house:

1. Many new customers exposed to catalogue though they know the names but have never seen the catalogue.

I am enclosing a copy I did some years ago that shows how I pictured the set-up. The numbers may not be appropriate for you today. But the bottom line is, the profit potential is tremendous. Equally important is that this island can be a great traffic builder as your customer will be coming to see and buy as the subsequent catalogues come out.

I would appreciate it if you would advise me on your thoughts on this 'marketplace for catalogues'.

Sincerely,

Mal Coven

P.S. You see by the Marketplace enclosure this was originally put together for Barnes & Noble. I found it impossible to reach Mr. Rossi with it. I hope I have more success with you.

P.P.S. I would be happy to assist you in contacting the retailers involved as I know some of them personally.

Enclosures

The Pinky Puppet

Sometime around 2005 Barb and I were in New York staying at the Algonquin Hotel on 44th Street. We had relocated there from the Plaza Hotel and the Regency because it was within walking distance of the theatre district. The hotel is well known because many famous writers of the 1920s and 1930s met and stayed there. Among them were Dorothy Parker and Robert Benchley. We received a special rate because Barbara had done some writing years before.

One morning at the corner of 44th and 6th Avenue I saw a fellow behind a stand selling animal finger puppets for $2 each. I always prided myself on being able to spot a good item and to me this looked like a winner. I asked the fellow a leading question.

"You don't sell many of these, I bet, not more than 10 or 12 a day?"

"How about 400 a day?" he said.

I was right. I asked him where he got them and he said his boss brought them in from Bolivia.

I invited his boss up to our hotel suite and told him I wanted a distributor's price to distribute them exclusively in Canada. He quoted me a price of 75¢ with the stipulation that I had to buy 5,000 puppets. I agreed, went to the bank machine, withdrew the money, and bought a suitcase to put them in. He had told me that they were hand-knitted by families in their homes, collected by his wife, and shipped to him in New York. Initially, we took only 2,500 – that's all we could get into the suitcase – but eventually we bought over 9,000.

The next step was to brand it and make an appropriate display stand. I went to the Yellow Pages (this was before I was computer literate). The first call I made was greeted with, "Mr. Coven, I know who you are – come on over." Don't think that didn't make me feel pretty good. The company not only designed and made a stand but also developed my character "Pinky" for Pinky Puppets.

I made a promotional business card and gave it to people with a free puppet. The card suggested they buy others at locations that were listed. The stand, filled with an assortment of 24 Pinky Puppets, sold well..

Eventually I decided to go to Sick Kids Hospital in Toronto with six containers of puppets to be distributed to the children, one container for each floor plus one for the emergency room. The hospital loved my idea. Eventually I hoped to sell them to the hospital gift shop, knowing it would be a good gift for visitors to buy for young patients. The two little old ladies who ran the shop turned me down without wanting to see the puppets or even asking the price.

Not too long after this I decided to donate the last 2,000 to the hospital. I kept 1,000 for myself to give away to children on my travels. I did this over many months whenever I came across little children with their parents. It always delighted me to see the happy look on their faces.

Besides giving them away in Toronto, I gave them to kids wherever Barb and I travelled, from Europe to Asia, Russia to Vietnam, France to China, and Singapore to Hong Kong, and of course the U.S. and other parts of Canada.

To this day in Toronto ladies have come up to me to thank me and tell me their children are still enjoying their Pinky Puppets.

Hand Knit Pinky Puppets

YOU NOW HAVE A GIFT FROM Pinky

You can find many more of his handmade puppet friends in:

- Chapters/Indigo
- The Toy Shop
- Mable's Fable
- Flying Dragon

The Pinky Puppets
were OK with these
Oklahomans.

Jon Patton

1120 North Duck Street, Suite B   Stillwater, Oklahoma 74075   (405) 372-3900 FAX (405) 743-8340

2-8-06

Mal —

    All is well in Stillwater America. Especially with your note and pictures from the trip.

    The finger puppets were a hit with the grandkids Daxton and Dylan. They send their thanks.

    Please give Barbara our best wishes and our sincere appreciation to you for thinking of us. Great trip!

               Jon : Nancy

Dear Mr. Mal Coven,

46.920.1499

With sincere gratitude
for your kindness.

We recieved your gift of
beautifully knitted hand puppets.
The baby, Cassius, absolutely
loves them. I meant to send you
an email, but there wasn't an address
on the bussiness card. However, we
love your gift. My favourite is the
monkey, with the mommy & baby. The
baby loves the duck. Thanks again.
♡ Baby Cassius, Daddy Chris,
Big Brother Ty & me, Marlena;

Elianne Neuman

Dear Mr. Coven,

Thank you very much for the very *cute* *puppets*! I really appreciate them and hope to enjoy and play with them. I wish you success on your new business.

Thank you very much.

Sincerely,
Elianne.

83 Glen Park Ave.
Toronto, ON
M6B 2C3
416-781-2344

PHILIP M. EPSTEIN
393 UNIVERSITY AVENUE, SUITE 2200
TORONTO, ONTARIO M5G 1E6

April 10, 2006

Dear Mal,

My grandchildren loved the finger puppets. I think they will be a great item and I wish you well with this new endeavour. Thank you for thinking of me and my grand kids.

Kindest regards,
Sincerely

ORDER SONS OF ITALY
IN AMERICA

ITALIAN AMERICAN BASEBALL HEROES

ITALIAN BASEBALL CARDS

I met Herbert Klein on a visit to the Jewish Historical Society building in New York City. The society documents all things Jewish for their archives. In their building on 16th Street they also have a fine Jewish museum. Herb was a volunteer who had just completed a project that he had developed for them, Jewish Baseball Cards. His marketing plan raised close to $2 million for the society. Barbara and I spent some time with Herb and his wife Gloria on subsequent trips.

At some point I suggested we do a similar project for The Sons of Italy, a prominent not-for-profit Italian organization that was well known for its charitable work. Herb had the experience, contacts, and expertise to duplicate what he had done for the society. So was born our project One Hundred Italian Baseball Heroes. Altogether there were over 200 to choose from. I knew the obvious ones. We left the balance of the choices to the National Italian American Sports Hall of Fame and others.

The executive at Sons of Italy were very enthusiastic about the project and invited us to some of their functions. One in particular was in Washington, DC, where we sat with or met many famous Italian celebrities. I had conversations of some length with both Nancy Sinatra and Gina Lollobrigida. They were both beautiful and charming. Gina, I'm sure, was into her 80s and didn't look it. Nancy was much younger, probably in her late 50s. I gave each of them some of my Pinky Puppets and they responded by inviting me to visit them in California. I also met with Frankie Valli and Yogi Berra.

The end product was first rate. Each card had a portrait of the player and on the back side not only their statistics but also what they accomplished after baseball. We put a price of $50 for a donation on them, much less than the Jewish baseball cards, which were priced at $100 and up.

At this writing we have sold over 4,000 but still have a way to go. It seems the Italian communities are not as enthusiastic about their players as the Jewish communities are theirs.

"Take Me Out to the Ball Game" with Chuck Weir

From the time the Blue Jays played their first baseball game in 1977 I always felt that they were dumb to not let the fans sing "Take Me Out to the Ball Game." Baseball is a traditional game and that song, and the poem "Casey at the Bat," have always been part of that tradition.

I went to Chuck Weir and told him I was going to try to persuade the Blue Jays to sing "Take Me Out to the Ball Game" but thought it would be fun to customize it with an extra stanza for the fans to sing.

I could picture the bouncing ball on the giant screen showing the words to another stanza and the fans singing along. I wrote a couple of stanzas myself but Chuck's were much better. He had one that was outstanding, with the word butt to be replaced by the fans singing "kick some ass" because it rhymed. After Chuck suggested it, he thought better and put in the word "butt," even though we both knew the fans would likely say "kick some ass" instead.

I submitted my proposal to have fans sing both the original lyrics plus our lyrics and it was rejected. Years later I tried again by approaching Paul Godfrey, CEO of the Jays at the time, but nothing happened. Finally the Blue Jay hierarchy did decide to sing "Take Me Out to the Ball Game." Only recently I tried my lyrics out on Paul Beeston, who was again president of the Blue Jays, to no avail. I believe if Paul ever got to sing our version he would like it and maybe I would get the result I was looking for.

Here it is:

Here we are at the Jays game
Here we are having fun
"High five" with your neighbours and raise a glass
Just sit back while the Jays kick some … butt
For it's root, root, root for the Blue Jays
Their guys are swinging in vain
For it's one, two, three strikes – they're out!
At the old ball game.

LOLA'S CUPCAKERY

Barb and I were waiting for a late flight at the Miami airport to take us back to Toronto. The delay was close to two hours. We got chatting with a gentleman sitting opposite us named Don Kaplan. He had a doctoral degree in computers from Stanford and had had been involved in several ventures in the restaurant business. He had been a partner in Mr. Greenjeans, an exceptionally successful restaurant concept.

As we talked, Don said he had developed a concept built around cupcakes with his wife Lola. I knew about several successful independent cupcake stores in Toronto and New York. He thought his concept could be the start of a chain. Initially I dismissed his idea because I didn't feel cupcakes had the legs to become a chain even though there was catering income potential.

He went on to tell me that part of the concept had a coffee and ice cream component with original recipes combining cupcakes and ice cream. Some were cup shakes and cup sundaes, among others. That intrigued me. Although he had very little money, he did have a close friend who would back him for $150,000. He was looking to raise a total of $600,000.

Don had a presentation to show any potential investors. His wife, a graduate of a culinary school, had helped him develop the concept and would be very active in the venture. He felt that Florida would be the place to start, once he had the money in place, because success with ice cream requires a warm climate.

I invited some friends and former business acquaintances to come to a presentation in my home. His close friend Barry Sutton, who was supporting him, also took part in the presentation. Besides me three other investors decided to go along with the project. To be fair, most of them went along because of my enthusiasm for it.

Then a tragic occurrence: Don's friend and major backer died from a sudden heart attack.

Even though we were short on capital, I thought that the money we had raised was more than enough to get the ball rolling.

I had spent much time in Florida and was very familiar with the mall landscape in the southern part of the state. I agreed initially to help Don find a location for his concept. Simon is the major mall owner in Florida. I tracked down the executive who was in charge of leasing. Though he worked out of the west coast of Florida, he was in charge of leasing in the Boca Towne Center, which we thought would be great for a startup. So off we went to see him.

He loved our presentation and said he would find some space for us. Even though Simon did not do the leasing at the Aventura Mall, they did have a financial interest and had suggested we see them, too. They also liked the whole concept but their leasing agent said he would like to be second. These two malls are premier malls in south Florida and are always fully rented so asking us in was certainly a vote of confidence.

The space that they would make available was next to the Food Court in the Boca Town Center and next to Bloomingdale's. It was ideal for us. Don had negotiated a lease and was ready to sign when the Simon's head office stepped in. They were moving someone to that spot who needed additional space and we lost it.

This was a setback. Don looked for other sites. He combed the southeast coast and finally settled on a location on Las Olas Boulevard in Fort Lauderdale. I had been on that street a few years before and remembered it as a bustling tourist shopping area. I didn't know where on the street his new shop was until I came down to visit it. It was farther east of the area I pictured. I wondered about the location. By that point Don had rented a home and had started to do catering business even before the store was ready to be opened. This would not have been my way of doing things, but he was very enthusiastic about the location and as the CEO he was the one to make the decision.

His idea was to make the place unique. The rugs and décor were very expensive. A lot of the money was spent before the opening. Initially it was going to serve cupcakes, with coffee and ice cream recipes to follow.

I came to visit and saw that he had hired two bakers to make the cupcakes. He and his wife had instructed them how to bake the cupcakes because their formula was unique. At that point I knew the concept was in trouble. In a startup, the principals do the work themselves. There was no reason to hire people: Don and his wife were more than capable. The special order fixtures that housed the cupcakes were very expensive. The money ran out before the coffee and ice cream recipes even appeared. No more money was forthcoming from the investors so the concept was doomed.

Don and his wife disappeared, never to have be heard of again.

There are many successful cupcake shops to this day and they probably started with less than half of the money Don had raised. Unfortunately, his grandiose idea sunk him and Lola's Cupcakery.

The potential for a chain was there. Crumbs Bakery in New York went public in the spring of 2011 and will be duplicating its concept in major cities on the east coast.

20

PROJECTS WITH COMPANIES

Filene's Basement

I was planning a trip to Boston with George Hartman to see a Celtics game. Bob Wolff, a classmate of mine at Boston College and the sports agent of Larry Bird, among others, got us tickets, which were not easy to come by otherwise. Around that time I received the current copy of Boston College's alumni magazine. Boston College was a Jesuit school. Although it had some Jewish alumni, they were few at this time. One of them, Sam Gerson, was on the cover of this issue of the magazine.

The article told of Sam's background, which was similar to mine. Like me, he was a graduate of both Boston Latin School and the Filene's executive training program. He had gone on to be president of The Gap and had returned to Filene's as CEO of its famous basement store. I felt I had to meet him and called him at his office. He knew my name as a Filene's alumnus and agreed to meet George and me for breakfast at the Four Seasons.

Even though he was pressed for time, he spent two hours with us. George was a retail analyst for a major brokerage house and was particularly interested in the fact that Sam was trying to buy the Filene's Basement store, which at the time was up for sale.

Filene's Basement had been bought by Canada's Robert Campeau as part of Federated Department Stores. Campeau had to sell the main Filene's store and Filene's Basement store downtown because he now also owned a large Jordan Marsh store right across from it. Sam had a partner in Thomas Lee, a well-known takeover artist, and the backing of Michael Milken, the junk bond king.

Sam and I agreed to get together with our wives on our next trip to Boston. Within two months Barb and I were having dinner in our hotel in Positano on the Amalfi coast of Italy. We started to chat with the couple at the next table, Beth and Josh Friedman, who were honeymooning. Coincidentally, Josh was senior vice president of Drexel Burnham, where Michael Milken ran the junk bond division. When I told Josh about my meeting with Sam Gerson he said, "That was my deal" and in fact Sam Gerson and his group had bought Filene's Basement.

I was not knowledgeable about these types of financial transactions so I asked Josh how this one worked. He said six or eight people participated in buying the $50 million worth of junk bonds. The interest on the bonds was 12% and each participant also received shares in Filene's Basement.

Because of my long history with Filene's and my faith in Sam Gerson as a superb merchandiser, I asked Josh if I could participate with about $250,000. He said that was not possible because the participants were buying $6 million or $8 million of the bonds – only investors in that league could participate.

It was the shares I really wanted; I considered the investment from the bonds secondary.

Three days later, just before our departure, I asked Josh as a personal favour to see what he could do about letting me participate this time. He said he would try and he did. After signing reams of papers I sent a certified cheque for $250,000 to the Toronto Dominion Bank in New York. I was very happy with my investment.

However, three days later my cheque was returned to me with a letter saying it is illegal for Canadians to own unregistered U.S. bonds.

I continued to keep in touch with Sam on subsequent trips to Boston. I toured the stores with him and marvelled at his hands-on approach, watching him delve into the stock room directing goods to be put on the floor. He made a trip to Toronto and I toured the main stores with him. He felt they were ten years behind the U.S. The only exceptions were the specialty shops Ira Berg and Holt Renfrew, which he liked.

BOSTON COLLEGE
CHESTNUT HILL, MASSACHUSETTS 02167

August 17, 1988

Samuel J. Gerson
Chairman and Chief Executive Officer
Filene's Basement Stores
40 Walnut Street
Wellesley, MA 02181

Dear Sam:

This is a response to your inquiry regarding Peter Mahovlich's son and his potential interest in playing hockey here at Boston College. I spoke to Bill Flynn and Len Ceglarski, head hockey coach, as well as to representatives in the Admissions Office.

Peter's son should write a short note immediately to:

> Leonard S. Ceglarski
> Head Hockey Coach
> Flynn Recreational Complex
> Boston College
> Chestnut Hill, MA 02167

stating his interest in Boston College and noting his high school hockey experience. He should include a telephone number so that Len and/or his colleagues can make arrangements to see him play during the coming season. Len would welcome a call at (617) 552-3028.

Concurrent to the above, the son should apply to the Admissions Office using an international student form. He can request this material by calling or writing to:

> Richard E. Escobar
> Program Director, Minority and International Students
> Undergraduate Admissions
> Lyons Hall 120
> Boston College
> Chestnut Hill, MA 02167
> (617) 552-4944

A completed application with a request for a campus interview date should be sent to Admissions as soon as possible.

Not too long after this, Michael Milken and the Drexel Burnham junk bond division were being investigated and it seemed they might be charged for illegal practices.

In spite of that, things were going well at Filene's Basement and Sam wanted to buy back the outstanding shares that the brokerage house owned at $11. This was not a public company and there was not a normal market for the shares.

I decided to try buying some of those shares myself. I called Jefferies, one of the brokerage companies that had participated. An executive told me he had 5,000 shares but wanted $18 for them. I knew he was trying to make a score on me because I knew that Sam wanted to pay $11. Nevertheless, I bought the shares. I had faith in Sam Gerson and the future of Filene's Basement.

I received a call from another broker who said he had 10,000 shares to sell at $18. The word was out that there was a live one out there. I declined, because I probably would have bought only 2,000 shares initially and I believed they wouldn't be interested in under 5,000 shares.

Six months or so passed and I received a call from my broker, Neil Nisker, telling me that Filene's had gone public, opening at $14 and quickly rising to $18, the exact price I had paid. I had neither gained nor lost and was happy with my position.

Then it happened. I received another call from Neil, this time to tell me there were 15,000 shares in my account because the shares had been split three-for-one before going public. Now I owned 15,000 shares at $6. The stock continued to rise. When it reached $24 I decided to sell most of them. Even though I had faith in Sam, I also had faith in the axiom, "Don't be greedy."

Of course as the stock continued to rise, reaching $34, I wondered how stupid I could be to sell so early.

Not long after, Filene's Basement ran into problems, some foreseen, some not. A number of their retail suppliers were opening their own outlet stores and it hurt Filene's. The value of the shares had plummeted to $14 when I sold my last 1,500 shares. It continued to fall and the company filed for bankruptcy. I had made a good profit but I was proud of the fact that I had faith in the operation and was determined to do everything I could to participate.

Sadly, Sam Gerson passed away a few years later, only in his early 60s.

MAJESTIC ELECTRONICS

It was the 1990s. I had just retired from Biway and was anxious to find a new place to hang my hat.

Jack Steckel, who was doing the advertising for Majestic Electronics, approached me to invest in that firm, a public company trading on the TSX. Jack wanted to buy the company. He had done their advertising for some time and had an intimate knowledge of its inner workings. The major shareholder wanted out.

He showed me a letter from investor Jack Stupp of Consumers Distributing, in which he committed himself to investing $600,000 if he could get an office and a secretary. I thought it might be a good place for me even though I knew nothing of the electronics business. I told Steckel I would invest $200,000 and all I wanted was an office, not a secretary. I never had a secretary in 28 years at Biway so I certainly didn't need one now. Two other businessmen invested $200,000 each. Steckel committed to $600,000.

We bought Majestic, which at the time was trading on the TSX at 55¢ a share, the price we paid the majority owner. Steckel became the CEO in the early 1990s and embarked on an advertising campaign featuring Stupp and myself in photos to show that Majestic had new people guiding them who had experience at Consumers and Biway and had a new plan for success.

The business improved as did the stock, which rose from 55¢ to $2.75. Not long after this, Neil Nisker was able to raise $7 million in a stock offering at $2.50, just below the current price of the stock exchange market, which was $2.75. One of the board members wanted to buy additional shares at $2.50 but because it sold out immediately he was shut out. Nisker told me he wanted to buy an additional 125,000 shares at the $2.50 price. I told Neil I would sell him 100,000 shares from my holdings. This was allowable; we were both insiders and could sell to each other but not to outsiders.

Things were going well and it looked as if the company was actually going to show a profit for the first time. We convened a meeting at the House of Chan restaurant on Eglinton Avenue. It was suggested during that meeting that we have the year-end meeting in Tucson at Canyon Ranch where Stupp had a home. My low-overhead Biway background and my sense of fairness to our shareholders told me this was not a good idea. A year-end meeting there would eat up a good portion of our profits. I took Steckel aside and said we should pay each member of the board $2,000 for their work and let everyone pay the balance of the costs of the trip themselves. He agreed to my suggestion.

I was not able to attend that meeting in Tucson some months later. I was told that we were in poor financial condition because the expansion had not worked out as planned. Business turned bad and we were short of cash. Subsequently, at a meeting with our lawyers at Fogler, Rubinoff, it was decided that we had no alternative but to declare bankruptcy.

I was fortunate because Eric Paul, who had left Biway, found some investors and bought the company. It went back on the exchange and I was able to sell my remaining shares at $.45. Lesson learned: It is better to be lucky than smart.

Saturday, August 24, 1991 **C3**

Majestic's boss to sell major stake to company seeking 65% of stock

By Bob Papoe
TORONTO STAR

Curtis Ramsauer, the head of Majestic Electronics Stores, is selling out and moving on.

Ramsauer, who owns almost 69 per cent of the retail electronics chain's shares, announced he has agreed to sell his stock to a numbered Ontario company.

Under the deal, which must still be approved at a special shareholders' meeting, 944890 Ontario Ltd. has agreed to buy 65 per cent of outstanding Majestic stock for 57 cents a share on or before Oct. 1.

Shareholders who take up the offer will receive a special dividend from Majestic of $1.71 a share.

A statement released by Majestic yesterday said that because the offer is for less than all of Majestic's outstanding shares, those tendered will be taken up and paid for on a pro rated basis, according to the number offered by each shareholder.

Ramsauer has agreed to make all his shares available to the takeover bid.

The Majestic statement said

Ramsauer, the company's founding shareholder and chief executive for 13 years, wishes to retire "from the day-to-day demands of running the business," but will continue to advise the new management on a part-time basis.

Ramsauer could not be reached for comment.

944890 Ontario Ltd. is owned by a group of investors including Jack Steckel, a Majestic board member for five years, Jack Stupp, founder of Consumers Distributing Ltd. and Mal Coven, a founder of Bi-Way

Stores.

The statement said Steckel is expected to be appointed president and chief executive of the company after the deal is completed. It said a fuller explanation of the new management's plans for the chain will be revealed at a special shareholders meeting on or before Oct. 1.

In December, 1989, a takeover deal for Majestic fell through when Roy-L Merchant Group Inc. and DCC Equities Ltd. withdrew a cash offer of $3.90 a share for the company's 5.2 million shares.

WE PUT OUR GOOD NAMES BEHIND EVERY PRODUCT WE SELL.

THAT'S OUR WAY OF DOING BUSINESS

On the box of most every electronic item available at Majestic you'll find a sticker with a toll-free telephone number.

That sticker is our way of showing that Majestic is the only place to shop for all your brand name consumer electronics, home and office equipment. We're the new executive management team. And over the years, we've introduced real value to the Canadian consumer.

Jack Stupp was the original founder of Consumers Distributing nearly 35 years ago. He was the first to discount national brands in Canada, creating a unique way for Canadians to save money. His idea was so successful, Consumers Distributing became a $1.5 billion business, with 400 stores across Canada and the United States. As Chairman of the Board, Mr. Stupp brings this expertise to Majestic.

Mal Coven was an original founder of Bi-Way. Bi-Way proved to Canadians that the cost of everyday needs could be brought down. Mal helped build Bi-Way into a giant chain with 250 stores across the country.

Jack Steckel, as head of a highly successful advertising agency, turned some of Canada's leading retail companies into household names. Together, we know the Canadian consumer. We know that today, more than ever, value, quality and price is important to you.

We know you want the widest possible selection and the lowest possible prices when you're shopping for a TV, VCR, camcorder, audio system, home computer or microwave. We know you want the dependability of brand names like Sony, Sanyo, Toshiba, Maxell, Pioneer, Canon, Panasonic, IBM, Epson and Aiwa. We know you expect expert help from knowledgeable sales people. For the last 20 years, that's exactly what Majestic has offered you. And today, we're prepared to back everything we say.

From now on, you've got our number!

PRIVATE & CONFIDENTIAL

March 30, 1992

Mr. Mal Coven
3100 South Ocean Blvd.
#504N
Palm Beach, Florida
33480

Dear Mr. Coven,

Enclosed please find an engagement letter between BBN James Capel Inc. and Majestic Electronic Stores Inc. for a $5-$7 million proposed financing. I have reviewed the letter with Jack Steckel and Jay Hennick and they have asked me to send a copy directly to you for your review prior to the board meeting scheduled for this Saturday.

As detailed in the engagement letter, BBN James Capel is prepared to underwrite the offering and will work with the Company's management during the next several weeks to determine the appropriate security being offered. Depending upon market conditions, the form of the security will likely be either Class B common shares or convertible debentures.

With respect to timing, we have already begun scheduling various investor meetings and have targeted a June 30 deadline to close the entire transaction.

Thank you for your attention and should you have any questions, please give me a call at (416) 947-2725.

Yours truly,

David G. Anderson
Senior Vice President
Corporate Finance

Encl.
DGA/gy

BBN James Capel Inc.

one financial place, 1 adelaide st. east, suite 2420, toronto, canada M5C 2V9
telephone (416) 947-2700, direct line montreal to toronto 871-9182
telex 065-24433, fax (416) 947-2730

CANADIAN TIRE AND MARK'S WORK WEARHOUSE

After leaving Biway in 1990 I wanted to connect in some way with another retailer. I had always been impressed with Mark's Work Wearhouse retail stores. I spent a lot of time with Mark Blumes, their CEO, going to a few of his stores with him. I was impressed with the great rapport he had with both managers and employees. I was also impressed with his private label business as well as the volume of sales he did with Levi's. (I marvelled that he could sell the same Levi's merchandise that we were selling at Biway at almost twice our price.)

The thing that most impressed me was something I had never seen or been exposed to before. Mark walked around the store with a computer and was able to keep track of his inventory in that store and others. He could transfer and make necessary adjustments very efficiently right on the spot. I compared this with our antiquated systems of taking stock lists in each store and sending them into the head office to distribute fill-ins from the warehouse or reorder additional merchandise.

I'm not selling Biway short because we had a great advantage: We always dealt in cases of 24, 36, or 48, not individual pieces the way he was. As I think back, even with my son David's urging it took me nearly 30 years to become somewhat computer literate.

In spite of the off-the-wall kind of guy Mark Blumes was, we got along very well. Shortly thereafter he needed to raise money to expand and I volunteered to help. I convened a meeting with a few retailers that I thought might be interested in investing in Mark's Work Wearhouse. In addition, I invited Alfred Tan, CEO of a large public importing company and a supplier of Biway. We were looking to raise $7 million and a few of those attending agreed to invest. Alfred Tan said he would take up the balance of the $7 million.

Mark's Work Wearhouse turned the deal down. Blumes was afraid they would be beholden to Alfred.

Sometime even before this I had met with the CEO of Canadian Tire, Dean Groussman, to see if he had any interest in investing in Mark's. His first reaction was

Mal Coven

August 9, 2000

Mr. Wayne Sales
President & CEO
Canadian Tire Corporation
2180 Yonge Street
Toronto, Ontario
M4S 2B9

PERSONAL & CONFIDENTIAL

Dear Wayne:

I want to take this opportunity to congratulate you on your new appointment. I was not at all surprised as I still have my ear tuned into the retail scene. In case you have forgotten, I am the co-founder of BiWay (1962-1990 – the good years) and, to further refresh your memory, we have had one meeting and a couple of telephone conversations.

In baseball, three strikes and you're out, but in retailing, when you think you have a good idea, you don't give up so fast (if you're me). This is true particularly when the timing gets better and you have added a new dimension to the plan.

The good idea is Mark's Work Wearhouse – revised (don't stop reading – hear me out). I have what I know are new exciting things to throw into the mix.

The street seems to think you need something to revitalize the stock price. That something could be Mark's Work Wearhouse Soft Goods department within your big box store. All the basics and key labels of Mark's Work Wearhouse. All working man's stuff. You have a similar customer base. I can close my eyes and picture the department. It would add a new dimension to Canadian Tire and help take you to a new level.

But there is more – much more.

I propose you have your selective private label merchandise in the 300-odd Mark's Work Wearhouse stores. Their big problem is adding store volume. This is what they need.

..2/

SUITE 514, THE PRINCE ARTHUR
38 AVENUE ROAD
TORONTO, ONTARIO
M5R 2G2

TEL: (416) 513-0101
FAX: (416) 934-1943

I can picture cut cases of your private brands. The types of goods you know better than I. Some of the names that have become institutions in Canada. They need the new dimension something beyond Soft Goods as volume and traffic builders. This is particularly true in the first three quarters where they lose money because of inadequate volume. This will help them. Now you have three hundred new outlets to wholesale to.

Sure I am prejudiced but this cross-branding will help you both.

How do you accomplish this, you ask (I hope). Buy Mark's Work Wearhouse 27 million shares @ $2 = $54 million for the whole company or, to control it, half that (approx. $400 million volume). They run a good store with a good CEO. With your clout you can make them really profitable and add a new dimension to your own stores at the same time.

I hope you're still reading this letter. Please give me your thoughts. I've thought this over long and hard and I am convinced it is a win/win situation. I would bet that the street would think that it's sensational!

Mark's Work Wearhouse has a good name for quality because they are sticklers for quality. In essence, Mark's Work Wearhouse would be your private brand.

Please let me know what you think. If you would like to meet again I am available.

Best regards,

Mal Coven

P.S. I have a good hot dog story for you that only another American could appreciate.

P.P.S. I own no shares of Mark's Work Wearhouse

to tell me that he was in the clothing business himself and didn't need Mark's Work Wearhouse.

"You only pretend to be in the clothing business with green pants and green shirts," I said.

His last words to me were, "I would like to meet with them and see if we can do business in some way together."

When I told the people at Mark's, I couldn't believe that they turned down any such meeting.

A few years later I contacted Wayne Sales, then a senior VP at Canadian Tire who came from Kmart in the States. As a former American I had a good rapport with him talking about retail in general both in the U.S. and Canada and other things dear to us, including hot dogs and smoked meat at various delicatessens in the city. We talked about Mark's Work Wearhouse, which I believe he was not too familiar with because he was relatively new on the retail scene in Canada. We had a lunch or two and saw a ball game together.

A few years passed when, lo and behold, Wayne was promoted to be the CEO of Canadian Tire. I immediately sent him a letter congratulating him on his promotion and pointed out in great detail the reason his company should buy Mark's. Among other things, I suggested that Canadian Tire set up Mark's Work Wearhouse departments within each Canadian Tire store. There was no question in my mind their customer base was the same.

Wayne called me soon after.

"Give me a chance," he said. "I've only had the job for two weeks."

The following December 2001, almost ten months later, I came back from a holiday in Florida to be greeted by the *National Post* headline "Canadian Tire Buys Mark's Work Wearhouse." I was delighted and called Wayne to congratulate him on the acquisition. I asked about remuneration but he said he felt nothing was due to me. I followed it up with a detailed letter pointing out that I had originally put the idea into his head. I called Norman May, an old friend and lawyer, who prepared a letter to Wayne insisting that I was owed a finder's fee.

The next day before the letter had been mailed I bumped into Wayne in Forest Hill Village. We talked at length, repeating our respective arguments. I thought more about it that evening and decided not to send the letter and to keep him as a friend. It was a good decision because not only has he gone out of his way to give me advice on several of my projects, but, at my request, he has also interviewed several people for positions in his company.

WINNERS AND T.J. MAXX

Mel Cabin was the very capable manager of the Biway store at Dufferin Mall in Toronto. He called to tell me he was moving to Florida. His daughter was ill and he said it would be best if they moved to a warm climate. He knew of my background in the States and thought I could help find him a position in Florida. As it turned out I was able to help not only him but myself, too.

I thought of T.J. Maxx, which had a large presence in Florida. The CEO was Ben Cammarata. Normally it is very difficult to get through to a CEO, but Ben took the call because he recognized my last name, which was not too common. He knew my cousin Dan Coven and had served with him on the board of Zayre, a large discounter. He said he would have someone meet Mel in Buffalo for an interview.

Then Ben made my day when he said he wanted to expand his company into Canada.

I put a plan together and took it to him. There were two off-price chains similar to his in Canada: Winners, a seven-store chain owned by David Margolis, and Willy Wonderful, a five-store chain. My plan was for T.J. Maxx to buy them both. Margolis was enthusiastic about joining with T.J. Maxx. Willy Wonderful went bankrupt in the interim. I told Ben at the time that there was room for 200 stores in Canada. As of this writing there are now 213 Winners stores.

I received $20,000 for my work in the acquisition.

MAL COVEN

March 9, 2009

PERSONAL AND CONFIDENTIAL

Ben Cammarata
Chairman and CEO
T.J. Maxx
770 Cochituate Road
Framingham, MA 01701

Dear Ben:

It has been many years since I suggested that you use Winners' seven stores as an entry to Canada.

This letter is to suggest to you an unusual opportunity that may well be available to you. Some of the things I am going to relate to you you are well aware of, others perhaps not.

Jay Schottenstein bought Filene's Basement in bankruptcy several years ago. They now have some thirty stores. They have recently (18 months) opened a "new look" store in Aventura FL which will be their prototype in the future. The store is doing exceptionally well even in this environment. Their plan is to duplicate it in Boca Raton and the Dadeland area. They are attracting a somewhat upscale customer, although obviously there is an overlap with your customer. It has a clean, uncluttered look with many brands - probably not available to you because of your size and scope. They are showing names like Bottega, Brioni, Malo, Piazza Sempione, Moschino, and Krizia.

In addition to these European labels, they are getting Eileen Fisher, Ellen Tracy, Vera Wang, Marc Jacobs as well as a substantial amount of Bloomingdale merchandise. In my opinion, with this look and assortment, when they re-open the downtown Boston Store, they will do "gangbuster business".

..2/

38 Avenue Road, Suite 514
Toronto, Ontario, Canada M5R 2G2
Tel: (416) 513-0101
Fax: (416) 934-1943

Filene's Basement is controlled through Retail Ventures Incorporated (RVI), currently trading at $1.70 with a range from $1.19 to $3.30.

I think there is an opportunity for you to do Winners and Marshalls all over again by buying the original great brand in the off-price business.

By coincidence, I have recently met Jay Schottenstein socially and have developed a good relationship with him. He is a baseball fan and through Steuben Glass, a company he owns, he has offered to make a glass replica of a Sandy Koufax baseball card in conjunction with our documentary "Jews and Baseball" which is nearing completion. This is a fundraiser for the Jewish Community Centres.

Separately, we have signed a letter of intent with NIAF, which you know quite well, to do a fundraiser selling Italian baseball cards. We are attempting to duplicate a feat my partner did for the American Jewish Historical Society (AJHS) in New York, that raised $2 million for them.

Our intention is to eventually have Steuben Glass duplicate high profile Italian players in glass. One idea we are kicking around is to do the DiMaggio brothers and their parents in Steuben Glass for presentation at your annual fall weekend in Washington. We were invited to attend the latter in 2008 as guests of NIAF. With your permission , I would be happy to sound out Jay Schottenstein on the things I have proposed as I will be meeting with him, anyway, in the last week in March.

Best regards,

Mal

THE TJX COMPANIES, INC.

BERNARD CAMMARATA
CHAIRMAN OF THE BOARD

April 28, 2009

Mr. Mal Coven
38 Avenue Road, Suite 514
Toronto, Ontario, Canada M5R 2G2

Dear Mal:

Thanks for your note dated March 9, 2009. As you can imagine, the TJX team keeps very current on the retail market generally--including off-price retailers--and even more so in this economic climate. As it happens, I have a good business relationship with Jay, and we know the Filene's Basement business quite well. Although I appreciate your thinking of TJX, we are not interested in your pursuing this on our behalf.

Sorry for the delay in responding, but I'm out of the office from December through May.

Best regards,

Ben Cammarata

as

MOXIE AND COTTS

Moxie, a cola-like carbonated beverage, has been part of my family in Boston since I was a child. Moxie started out as a medicinal drink in the early 20th century and became popular in New England in the 1930s. It was Dad's favourite drink. I hated it.

Moxie lost its popularity by the 1940s because sugar was being rationed. It fell by the wayside even with Ted Williams promoting it.

There are many books in the public library in Boston about Moxie and today anything to do with the drink is a collector's item. Moxie became part of the language, meaning lots of energy, pep, and nerve. It was an ideal name, in my opinion, for a carbonated beverage.

When I moved to Toronto in 1962 I brought a few bottles with me. As I suspected, it did not go over well. My friends said that "it tasted like carbonated cough syrup."

Moxie was owned by an Atlanta company that also owned and distributed Dad's Root Beer among other beverages. I spoke to their people and found it was a marginal product, selling for the most part in Maine. My idea was to market the name but with another fill.

Gerry Pencer, a neighbour of mine whom I had never met, was in the bottling business under the name of Cott, a public company. The Cott beverage was at one time very popular in Canada and New England because it was the first to introduce a carbonated beverage with artificial sweetener and thus with no sugar and no calorie count. They were a very large private label bottler, with Wal-Mart as their largest customer. I knew Wal-Mart's cola fill was actually Royal Crown Cola, an excellent product but a name far behind Pepsi and Coca-Cola in public recognition.

Gerry invited me to come down to his office at Harbourfront and I came in a few days later armed with a book about Moxie that I had borrowed at the main Boston Public Library in Copley Square. Gerry was very familiar with the Moxie name and product because his family often vacationed in New England in the summer.

He thought for a moment and then said, "You might just have a good idea."

He mused that it could probably be bought very reasonably because no more than two or three thousand cases were sold each year.

"I'll change the packaging to a beer bottle and market it in a six-pack," he said. "I have just the fellow to do it. He ran Dr. Pepper recently with great success and I think he is available."

I was ecstatic. He liked my idea of using the Royal Crown fill. I left behind the Moxie book I had borrowed and said he would get back to me. A few weeks went by and I had not heard from him. I called his office and found out that he was ill. I sent him a book I knew he would enjoy about Abe Cohen. This colourful character was originally from Eastern Europe and had moved to London, then Montreal, and then Calgary. While in Calgary, he broke up a fight in a Chinese restaurant and was thanked by the owner, a woman who knew Mao Tse Tung. She introduced Abe to the Chinese leader when he toured Canada and he went on to become a General in the Chinese army.

Tragically, Gerry passed away of brain cancer soon after. We both thought the plan was viable, but it was not to be.

Moxie Leads The Soft Drink "Spirit of America"

Q-TIP AND KLEENEX have become nouns we use every day to refer to any brand of swab or tissue. But Moxie is a brand name that refers to an entire *attitude*. As such, it has also made its way into American vocabulary.

The "spirit and verve" that Moxie describes was the inspiration for Dr. Augustin Thompson's beverage. But it was his entrepreneurial spirit and marketing genius that fueled Moxie's journey to popularity and market share. In every respect, Moxie became "the spirit of America. . .the audacity of the movers and shakers who continue to change the world."

Originally created in 1876 as Moxie Nerve Food, Thompson's medicinal formula predates Coke by about 10 years. Concocted from Gentian root extract, cinchona, sassafras, caramel and other ingredients, Moxie Nerve Food claimed to recover exhaustion, improve energy and motor response. Named for the American Indian Moxie Falls in Maine, Moxie Nerve Food was not the first herbal tonic.

Believing water could treat ailments, the Greeks and Romans espoused steam rooms and hot and cold baths in the curative process. Europeans centered spas at natural hot springs for the therapeutic benefits of water. And people began to consume the naturally carbonated spring water as well. After the Civil War, pharmacists would enhance these "tonics" with medicinal roots and herbs. Sugar or other ingredients might also be included to improve taste.

Thompson began bottling his Nerve Food soft drink in 1884, the date printed on every Moxie can. Here's where the Moxie spirit kicks in. Thompson and Frank Morton Archer were forward-thinking revolutionaries for their time. Their ground-breaking strategies for market share have been imitated ever since and are commonplace today.

Archer sent 8-foot model Moxie bottles around the country, drawn by horses or on trucks. These eye-catching novelties, and the eventual "Moxiemobile" (a mechanical horse mounted to a car chassis so that the "rider" could drive from the saddle) are pre-cursors to today's inflated, larger-than-life, on-site beverage POPs.

Moxie's bitterness was addressed as a point of difference in early ad campaigns. "It's the flavor for those who are at all particular," was one headline. Other soft drinks, such as Proxie, Noxall, Modox, Rixie, Noxie, No-Tox and Toxie tried to piggy-back on the synonymous association Moxie carved out as a tonic soft drink. None were successful.

In the 1960's, Thompson's sons Frank and Harry led the sugar-free soft drink era when almost half the company's output was Diet Moxie.

Today, Moxie is owned by The Monarch Company, which manufactures several formulas for the company's regional niche brands, including Dad's Root Beer, NuGrape, Nesbitt's Honey Lemonade, Frostie Root Beer, Bubble Up, SunCrest Lemonade, Dr. Wells, and Deli's Milk Shake.

Hudson's Bay Trading Company

Since leaving Biway I have written scores of letters to prominent figures, most often to retail executives. One such letter was to Jeff Sherman, who had just been appointed CEO of the Hudson's Bay Trading Company, the oldest company in North America with over 300 Bay stores and a similar number of Zellers stores. Jeff Sherman had been a prominent retailer in the U.S., having been president of Bloomingdale's.

I wrote Jeff with my suggestion for improving the Bay and Zellers. I am batting .500 in letters that receive replies. In this instance he was impressed enough to ask Lorraine Fiset, his executive assistant, to arrange a lunch date.

At lunch we talked about the retail scene in the U.S. and Canada. We knew many people in common, including Hal Leppo, who worked with me many years before and went on to become president of Lord and Taylor, and Hal's son Dan, who worked under Jeff when he was president of Bloomingdale's. We got along quite well.

At a subsequent lunch Jeff asked me to give him an opinion on some changes they had made at the flagship Bay store and to look at a particular Zellers store they had just revamped. I did the former myself but asked my son David to check out the Zellers store for me. David wrote a five-page report that not only impressed me but Jeff, too. Jeff asked David to join us at lunch.

Jeff was new in Toronto and knew few outside the Bay environment, so I invited a few friends and acquaintances to the Four Seasons to meet him. Among them were Paul Godfrey, then president of the Blue Jays; Andy Giancamilli, CEO of Katz Group of Companies; Joe Mimram of Joe Fresh fame; Harry Rosen; Mark Sarner, president of Manifest Communications; and Les Mandelbaum of Umbra. It was a great lunch. I did a favour not only for Jeff but also for those I invited.

When Jeff left the Bay, Lorraine was kind enough to arrange a lunch for me with Don Watros, who became the Bay's COO. I have stayed in contact with Jeff both at lunch in New York and by email, and consider him a friend.

I made these contacts not for any direct financial gain but because I like to meet successful retailers and keep abreast of the industry in which I toiled for 60 years. I think they and I have something to offer each other.

In addition, some of the retail connections that I have kept current with have been a great help to Barbara's son Adam. In several instances they have paved the way for him to an introduction to a retail executive he wanted to reach in his business ventures.

Ironically, many years before Biway's association with Dylex, Joe Siegel, former chairman and controlling shareholder of Hudson's Bay Company, said to me that one of the biggest mistakes he made was not buying Biway.

HUDSON'S BAY CO.

JEFFREY B. SHERMAN
President and Chief Executive Officer

Tel: 416 861 4871
Fax: 416 861 4440
Email: jeff.sherman@hbc.com

February 23, 2009

Mal Coven
38 Avenue Road, Suite 514
Toronto, ON
M5R 2G2

Dear Mal,

I want to thank you most sincerely for taking the time to arrange the luncheon last week at the Four Seasons with a number of Toronto's business leaders. I very much enjoyed the opportunity to meet some great people and share inspiring conversations. You have some great contacts, and what is most obvious to me is that you are also held in very high regard.

I look forward to touching base with you again soon.

With best regards.

Jeff Sherman

Hudson's Bay Company 401 Bay Street, Suite 500, Toronto, Ontario, Canada M5H 2Y4

MAL COVEN

August 14, 2008

<u>**PERSONAL AND CONFIDENTIAL**</u>

Bonnie Brooks
President & CEO
The Hudson Bay Company
Executive Offices
401 Bay Street
Toronto, Ontario M5H 2Y4

Dear Bonnie:

I want to congratulate you on your appointment at The Bay and wish you much success in your new and exciting adventure. You may not remember my name as a founder of BiWay stores. We were a part of Dylex during your time at Town and Country. Nathan was a good friend and always spoke well of you and your merchandising talents when you were associated with him.

I want you to know I am not looking for employment. I have more than enough to keep me busy with several original projects with which I am currently involved.

Before moving to Canada in 1962 I spent ten years at Filenes (a part of Federated at the time) as a buyer and merchandiser in several departments. Filenes, though a departmental store, billed itself as "The World's Largest Specialty Shop" (no hard goods). I made my reputation there with innovative thinking, many times against the grain (10,000 snowsuits in July at Filenes) also at BiWay. We registered Bloomies label before they did as it was only a nickname in those days. We were the first discounter to carry Levis and Lee We were the largest user in Canada for boys' wear and third largest user of men's Levis.

..2/

38 AVENUE ROAD, SUITE 514
TORONTO, ONTARIO, CANADA M5R 2G2
TEL: (416) 513-0101
FAX: (416) 934-1943

I have an avocation as a consultant, I think you would call it that by some stretch. But an unpaid one. I offer my opinions and advice completely unsolicited and have made friends in doing so. I wrote to Wayne Sales and bugged him to buy Mark's Work Warehouse from the time he was Senior VP and then when he was CEO at Canadian Tire. I approached Ben Cammarota, CEO at TJ Maxx, to enter the Canadian market with a plan to buy Winners (that I got paid for). I met with Tom Stenberg (Staples founder). I did a Toronto survey for him four years before he came. Unfortunately for me, the Board turned him down as being too premature.

I am telling you all this to lend some credence to what I have to say. I think there is a great opportunity at The Bay to reawaken a sleeping giant. You were quoted in Marina Strauss' Globe and Mail column as doing it with new prestige labels. There may be some that might help but, frankly, I don't think that will do it.

Canada is a blue collar country with white collar workers making blue collar incomes. As you well know, department stores have been on the decline in Canada for many years (down from 5 to 2) . The remaining two have had mixed results.

I am going to give you a few different ideas that might be helpful to wake up the sleeping giant.

I feel the department store image is wanting, with the trend toward discounted box stores and specialty shops. I would go to Filenes' old handle:

The Bay
The World's Largest Specialty Shop

- It gives The Bay a new contemporary image your customers understand specialty shop. That's where they shop. I would not stand for your important key brands (Nautica, Tommy Hilfiger, Calvin Klein) in Winner stores.

- I would go after high school and universities. Have representation there. Give them current clothes to wear at appropriate seasons. It may be old hat but can be effective. Lululemon put yoga wear on the map using a form of that technique.

- Have a special day for different high schools, public and private.

- Have events scheduled on an ongoing basis, every two weeks something going on. Make The Bay a part of your customer's life.

Offer: Free make-up classes (high school and young adults)
    Free modelling classes
    Free yoga classes
    Celebrity appearances your customers or potential customers can relate to.

I am sure there are many more possibilities. You must change the stodgy image that both The Bay and Sears have with teens and young adults.

These are a few random thoughts off the top of my head. I am sure that, if given time, I could think of a few more. For sure you can too.

If you would like to meet me for lunch (I live across the street from the Four Seasons) I would be happy to oblige. To repeat, I am an unpaid consultant.

Good luck.

Sincerely,

Mal Coven

PS   I have run "World's Largest Specialty Shop" by a few knowledgeable people and they really like it too. Please do the same. This letter is between me and you.

MAL COVEN

PERSONAL & CONFIDENTIAL   May 11, 2011

Bonnie Brocks
CEO
The Bay
401 Bay Street, Suite 500
Toronto ON M5H 1Y4

Dear Bonnie:

Enclosed is a picture of the shoeshine stand. It does me justice but not the shoeshine stand. It will have to wait until you get to Istanbul at the Palace Hotel.

Like all good retailers, you are always looking for new ideas no matter where they come from. Sometimes it is from people that work for you, sometimes it may be from other retail outlets. It can also come from a retired retailer who built a business always thinking out of the box.

If you have ever been to the Edmonton Mall you would have seen a street that looks like Paris with appropriate stores along that strip. If you have never been there, take a walk along Queen Street West, west of Bathurst Street. There are a lot of funky stores, small and very successful. Look at those walking on the street, probably mostly in their 20s and 30s - just the customers you would like to entice into your Queen Street store. Look at Kolkid, 674 Queen Street West. It is a great store in my opinion. I think you will agree there are others just like it for adults.

My plan is to brand one floor, or most of it, 'Queen Street West'. Give four or five of these stores 1,000 ft. at a very cheap rent. They will put in their own people to run it and collect their own money. The balance of the floor will be your own Queen Street West departments with appropriate merchandise. Promote the whole floor – all the small shops along with your own.

That is the general idea. Queen Street West could be a great label for you. It is a big undertaking but you have the space to burn. A lot better than a floor full of furniture and rugs, electronics, etc., and potentially more profit than all that restaurant space.

UJA invited me to hear Baker speak, 7:30 am June 7th in the Simpson Tower. By then you should be able to tell me I am a genius or nuts. Maybe even sooner.

Regards,

Mal

38 AVENUE ROAD, SUITE 514
TORONTO, ONTARIO, CANADA M5R 2G2
TEL: (416) 513-0101
FAX: (416) 934- 943
malcoven@rogers.com

Shayne Tryon
Senior Manager Service Excellence
Office of the President
Email: shayne.tryon@hbc.com
Tel : 416.861.4643

May 25, 2011

Mr. Malcolm Coven
514-38 Avenue Road
Toronto, ON
M5R 2G2

Dear Mr. Coven,

Thank-you so much for taking the time to write Bonnie Brooks with your ideas! I work closely with Bonnie and she asked that I reply to your letter.

You are right, as part of our effort to improve the Bay, we are taking steps to attract younger shoppers. To do this, we have introduced many new brands like Juicy Couture, Free People and Ben Sherman. We will continue to expand brands for our younger demographic based on sales and how our customers respond to new merchandise.

With respect to creating a "Queen Street West" area in our store, I have shared your idea with our General Manager of Store Planning and our Senior VP of Operations. Your idea is similar to the strategy we're rolling-out to have more "shops within a shop" in our stores. For example, at the Bay Queen Street, you'll notice branded shops, some operating with a greater degree of autonomy than others (Coach on the main floor being one that has a contained experience with dedicated staff). The feasibility of working with more independent, local retailers needs to be explored for business viability, but could definitely resonate with some consumers.

Thank-you, again, for taking the time to share your ideas. We certainly appreciate your enthusiasm and support of the Bay! I sincerely hope we have the chance to earn your patronage very soon.

Kind regards,

Shayne Tryon
Senior Manager, Service Excellence

The Bay, 401 Bay Street, Suite 700, Toronto, Ontario, M5H 2Y4

The Muppet Stuff Stores

I had met Lorne Solish at various family functions. Lorne was an accountant with experience in the franchise business and a former partner in the Golden Griddle Pancake House. He had a franchise to open Muppet Stuff stores. When he had several stores I went to look at the one in the Promenade Shopping Centre in Thornhill. He was selling various items of Muppet merchandise with some success. I thought the concept was very good but that he was missing one thing: children's clothing bearing the Muppet logo. In other words, the store should be expanded into a children's clothing store featuring that logo. There was potential for building a large chain of stores set up this way, I thought.

At the time Lorne needed additional financing and was looking for a new investor. I decided to invest $75,000 and help him with my plan, which he thought was a good one. We developed some new items that included T-shirts, sweatshirts, and other basic clothing items from appropriate resources. We generated additional volume to help cover his overhead, which was onerous because he was located in premium malls.

Jim Henson, the Muppets founder, came to town and invited me for breakfast at the Sutton Place Hotel. I gave him two Muppet sweatshirts for his daughters. He was delighted with both the sweatshirts and the concept we were developing.

During most of this time, I was still at Biway. I received a call from Lorne when I was in the middle of a meeting in my office. I told him I couldn't speak to him right then unless it was very important.

"Disney wants to buy us," he said.

"That's important," I said.

About this time, around the end of the 1980s, Disney had made an offer to buy Henson, not only to get all the rights to the Muppets and the other characters he was developing, but also to get Henson's own expertise.

Disney didn't want anyone else to own the Muppets franchise so they wanted to buy us out.

Even though Disney's deal with Henson had not been finalized, they wanted to approve any new items we were developing with the Muppet logo. We kept sending new proposed items to Disney's lawyers for approval but either the approval came very slowly or we received no response at all. Our progress slowed to a standstill.

Disney and Henson negotiated for some time. The deal was never struck because Jim Henson died in 2004 at a very young age. The Henson heirs decided not to go through with the sale at that time. (Disney did buy the Muppet rights many years later.)

We sued Disney because its interference in our operation stymied our growth. After a few years the lawyers' fees had added up to a significant sum so Lorne decided to settle. He ended up just recouping our original investment.

Even at this writing, many years later, I think such a venture could be a success. I'm surprised that Disney has not followed through on the plan that Lorne conceived. In my opinion it would have more legs than the Disney Store, the novelty of which has run its course.

THE TORONTO TERMINATORS

In 1990 Russ Jacobson and I thought it would be great fun to get a minor league franchise for Toronto as there was no NBA team in Toronto at that time. We approached Ted Stepien, owner of the Cleveland Cavaliers in the NBA, who also owned a minor league basketball team in Toronto called the Tornadoes.

After a few conversations we dropped the negotiations because we found him too difficult to deal with. The Tornadoes left the city soon after. In 1992 I decided to revive the idea. The team was to be called the Toronto Terminators. I contacted the United States Basketball League, which had the franchise in Winnipeg and many cities in the U.S. The league was very excited to accept Toronto as the site for a team because all of their franchises were in smaller cities, given that the larger ones had NBA franchises.

I received an unsolicited call from Richard Peddie, who was then running the SkyDome and later would become the president of Maple Leaf Sports and Entertainment, owners of the Toronto Maple Leafs and the Toronto Raptors. He was

TORONTO TERMINATORS TO JOIN 'LITTLE' LEAGUE

Pro hoops coming to town

By MIKE SIMPSON
Toronto Sun

It may have to stand on tip-toes, but the World Basketball League should be stretching into Toronto in 1993.

The WBL, which mandates no player can be more than 6-foot-5, and Toronto entrepreneur Mal Coven are scheduled wrap up an agreement next Tuesday, the same day a news conference has been called to announce the new franchise.

Sources said Coven, a founder of the Bi-Way stores and a co-owner of Majestic Electronics Stores, is hoping to house the team — the Toronto Terminators — in Maple Leaf Gardens for its 27 home games in the non-hockey months of May to October.

Other investors in the project include lawyer Eddie Greenspan and Toronto

businessmen Phil Dezwirek, Leonard Simpson and Phil Litowitz.

The price of a franchise in the five-year-old league is $500,000 US, of which $200,000 is put up by local investors. The league guarantees the rest, making it a 60% partner in each team.

Besides the height limit, the 10-team league also operates with a $150,000 salary cap for players.

Jon Havelock, the WBL's vice-president of Canadian operations and co-owner of the Calgary 88's, said there are a few hurdles to clear, but including Toronto on the league map is an attractive prospect.

"Toronto would be a great addition, if only for the instant rivalry it creates," said Havelock. "You know how every other city in Canada loves to hate Toronto."

There will be five Canadian cities in the WBL next season — Calgary, Hamilton, Halifax, Saskatoon and Winnipeg — and Havelock said he hopes to expand to eight in the next three years. Other franchises are located in Boca Raton, Fla., Memphis, Erie, Pa., Dayton, Ohio and Youngstown, Ohio.

The Hamilton Skyhawks, which begin play in '92 out of Copps Coliseum, own the territorial rights to Toronto, but owner Ron Foxcroft expects an easy settlement.

"Hey, I encouraged this," said Foxcroft. "It will be a great for both cities and with quality owners like Mal, I think this takes our league to another level."

Havelock said the great advantage a Toronto team would enjoy is the opportunity for local sponsorships. Foxcroft, who budgeted for $200,000 in corporate help, said he has already reached the $400,000 level.

The target for season tickets is 3,000 — the break-even point — and ticket prices will range from $4.25 to $16.

The Skyhawks are negotiating with Hamilton's Ch. 11 for a game of the week and sources indicate TSN will be approached for league rights.

---

kind enough to offer to help me find a venue for the team and even with the negotiations. We decided on two possibilities: Ricoh Coliseum at the CNE and Varsity Stadium on Bloor Street where the University of Toronto team played.

Our plan was to sell a family package of season tickets very inexpensively. We were looking for a venue with a capacity of 2,000 people and we thought we could sell many season's tickets to the many families we knew to be basketball fans. I approached some friends, including the Knights of the Round Bagel (more about them later), and they reacted positively, pledging $10,000. Others were Eddie Greenspan and Miles Nadal. We sold out the ten units needed very quickly.

Now to find players. I knew I needed some Jewish players as a draw for the Jewish community. I also knew that Israel was an enthusiastic basketball country and that some of their players were a possibility.

Then I got lucky. I was spending part of the winter at our home in Palm Beach when I read in a local sports page that a team from Tashkent in Russia was coming to Boca Raton to play an exhibition game with Florida International University. I thought there might be some Jewish players from the millions of Jews still in Russia. I was friendly with a salesman from Saks Fifth Avenue who was a Russian immigrant. He volunteered to come to the game as my translator.

At the game we bought the program, and, lo and behold, we saw what could be a Jewish name on the Russian team. At half-time I approached a gentleman who was sitting on the team's bench with a jacket and tie.

In my best Yiddish, I said, "Recht Yiddish?"

Pulling out a Magen David (Star of David) on a necklace from under his shirt, he answered, "Yes, yes."

The next question I asked in half Yiddish and half English.

"Are there any Jewish players on the team?"

World basketball loop expanding to Toronto

DEC 1 1991

By Chris Young
TORONTO STAR

The basketball league that made a liar out of pop star Randy Newman is coming to Toronto.

Beginning in May 1993, the Toronto Terminators are scheduled to take to the court as pro hoops once again tries to make inroads with Metro's hockey-mad citizenry.

Whether those fans will go for the World Basketball League, of which the Terminators would become the 12th member, remains to be seen. The WBL is a league created for short guys — 6-foot-5 and under — and lacks the NBA's glamour appeal. It was Newman who satirically noted "Short people got no reason to live" — which may explain life in the big-bucks NBA, but not in the WBL.

Maple Leaf Gardens is the target site for homegames, although nothing has been set yet and, indeed, no deal has been signed. Boston-born Toronto businessman Mal Coven is the point man for a group of about 40 investors, all of them Toronto businessmen.

Coven, founder of the Bi-Way discount store chain and among a group that acquired Majestic Electronics in September, said Jon Havelock, vice-president of WBL Enterprises Canada, is to fly in from Calgary next Tuesday to join Coven and some of his partners in unveiling the new team.

Although Coven would not talk money, he did say the total cost of the team is a little less than the figure of $850,000 outlined in a league information sheet.

"It's pretty well complete," Coven said. "The money is not a problem. I'll put it up myself if I have to. There's nothing I know that could stand in the way of it."

Will Toronto go for a team that is anything less

What is the WBL?

WORLD BASKETBALL LEAGUE

1991 lineup: Calgary 88's; Dayton (Ohio) Wings; Erie (Pa.) Wave; Florida (Boca Raton) Jades; Halifax Windjammers; Memphis (Tenn.) Rockers; Nashville (Tenn.) Stars; Saskatchewan Storm; Youngstown (Ohio) Pride.

1992 additions: Hamilton Skyhawks.

Possible 1993 additions: Toronto, Winnipeg.

Canadian teams and sites: Calgary (Saddledome, avg. '91 attendance 5,300); Saskatchewan (Saskatchewan Place, Saskatoon, 5,900); Halifax (World Trade and Convention Centre, 4,700); Hamilton (Copps Coliseum).

League history: With headquarters in Memphis, the WBL was created in 1988 and overhauled to players under the height of 6-foot-5. In 1991, nine teams including three in Canada completed the league.

Top players: Keith Smart (Halifax), '87 NCAA hero with Indiana; Dudley Bradley (Saskatchewan), former NBA journeyman; David Rivers (Memphis), former Notre Dame star.

than the NBA, especially head-to-head with the adored Blue Jays?

"You have to take it in a different way," Coven said. "Take it as first-class entertainment. It's an exciting game."

The WBL has four Canadian entries. The Hamilton Skyhawks are set to join the league, which operates from May through September, this spring. They join WBL teams in Calgary, Halifax and Saskatoon. In Calgary at the Saddledome, crowds for the WBL average 5,300.

A Winnipeg franchise may be joining Toronto for a 1993 christening, which would bring the Canadian content to six teams, or half of the league.

Teams played a 51-game schedule last season, including matches against visiting international squads, among them the Canadian national team. With the cap on size and European rules, it is very much a guard-oriented, ball-handling sort of game that lacks the brute strength and towering presences of the NBA.

Toronto has a roundball history of note, most of it unsuccessful. Although the game has enjoyed huge popularity in Metro high schools, pro teams have never made a go of it. The Toronto Huskies were a charter member of the Basketball Association of America, later the NBA, in 1946 and lasted one season.

In the early 1970s, the NBA Buffalo Braves played regular-season games at Maple Leaf Gardens. And in the early '80s, the Tornados of the minor-league Continental Basketball Association played out of Varsity Arena for a few seasons to tiny crowds. NBA exhibition games regularly have been played here and in Hamilton's Copps Coliseum, where the Skyhawks will play.

Bi-Way basketball may have a market in Toronto

CRAIG DANIELS

Maybe I was wrong

PERHAPS I AM P.T. Barnum's natal choice of the minute.

And perhaps "sucker" is a pretty tame risk when it's for something this important.

All I can tell you is that I began an hour's tug of war yesterday with Toronto's newest pro franchise owner, and by the end I wanted pull for the voice on the other end of the phone — a voice belonging to 62-year-old Mal Coven, financial point guard for the Toronto Terminators of the World Basketball League.

I'm paraphrasing, but I said last Friday that any man willing to start a WBA franchise in this city had shot a mental rod.

After all, *everything* is wrong with the idea. Toronto is too big a city, Toronto wants an NBA team and nothing else. Toronto won't support minor-league anything, and had proven it in the past with the Tornados, if nearly not with the Argos. Toronto is obsessed with the Blue Jays from May to October, the months the WBA plays.

Toronto is this, Toronto is that.

And yet, and this is where Mal Coven begins to make sense, Toronto's sports teams have abandoned, deserted the average wage earner. The working guy. The kind of guy who works *for* the guy who buys this paper. The guy sport used to be for.

"I don't *want* the guy in the SkyBox," says Coven, "I want the man on the street. What we're delivering is a quality entertainment package for the working guy.

"Look, you want to be a big shot, you can buy a season ticket package [from me] for 100 bucks and *pretend* you're a bigshot.

"*I guarantee* that you'll be able to sit in the reds at Maple Leaf Gardens for $5. Where else can you take a family of four out in this city for $20?"

He talks earnestly, sounding like a born salesman, a man by reflex on the lookout for an undervalued quantity and a man willing to bring it to a customer. For a price? Sure, one the customer and retailer are both interested in.

Coven is a founder of the Bi-Way stores. He came from Boston 30-or-so years ago, started with one store, and when he left two years ago, there were 255.

He's now part owner of Majestic Electronics, a guy cut from the cloth of an Ed Mirvish, a Steve Stavro: sell cheap, sell quality, most of all sell lots. Love your customer, give him a fair deal, and he'll come back.

He wants to sell basketball the same way — to the very people who buy at Honest Ed's, at Knob Hill Farms and, sure, Bi-Way.

"I want to do this grass-roots," he says. "Do you know how many guys I know in this town? I want 50 guys to invest with me. Each one knows six people who are basketball nuts. That's the way we're going to do this. We're going to sell to the high school kids. We're going to market the stuff kids want. In black and silver — those colors are hot. I *know* this stuff, okay?"

He talks too quickly. He may well be the antithesis of the style, if not the substance, of a Bruce McNall, a Richard Peddie, a Larry Ryckman.

But think of the people who *fill* Mirvish's, Knob Hill, Bi-Way, every weekend, the people with two kids, mortgaged to the hilt, or more than likely unable to even afford a house — maybe they are recent immigrants — and are looking for something decent to take their kids to.

Think of them and maybe you'll think Coven's got something the prevailing thinking has missed.

It's true that Mirvish and Stavro have not exactly starved on their way to bringing bargains to their customers, but somehow you can respect somebody *willing* to bring a bargain to the customer. There aren't many to be had from the other pro teams in this city.

Sure, you can still buy a Jays' ticket for $4 bucks — there are all of 3,000 of them in the nether reaches of a stadium of 50,000. You almost have to buy that seat in April to see a game in July.

And the product? No, the WBA is not the NBA, but it is *very* good, so good that on a given night a WBA team could beat an NBA team. It is played by men no taller than 6-foot-5 — all of whom can dunk — but is much faster, and in some ways more skilled, usually more exciting than the NBA. Remember that fast men can run tall men *ragged* on a basketball court.

"Look," says Coven, "we both know that this city is ripe for the NBA. But if they are too stupid to put a franchise here, what am I supposed to do about it?"

With a salary cap of $150,000 per team, with a sweetheart Gardens rental deal from Stavro — why not when your building is dark during those months anyway? — it would only take — a guess — five, six thousand to make a team fly — particularly with the league willing to swallow 60% of any loss.

Have I been conned by a good salesman?

For the sake of all the people who have been left watching from their TVs instead of a box seat, I hope so.

He pointed to the program and showed me that most of the players were Jewish.

What a find! I arranged to meet him at the Holiday Inn on Glades Road after the game. I met many of the Jewish players and found out that even the trainer was Jewish. I told the manager about the Toronto Terminators and asked if some of his players might want to play for the team. He told me it was possible but complicated because I would have to get permission from more than one faction in Russia. I said I would get back to him.

When I got back to Toronto I discovered that the complications existed not only in Russia but also in Canada and were beyond my capabilities to arrange. My dream of incorporating these players didn't come true but I sure had a great experience in the process.

Using the letterhead from a note the Russian coach had given me, I had my Saks Fifth Avenue translator write a letter in Russian to Eddie Greenspan telling him that he had heard of his prowess as a basketball player at his Niagara Falls high school and that he wanted to meet him. I don't know if Eddie ever had the letter translated. He never mentioned it to me any of the infrequent times I have seen him since. Perhaps he wasn't as curious as I expected.

SEASON TICKET COMMITTEE:

GORO ATLIN	AUBREY GOLDEN	NEIL NISKER
JOE AZZIZ	MURRAY GOLDMAN	RON OTIS
MICHAEL BASEN	HARRY GORMAN	VICTOR PROWSKY
ALLEN BLACKSTIEN	PHIL GOTTLIEB	LARRY ROBBINS
IRVING BLOOMBERG	EDDIE GREENSPAN	IAN ROHR
DUSTY COHL	SYD GREENSTEIN	AL SANDLER
BARBARA COVEN	ADAM GRIFF	MENDY SHARF
MAL COVEN	GEORGE HARTMAN	ALAN SILBER
DAVID CRAVIT	KEN HITZIG	SYD SILVERBERG
PHIL DEZWIREK	RUSS JACOBSON	LEONARD SIMPSON
PEGGY DEZWIREK	HAROLD D. KAMIN	HERB SOLOWAY
HERBIE FINKLESTEIN	RALPH LEAN	SOL SPEAR
MICHAEL FIRESTONE	LAWRIE LIPTON	JACK STECKEL
MICKEY FIRESTONE	PHIL LITOWITZ	DEANIE STULBERG
ABE FISH	SHARON LOKASH	JACK STUPP
NORM FREEDMAN	DR. DONNY LYONS	STEVEN TITLE
ADAM GILBERT	SYD MANDEL	DAVE USHER
CECIL GILBERT	MICKIE MOORE	AMNON WAKSMAN
GARY GLADMAN	MILES NADAL	

17 Old Forest Hill Road
Toronto, Canada M5P 2P6
(416) 484-4407

David Stern, Commissioner of the NBA (left), extends congratulations to the Terminators
with his autograph on a first day cover on the 100th anniversary of basketball.

I arranged a party at the Primrose Club and invited friends, family, and potential season ticket holders to meet some of the league people who were coming to Toronto to meet their new partners. The financial arrangements were that the team would be responsible for half the losses, if there were any, which left us a bit of a safety net.

At a Miami Dolphin game a year before, I ate a delicious foot-long kosher hot dog from Hebrew National. I knew I had to serve them at my party.

I called Michael Klein at Nortown, the distributor of Hebrew National in Toronto. He told me they were not available in Canada because of the labelling but gave me the name of the sales manager in the U.S. who would probably assist me.

The sales manager said he could help but only if I picked the hot dogs up in the States. However, who did I know in Buffalo who could take delivery? Then it came to me. I remembered that Harry Rosen he had a store in Buffalo. Harry consented to receive my shipment at that store. I'm sure it was the only time a fine men's store – or any men's store – ever received a delivery of 150 foot-long kosher hot dogs.

I drove to Buffalo in a snowstorm and returned to Toronto in a snowstorm. At the border upon my return I explained that the hot dogs were for a special diet for a "fairly" religious group attending a basketball event. The border guard laughed and waved me through without inspecting my valuable cargo.

Ralph Lean, a well-connected lawyer, introduced me to Mayor June Rowlands, who arranged a press conference for us. Craig Daniels, a columnist at the *Toronto Sun*, wrote an article saying he thought we were unlikely to succeed.

I called Craig and told him about our marketing plan, after which he wrote another article that said, "After listening to Mal Coven's marketing strategy, they might have a good chance to succeed."

I went to Bata, a supplier of Biway, and they were nice enough to make me samples of high top canvas children's running shoes bearing the Terminators imprint.

Then it happened. The financial backer of the U.S. Basketball League, who owned a chain of discount drugstores, was indicted for cooking the books and subsequently went to jail. The league collapsed, along with the Terminators.

Was it worth it all? It sure was. To quote Jay Landesman, a writer, editor, and

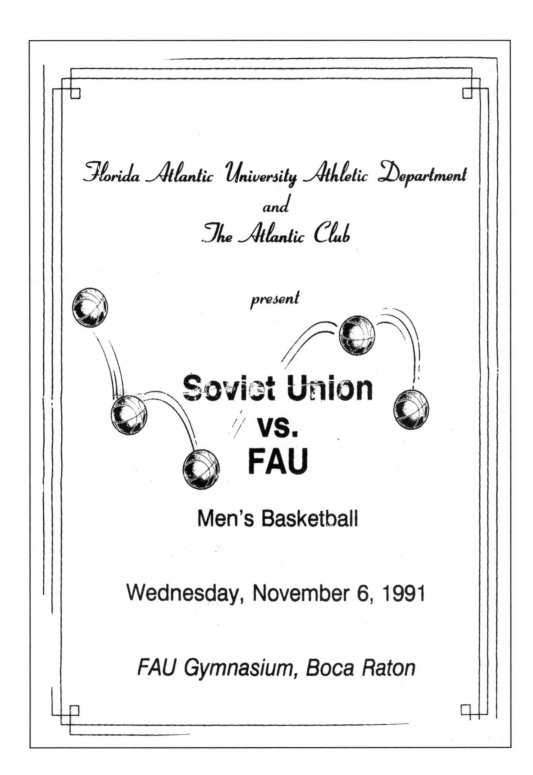

Florida Atlantic University Athletic Department
and
The Atlantic Club

present

Soviet Union
vs.
FAU

Men's Basketball

Wednesday, November 6, 1991

FAU Gymnasium, Boca Raton

playwright who has had many successes and failures, "Sometimes there is even fun in failure."

As an entrepreneur, I have to agree.

MAL COVEN PRESENTATION

TORONTO TERMINATORS

FIRST PARTY – DECEMBER 3, 1991

Hotdog lovers of Canada, welcome. Thank you for coming. Welcome John Havelock and Ron Foxcroft – thank you for being here. I'll be introducing you shortly.

By the way, before I forget, we will have a little draw for ten of these [show basketball] so get your business card in the bowl out front. [Put on T-shirt]

Thirty-three years ago my friend and partner Russ Jacobsen and I lived with our families in Framingham, Massachusetts. We organized a sports night for our fledgling *shul*. We had a limited budget and spent most of it on the speakers. We invited Mike Holovak, who was the coach of the New England Patriots. He spoke for free. We also invited Red Auerback, Bill Sharman, and Bob Cousy. They weren't free.

We awarded the Framingham High School football team 1 win and 12 losses "Comeback of the Year" Award because they beat Natick 12 wins, 1 loss (Doug Flutie's school). Red came to the podium and just murdered us. It went something like this: "Whoever heard of giving an award to a 1 and 12 team? What a chintzy statue! And whoever heard of hotdogs and beans at a banquet like this?"

Thirty-three years later … no beans.

This past Friday I was returning from Buffalo – with the two cartons of hotdogs you devoured this evening that Harry Rosen kindly received for me in his Galleria store – when my car phone rang. It was Donny Lyons. It went something like this: "Mal, I want to apologize, I can't come to your party. I really want to be there. My wife made other arrangements and I can't get out of it. Please do me a favour – bring me a couple of those 12-inch hotdogs to Benny's restaurant tomorrow morning for breakfast." Five minutes later I got another call from Bill Ballard. "If you're bringing

Uzstroymekhanizaciya
Coach - Alexander Vlasov

Uzbekistan

	Field Goals		Free Throws	Fouls	Points
Valdimir Telegin (203 cm, 87 kg, F)	3 3 3 3 3 3 3 3 3 3	2 2 2 2 2 2 2 2 2 2 2 2 2 2 2 2	1 1 1 1 1 1 1 1 1 1 1 1		
Andrei Kavardak (205 cm, 77 kg, F)	3 3 3 3 3 3 3 3 3 3	2 2 2 2 2 2 2 2 2 2 2 2 2 2 2 2	1 1 1 1 1 1 1 1 1 1 1 1		
Andrei Firsov (209 cm, 89 kg, C)	3 3 3 3 3 3 3 3 3 3	2 2 2 2 2 2 2 2 2 2 2 2 2 2 2 2	1 1 1 1 1 1 1 1 1 1 1 1		
Alexander Vilgeim (209 cm, 82 kg, G)	3 3 3 3 3 3 3 3 3 3	2 2 2 2 2 2 2 2 2 2 2 2 2 2 2 2	1 1 1 1 1 1 1 1 1 1 1 1		
Oleg Lavin (184 cm, 84 kg, G)	3 3 3 3 3 3 3 3 3 3	2 2 2 2 2 2 2 2 2 2 2 2 2 2 2 2	1 1 1 1 1 1 1 1 1 1 1 1		
Alexander Cherkov (193 cm, 87 kg, G)	3 3 3 3 3 3 3 3 3 3	2 2 2 2 2 2 2 2 2 2 2 2 2 2 2 2	1 1 1 1 1 1 1 1 1 1 1 1		
(190 cm, 86 kg, G)	3 3 3 3 3 3 3 3 3 3	2 2 2 2 2 2 2 2 2 2 2 2 2 2 2 2	1 1 1 1 1 1 1 1 1 1 1 1		
Andrei Ryazahov (197 cm, 100 kg F)	3 3 3 3 3 3 3 3 3 3	2 2 2 2 2 2 2 2 2 2 2 2 2 2 2 2	1 1 1 1 1 1 1 1 1 1 1 1		
Serge: Demyrin (204 cm, 102 kg, F)	3 3 3 3 3 3 3 3 3 3	2 2 2 2 2 2 2 2 2 2 2 2 2 2 2 2	1 1 1 1 1 1 1 1 1 1 1 1		
Dimitri Schiglinsky (196 cm, 80 kg, G)	3 3 3 3 3 3 3 3 3 3	2 2 2 2 2 2 2 2 2 2 2 2 2 2 2 2	1 1 1 1 1 1 1 1 1 1 1 1		
Valori Filyushkin (205 cm, 105 kg, C)	3 3 3 3 3 3 3 3 3 3	2 2 2 2 2 2 2 2 2 2 2 2 2 2 2 2	1 1 1 1 1 1 1 1 1 1 1 1		
Grigori Kazansky (207 cm, 100 kg, C)	3 3 3 3 3 3 3 3 3 3	2 2 2 2 2 2 2 2 2 2 2 2 2 2 2 2	1 1 1 1 1 1 1 1 1 1 1 1		

Don't drop the ball . . .
get your season tickets now!

For more information, call 367-3710

them for Lyons, bring a couple for me for breakfast." The former was a request. The latter was an order.

I've asked you to come to our party to expose you to the best-kept secret in sports in Toronto – THE WORLD BASKETBALL LEAGUE. John Havelock will tell you more about the league. I want to talk about the TORONTO TERMINATORS.

As many of you know, my background is Biway and the marketing of mass market merchandise. We have here a similar situation.

We have the fastest-growing sport in the world.

We have a market of three million plus within easy reach of the store.

We're the only store in town with our wanted merchandise.

We have a city where most play basketball in high school and enjoy watching the game.

We have a time slot May to September where people are anxious to get out of the house for activities.

We have a generous supply of talent for the team with a salary cap of $150,000 … for the whole team!

We know we can tap this market.

There will be a first-class facility available to us, I'm sure, at a reasonable price because of the May to September scheduling. The only other merchandise being sold at that time is the Blue Jays and their prices are nowhere near ours, and we'll schedule our home games when they're on the road.

Ladies and gentlemen, we will deliver a first-class entertainment package to a multicultural city that knows and loves basketball AT AN AFFORDABLE PRICE. Yes, ladies and gentlemen, a family of four will be able to sit in a good seat in a first-class facility for under $20. How many things can a family of four do for less than $20? We will have hundreds of good seats at $5. I promise you we will be Biway, Knob Hill and Honest Ed all rolled into one.

There are some people who have doubts. It has been written recently "In 1946 the Huskies died." Timing is everything. I have a friend that passed up 100 acres just north of Wilson Avenue for $500 an acre in 1946. Timing is everything. The Huskies argument doesn't make too much sense to me. It's been written Ted Stepien tried it and failed with the Tornadoes and that's why we won't succeed. There is no outsider who could come into this city and be successful in Toronto in this situation. I owe a debt of gratitude to Ted because he first exposed me to professional basketball in the 80s. This whole thing started three weeks ago when I answered an ad he put in The Star.

This has to be a grassroots thing. You all being here will attest to that.

In Hamilton I understand Ron budgeted for $200,000 in sponsor money. I understand they are over $400,000 to date. We think we can do better.

This is Toronto, remember, with a population base over ten times the size of Hamilton. Three major corporate sponsors have approached us already, unsolicited, and two of them are here tonight.

It's not just for the hotdogs.

Now for merchandising. That's something people say I know something about. T-shirts, sweatshirts, athletic shoes, you know the sort of thing. We think there's a tremendous potential for licensed products in the Toronto market. The logos on shoes and sweatshirts would sell even without a team and we will be ready to distribute licensed merchandise next Fall.

We have a goal. We may not get there right away but it's our goal. If the Blue Jays can draw four million fans we think one day we can lop off a few zeros and draw 400,000.

That's our story, what I think we can do, but we need your help. We're looking for a lot of participation, $40, $50, $60 or whatever. If we have more people than that, I promise you we'll find room for everybody. We can't guarantee you a huge return on your money but we can guarantee you'll have more fun than you ever had in your life with basketball. But we may just fool you. I find many times you make more money when you're not trying – and we didn't go into this for the profit. I think it was Dusty Cohl who said, "This is sort of like the House of Chan."

A word to the media – this team is good for the city, the economy. It's good for morale and G-d knows we need a lot of things like that. Please don't ignore us. We expect criticism – and rightly so. We can have differences of opinion. Please try to think positive. This room is full of people who spent their lives thinking positively – and succeeded.

You've already seen this past season's championship game on the big screen while you were eating your hotdogs. Shortly we'll be showing you a film about the WBL to give you a little of its flavour. It's a couple of years old (the new one wasn't ready yet) but I think for our purposes it will do the trick.

There may be some shots of the Las Vegas team in it that moved to Tennessee. The other pro team, UNLV, I guess, squeezed them out.

Thank you, and I'm glad you were able to be here tonight. Now the video.

VIDEO RUNS: (5 minutes)
MAL: Introduce Ron Foxcroft
RON FOXCROFT: 4-5 minutes
MAL: Introduce John Havelock
JOHN HAVELOCK: 10 minutes
MAL:Thanks and set up signing
Introduce Eddie Greenspan
EDDIE GREENSPAN: 2-3 minutes
MAL:Introduce partners to do the draw
MAL:Closing remarks (following page)

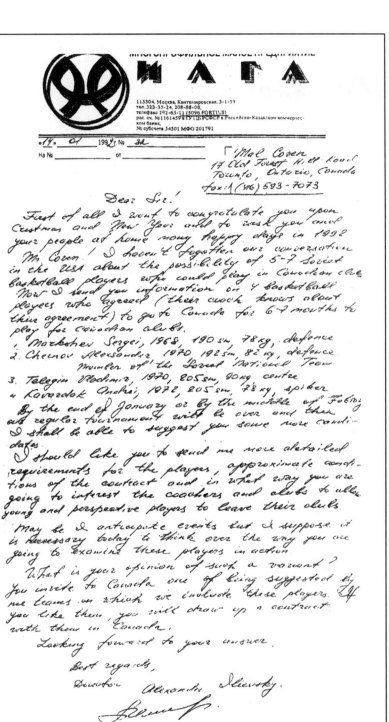

МНОГОПРОФИЛЬНОЕ МАЛОЕ ПРЕДПРИЯТИЕ

ИАГА

115304, Москва, Кантемировская, 3-1-59
тел. 323-35-24, 208-88-08,
телефакс 292-65-11 (5096 FORTIUS)
рас. сч. №116145918 (ГУ ЦБ РСФСР в Российско-Казахском коммерчес-
ком банке,
№ субсчета 34501 МФО 201791

«14» 01 1992 г. № 32
На № _____ от _____

⌐Mal Coven
17 Old Forest Hill Road
Toronto, Ontario, Canada
fax:1 (416) 593-7073

Dear Sir!

First of all I want to congratulate you upon Cristmas and New Year and to wish you and your people at home many happy days in 1992

Mr Coven! I haven't forgotten our conversation in the USA about the possibility of 5-7 Soviet basketball players who could play in Canadian club

Now I send you information on 4 basketball players who agreed (their coach knows about their agreement) to go to Canada for 6-7 months to play for canadian clubs.

1. Markshev Sergei, 1968, 190 sm, 78 kg, defence
2. Chernov Alexsander, 1970, 192 sm, 82 kg, defence
   member of the Soviet National Team
3. Telegin Vladimir, 1970, 205 sm, 90 kg, centre
4. Kavardak Andrei, 1972, 205 sm, 78 kg, spiker

By the end of January or by the middle of Febru I at regular tournament will be over and then I shall be able to suggest you some more candidates.

I should like you to send me more detailed requirements for the players, approximate conditions of the contract and in what way you are going to interest the coachers and clubs to allow young and perspective players to leave their clubs.

May be I anticipate events but I suppose it is necessary today to think over the way you are going to examine these players in action

What is your opinion of such a variant? You invite to Canada one of being suggested by me teams in which we include these players. If you like them, you will draw up a contract with them in Canada.

Looking forward to your answer.

Best regards,

Director   Alexander Ilievsky.

norimco

December 13, 1991

Toronto Terminators Ltd.
17 Old Forest Hill Road,
Toronto, Ontario
M5P 2P6

Dear Mr. Coven:

Just a short note confirming our discussion on the Footwear
License for Canada on the Toronto Terminators.

The guarantee of $15,000 (Canadian) against a royalty of 6% of
net sales, is acceptable.

As we move closer to the "tip-off", Norimco, Bata's
manufacturing and wholesale division in Canada, looks forwards to a
successful partnership with . . . . . . The Terminators.

Yours truly,

NORIMCO, Division of Bata Industries Ltd.

Phil Zwibel
Vice President & General Manager

PZ/bew

MILLENNIUM COMPLEX INC.
P. O. Box 716
Postal Station "Q"
Toronto, Ontario
M4T 2N5

Mr. Mal Coven
17 Old Forest Hill Road
Toronto, Ontario   M5P 2P6

December 18, 1991

Dear Mal:

I want to congratulate you on your success in winning the rights for the WBL franchise for Toronto. I have great confidence that you have a winner.

Of course, we want to be involved in owning a share in the WBL team, and we are prepared to sign on once the final documentation is prepared. We think that a "half share" would be appropriate as you suggested with our investment to be $7500.

More importantly, our interest is high on securing preferred prestige seating. We would like:

**10 seats in a row (including the aisle seat), CENTRE COURT,
right behind the Terminator bench**

We really like basketball, we're vocal, and we really appreciate the best seats. We will advise you the names in which to register the 5 pairs of seats when you equest that information.

You explained that you are looking for $100 deposit for each pair, and we et to approve the actual choice of seats. If you want, consider this to be your ithorization to charge $500 deposit money to my Master Card:

5420 3272 0296 6808   Expiry 08/93

We support what you are doing and we are happy to be a part of it.

Sincerely,

Millennium Complex Inc.

Per: **J. GARY GLADMAN**, President

np

PART FIVE

HAVING FUN

December 18, 2000

Barbara Walters
c/o ABC Television
147 Columbus Avenue
New York, NY 10023 USA

Dear Barbara:

A few years back you wrote in your biography that one Lou Chesler, a friend of your dad, helped you out with a loan of $15,000.

I am a friend of Lou Chesler's youngest daughter, Joanne Chesler. Joanne has always admired you and would like to meet you when she is in New York. However, unlike her father, she is too shy to ask. She is a lovely personable lady and I am sure you would enjoy her company. Her address is:

> 561 Avenue Road, Apt. 1406
> Toronto, Ontario M4V 2J8 Canada
> Res: (416) 966-2606
> Fax: (416) 966-2316
> Cell: (416) 706-6262

For the record, I am a former Bostonian (Boston Latin, B.C. and Filene's Graduate), a retailer in Toronto for many years.

Sincerely,

Mal Coven

21

BARBARA WALTERS

JOANNE Chesler is a friend of Barbara and mine. The Chesler family, in particular Lou Chesler, Joanne's father, is a colourful one. Joanne was the youngest of three beautiful daughters and Lou was famous for his many ventures. At one time or another he owned a night club, a movie studio, and a gambling casino. The Cheslers lived not only in Toronto but also on Long Island and in Miami. Joanne's parents shipped her off to boarding school in Switzerland when she was 14, which was the start of a somewhat troubled life.

When I met Joanne she was divorced from Richard Fogler and did various things including interior decorating.

I noticed a reference to Lou Chesler in a book by Barbara Walters. Barbara's father owned The Latin Quarter in New York. With the advent of television, he had found himself in financial trouble. Lou Chesler and Barbara Walters' father knew each other because both had night clubs and hung around with many of the same people. Barbara mentioned in her book that Lou had sent her father $15,000 unsolicited to help him out financially with no strings attached. That was serious money in the 1950s, easily equivalent to over $140,000 in 2012.

I had lunch with Joanne occasionally and spoke to her on the phone frequently on my way from the Bagel World restaurant to my office. There were three phone calls I always made for quite a few years on my way to my office at home. The others were to Maxine Cooper and Barbara. At one point I suggested to Joanne that if Barbara

Walters thought enough of her dad to mention him so glowingly in her book then she, Joanne, should write to her. It might lead to something worthwhile.

Joanne, although beautiful and personable, was very shy and refused to make write the letter. I pressed her, to no avail. I decided to write to Barbara Walters myself on her behalf. Within a very few days I received a response. She said that she would be delighted to meet with Joanne in New York but it was awkward for her to call since it was I who had made the contact.

Unfortunately, Joanne was probably the one lady in a thousand who would turn down a meeting with Barbara Walters. This letter is one of many that I have saved. I particularly remember the last line that Ms. Walters wrote: "Mal, you are a most thoughtful friend."

I am happy to say that Joanne was remarried recently to an architect and is now living in Westport, Connecticut.

While driving back from Detroit after a basketball tournament that my grand-daughter Nomi was participating in, I played an audiobook of Barbara Walters in the car. I told friends that I felt as though she was sitting beside me as I listened to her for four hours on the tape. She is quite a lady.

ABC News

Barbara Walters

December 22nd 2000

Mr. Mal Coven
38 Avenue Road, Suite 514
Toronto, Canada

Dear Mr. Coven,

Thank you for writing to me. Why don't you have Joanne Chesler give me a call when she is coming to New York, and I will try to see her. I think it would look strange if I wrote to her out of the blue.

You are a most thoughtful friend.

Sincerely,

Barbara Walters

22

PAUL GODFREY AND
MORT ZUCKERMAN

I had an idea to sell a package of several magazines to new subscribers, a bundle of three or four monthly. The likes of *Vanity Fair, New Yorker*, and so on would be offered for delivery one day after the current issue was pulled off the newsstands. Even though they were out of date, they would be new, fresh magazines. The bundle could be sold very inexpensively. The quantity distributed in this way could be added to the sales count and would be of benefit to both the magazine and the advertisers.

I didn't know anyone in the business to run this by for an opinion. Then it came to me. I remembered that my brother-in-law Morris Fish, on his frequent visits to my family in Framingham while travelling with the McGill debating or water polo teams, visited a friend and classmate of his at McGill, Mort Zuckerman, who was working for Cabot Co. in Boston.

This same Mort Zuckerman now owned both the *Atlantic Monthly* and *U.S. News & World Report*, a weekly magazine, as well as the *Daily News*, a New York tabloid.

Of course he did not know me and normally would not take a call from me. I decided to use Morris' name to get through to speak with him. I told the lady who answered the phone that I was Morris Fish's brother-in-law and wanted to ask Mort for some advice or direction.

She checked her Rolodex and said, "Oh, yes, I have Morris' name" and put Mort on the phone.

I introduced myself and quickly said I was not looking for money but only wanted some direction to see if my idea was plausible. He listened to what I had to say and thought enough of it to give me the names of two people in New York who could be of some help to me.

I went to New York and met one of them, Chip Block, who owned six or eight specialty magazine publications. I stupidly made the joke he must have heard hundreds of times: "You must be a chip off the old block." In spite of that, Chip gave me an hour of his time explaining why my idea could not work. I thanked him and went on my way.

Less than a week later I received a call from Paul Godfrey, at the time publisher of the *Toronto Sun*. Paul knew me only from the time I spent with him once while waiting to retrieve our cars at the Sheraton Hotel. We were commiserating that it was going to cost us $33 for parking there for two hours.

Now, on the phone, Paul said he understood I was a close friend of Mort Zuckerman in New York. I remember replying that seven minutes on the phone with him did not exactly classify me as a friend. In spite of that, Paul asked if I would contact him on his behalf.

At the time, the *Toronto Sun* was in play. Quebecor had put in a hostile bid to buy the *Sun*, and Paul, publisher and CEO at the time, was looking for a white knight – someone friendlier to him and his company who would make a counter bid. Mort Zuckerman's *Daily News* was a tabloid similar to the *Sun*, and we knew Mort had Canadian origins, this being an important factor in controlling a newspaper in Canada.

I said I would call "my close friend" for him. Before I did, I prepared a package of information about the hostile bid and anything else about the *Sun* I could find that might be useful. I placed the call and explained to the nice lady guarding Zuckerman's time that I was calling him on an entirely new subject.

I told Mort the story about the *Sun* and the hostile bid. He knew a bit about it and said he was interested in knowing more. I told him I had a package ready to send. He thanked me and said because it was late in the week I should send it not to his office but to his place in the Hamptons. I readdressed it and did just that. I also gave him Paul's phone numbers and said he would contact him on the weekend.

I felt pretty darn good that I could be the intermediary in this potential transaction. I called Paul, who was of course delighted with the progress I had made. However, he called me a few days later and told me the deal could not be made because Mort Zuckerman was not still a Canadian citizen.

However, for my efforts, Paul said, "My door is always open to you" and it has been ever since, when he was president of the Blue Jays and now as CEO of Postmedia Network. He always replies phone call for phone call and letter for letter. He came to my 79th birthday party at a box at Rogers Stadium, and went out of his way to come to my 80th at the Four Seasons, leaving the Brazilian Ball to appear.

He has helped me on several occasions. I know he was pleased that I invited him to the lunch I organized for Jeff Sherman, then CEO of the Hudson's Bay Trading Company.

Even though my magazine idea was not workable, it did end up by making me a great new friend.

23

JACKIE MASON AND THE CORKY AWARD

I was browsing in a hardware store with Mendy Sharf, one of the charter members of the Knights of the Round Bagel (more on them later), and happened to notice a table stacked with corks from small to very large. Even though I knew what they were for, I decided to ask Mendy, a connoisseur of inexpensive wines, a question about them.

"Do you know what the large ones are for?" I asked.

"They're for wine casks," he said.

"No, you're mistaken. They're for big a-holes."

So was born our Corky Award for the A-Hole of the Year.

Al Green was a noted developer and is a serious sculptor and a friend. He joined the Knights of the Round Bagel for breakfast at Bagel World, bicycling from his home on Forest Hill Road to join us most weekday mornings.

The Corky Award was on my mind. Of course we needed an Oscar-type statue. I naïvely asked Al to make one for me.

"Are you crazy?" he said. "All of my pieces are struck in Israel. That would be almost impossible."

He then went on to tell me about all the steps needed to make a statue.

Not to be discouraged, I explained to him exactly what the award was for.

He drew a sketch on a napkin. Of course, the purpose of the award was the thing that did it – a statue to be given yearly to the A-Hole of the Year.

Some months later he showed me the results of his work. It was green and bent over at a 90-degree angle. I looked at it from the back side and said, "Great!" His name and the name of the award were scratched onto the base.

"No, no, the wax melted and that caused the bend," Al said. "The bend was a mistake."

Not too much later he showed me the final version. Looking like a version of the Oscar, it was a magnificent piece of work in my eyes. He made three of them.

That was the year 2000. The plan was to have a dinner and a roast each year in honour of the a-hole of that year. We kidded around and came up with many candidates. The competition was keen.

It seemed that we would never come to an agreement until Jackie Mason came into the picture. Jackie was appearing for an extended booking at a theatre in North York and he was staying at the Four Seasons Hotel across the street from my apartment on Avenue Road.

The Knights of the Round Bagel with Jackie Mason in absentia.

I came up with an idea.

I knew that like all New Yorkers of his generation, he loved delicatessen.

Hands down my favourite deli sandwich – and any connoisseur's – was a hand-cut smoked meat sandwich on an onion bun from the Centre Street Deli in Thornhill. The owners, Cheryl and her partner Sam, learned their skills in Montreal where Cheryl's dad owned the Snowden Deli. Whether you wanted it lean, medium, old-fashioned or not, to me it was the best in the whole world. Smoked meat was unique to Montreal and the way the meat was stacked and hand-cut at Centre Street Deli was even better than the ones served in Montreal.

The Toronto Sun, Tuesday October 3, 2000

Jeff HARDER

Comedian **Jackie Mason** has received the ---hole of the year award from the Knights of the Round Bagel.

The Knights are a loosely knit group of rich Torontonians who would rather honour than ridicule famous people. In the past, they have hosted **Mel Brooks** and **Carl Reiner.**

They wanted to do the same for Mason, who is bringing Broadway's *Much Ado About Everything* to the Toronto Centre for the Arts, starting Nov. 14.

He is supposed to be staying at the Four Seasons Hotel, which is directly across the street from the home of Bagel Knight **Mal Coven,** of BiWay fame.

"We thought we'd fly in some Montreal smoked meat for Jackie," Coven explained. "But when we called his agent to invite him, to make him an honorary member, the guy asked for an appearance fee. An appearance fee for a party, can you believe that?"

Agent **Roland Scahill,** reached at his New York office, confirmed the story, noting that Mason is a performer who makes his living on public appearances. "Mr. Mason knows about this. He is not upset at all. There are no hard feelings."

The Knights had their little ceremony anyway. Mason missed the kosher meal and his Korkee award, which will now be given out annually, to the biggest, well, you know.

● ●

Liberal Leader **Dalton McGuinty** has been short one policy director since the passing of former Liberal prime minister **Pierre Trudeau.**

Policy guy **Gerald Butts,** a friend of Trudeau's son, **Justin,** has been in Montreal helping provide comfort for the grieving family.

Justin also stood up for Butts when he needed a friend. The young Mr. Trudeau was a member of Butts' wedding party.

● ● ●

Toronto mayoral candidate **Tooker Gomberg** is scheduled to be in an Alberta courtroom tomorrow.

He is facing mischief charges after allegedly chaining himself to a truckload of oilfield equipment.

The hearing was to be held in Fort Saskatchewan, the petro-chemical and smokestack capi-

JACKIE MASON
It's not kosher

'When we called his agent to invite him, to make him an honorary member, the guy asked for an appearance fee. An appearance fee for a party, can you believe that?'

tal until a closed-door meeting in February put an end to the professional relationship.

"We sat down and said this is not working," Nadeau explained. "I decided to leave. I was not fired. It was a common agreement. It was time for me to go. After 10 years, it was too much."

The common agreement led to a city-sponsored severance package, Nadeau confirmed. However, he didn't disclose the dollar amount.

Now, he is selling $100 tickets to Jakobek's going-away party. It will be held Oct. 26 at Pier 4, 245 Queen's Quay West.

"We are going to have 300 people," Nadeau said. "There will be food and complimentary beer and wine."

All of the proceeds go to the charitable arm of Jakobek's new employer, the Toronto East General Hospital. Guests are free to pay more than $100 for admission, Nadeau said.

"They get tax receipts from the hospital."

● ● ●

Ontario's Conservative government loves to rant and rave about federal misuse of the burgeoning surplus in the nation's employment insurance account.

At the same time, the province's own money-losing television station, TVOntario, uses the EI system to facilitate its routine, annual layoff of staffers dedicated to *Studio Two,* a public affairs program.

"It's built right into your contract," said one person who has read the finest of print. "There's a four- or six-week layoff in every contract. You go on employment insurance for that period, typically in the summer."

Premier Mike Harris has repeatedly called on the feds to trim EI premiums, which he equates to a payroll tax.

"I'm going to do everything I can to embarrass Ottawa because I legally can't force them (to act)," Harris has said. "This money belongs to the workers, it belongs to employers and this nonsense has to stop."

● ● ●

Some girls just wanna be downloaded, over and over again.

Internet pinups **Danni Ashe** and **Cindy Margolis** are fighting over the *Guinness Book of Records* title for "most downloaded woman."

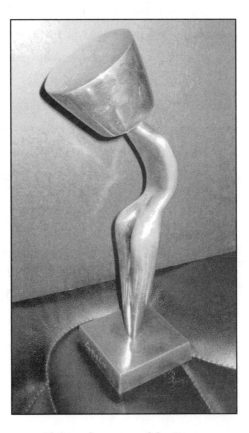

Al Green's version of the Oscar.

My idea was for all the Knights to gather at my place, buy smoked meat, and invite Jackie Mason to join us. I contacted his agent at the William Morris Agency on the phone to tell him that I wanted to invite Jackie to join us for an orgy of delicatessen. I mentioned that it would be very convenient for Jackie because I lived a few steps away from his hotel.

A few days later I was told that Jackie would come but that he wanted an appearance fee. I was shocked. I thought it was a mistake. I couldn't believe that Jackie had made that decision himself. His agent said that it came directly from Jackie. I immediately withdrew the invitation.

Thus was chosen the first winner of the Corky A-Hole of the Year Award.

We had the party with a large blowup of Jackie's picture sitting in his stead. There was no way I was going to give him that statue, one of only three in existence. In its place I made a framed certificate from the Knights that told the story of the reason that he received this dubious award and sent it over to him at the Four Seasons Hotel.

A few days later Joanne Chesler's son saw Jackie at the Windsor Arms Hotel and mentioned my name. If I printed his response, this book would never pass censorship.

Some ten years later I was on Lincoln Road in Florida and spotted Jackie sitting with friends at an outdoor café. I went over and introduced myself. I told him I was from Toronto and lived across the street from the Four Seasons Hotel.

He turned an angry red and said, "I don't have to go anywhere I don't want to."

That's quite true. Of course he did not have to attend. If he had just declined our invitation I would have understood and moved on.

(P.S. There were so many nominations for candidates in the future we could never agree on a recipient and never gave another award.)

Mal Coven

Bill Maher
Politically Incorrect
7800 Beverly Boulevard
Los Angeles, CA 90036

January 9, 2001

Dear Bill:

WE NEED YOUR HELP!

𝕿𝖍𝖊 𝕶𝖓𝖎𝖌𝖍𝖙𝖘 𝕺𝖋 𝕿𝖍𝖊 𝕽𝖔𝖚𝖓𝖉 𝕭𝖆𝖌𝖊𝖑 must find someone worthy of this year's Corky Award for the Asshole Of The Year (A/Hole if you prefer).

In Canada we have lots of shmucks but alas, no assholes.

WE NEED YOUR HELP.

We need nominations, also maybe a venue for our annual Corky Award (sculpture enclosed).

Should we have categories, re: politician, lawyer.

The Corky Sculpture was struck by a famous Canadian (Al Green) from an idea by a genius (me). It was decided a large cork was more fitting (no pun intended) for a large A (hole) more so than a wine keg.

WE NEED YOUR HELP!

Enclosed is certificate given last year (no sculpture) to Jackie Mason for the A/Hole Of The Year 2000. Also note certificate given to Mel Brooks and Carl Reiner 1999, our Honorary Members.

Regards,

Mal Coven

P.S. The Larry King Show was sensational.
P.P.S. We could use another M.C. too.

THE PRINCE ARTHUR
38 AVENUE ROAD, SUITE 514
TORONTO, ONTARIO M5R 2G2

TEL: (416) 513-0101
FAX: (416) 934-1943

FAX NO. (212) 903-1446

TO: MR. ROLAND SCAHILL:

This is a follow up to our conversation last week ie: JACKIE MASON IN TORONTO last May. The Knights of the Round Bagel organized a breakfast, 7:00 a.m. for the express purpose of Knighting him (no kneeling please!). I am enclosing the certificate of that day. I did speak with him briefly before his show, he said "He didn't know", "he forgot", "he's sorry", "he can't make it." He literally cost our organization **"Tousans"** U.S., however, in Canadian funds it was only $8.50, so it wasn't so terrible.

Not to be deterred so easily (opening 250 stores was not easy either), here we go again. This time it's different. Jackie is coming here for two weeks to give us a new opportunity and we are making him an offer he won't refuse.

First, for him I moved across the street from the Four Seasons Hotel (25 steps).

Second, we have prepared a deli delight of hot Montreal Smoked Meat, hand cut on the premises by Master Cutter "Knight Ian" (he learned his trade as a garment cutter in the needle trade.

Third, The Brisket will be flown in courtesy of Air Canada. Believe me its got Carnegie and Second Avenue beat by a kilometer. (Eh!)

Fourthly, of course there will be a fitting Knighting ceremony (No kneeling please!),

Lastly, in addition we would like some advice as we have a new annual award we will be giving, no, not the Emmy, not the Oscar, but the "Corky", to be given to the "Asshole of the year." One of our guys is a serious sculptor (Al Green, no kidding) we have the first one in hand. It's a beautiful bronze statuette with corkhead with tushi protruding, struck in Israel.

Please fax me the date and time Jackie will be available.

Best Regards!

MAL.

PS. Roland you asked me to put this tid bit:

Jackie you called me over to your table at the Park something restaurant near Carnegie Hall. I think its more of a Diner type place. We chatted about Toronto and when I told you they had stolen my Mercedes in my driveway, you looked at the man and woman you were sitting with in disbelief that they stole cars in Toronto. As I was leaving I have you my card and offered you a home cooked meal when you came next. Then I broke you up by turning and saying "Don't worry I'll remember you!"

PPS. Enclosed fax came by coincidence (I kid you not) separately from a friend in Ottawa. Thought you would get a kick out of it.

Mal Coven
38 Avenue Road, Suite 514
Toronto, Canada M5R 2G2
Tel: (416) 513-0101   Fax: (416) 934-1943

Press Release
Jackie Mason "Honoured"
1st Annual
Corkee Award Dinner

This Past Wednesday, The "Knights of the Round Bagel   a group of prominent Toronto businessmen dined at the home of Mal Coven to "Honour" Jackie Mason in absentia with only a huge poster of Jackie's picture present. A sumptuous (kosher) nine course deli meal was served. The climax of the evening was the presentation of the **Corkee Award**, a beautiful bronze sculpture by Al Green, prominent Candian artist who was commissioned by the group.

The Award is for a person who is best qualified for the title:

Asshole of the year
Or
A—hole of the Year
(your preference)

An earlier unanimous vote of the Knights selected Jackie Mason 10-0 (no abstentions) for the award. Jackie will be appearing in Toronto Nov 15- Dec 3. He was invited to the apartment home of one of the Knights (20 yards from the Four Seasons Hotel where he stays) to be "Knighted" as an honourary member of the "Knights of the Round Bagel" and for a multi course deli meal. Other past honourees were Mel Brooks, Carl Reiner, Adam and Jodi Cooper. He asked for "Appearance Money" and of course the invitation was withdrawn.

For this request for "Appearance Money" to enter one of our homes for dinner we have voted him

THE ASSHOLE OF THE YEAR 2000

His name will inscribed on **"THE CORKEE"** as will other subsequent "Honourees". A framed copy of the enclosed proclamation will be sent to him.

The Corkee Award will be given annually to finally give to person (or persons) who's deed has never been properly spotlighted before.

THOSE PRESENT FOR THE OCCASION

Adam Cooper	Thomas Levie
David Coven	Phil Litowitz
Mal Coven	Ian Roher
Leo Goldhar	Mendy Sharf
Al Green	Moe Smith
	Sid Silverberg

The Menu

Lambino Tomato & Onion Salad
Kishka Marky
Julie Potato Pudding
Julie Kasha & Bows
Button Deli Sandwiches
Deep Brown Beans with Knucker Slices
Empire 12" Hot Dogs & Buns
Fresh Pineapple & Strawberries
Fresh Blueberries Buns

Wine—1995 Chateau Siaurac

Requests for photos contact Mal Coven

Proclamation
of the
Knights of the Round bagel
(We barely have a minyon)

here As One Jackie Mason was invited to the home of one of our knights to partake in a sumptious 9 course deli meal with our members.

here As The purpose of this gathering was to make one Jackie Mason an honorary member, joining other honorary members Mel Brooks and Carl Reiner.

here As The apartment where this was to take place was across the street from the Four Season Hotel where one Jackie Mason will reside Nov. 14 – Dec. 3, when he will be performing in Toronto.

here As A fax was sent at the request of one of his agents, Roland Scahill and passed over to one Jackie Mason thru his other agent Jill Rosenfeld.

here As The reply via telephone from agent Scahill passing along Jackie Mason's reply that, in order to come to the dinner at the knight's home he would need "appearance money."

here As We called back to tell them we withdrew the invitation.

In light of the foregoing Where As's
By unanimous vote 10-0-0 (no abstentions)
we have declared this foregoing conduct by Jackie Mason
the winner of
"The Corkee Award"
For the Year 2000
For the biggest asshole of the year

This award will be given in absentia, suitably framed
His name will be the first to be engraved on the Corkee statue.

Sept 27, 2000

24

WILL HECHTER, JEWS, BASEBALL – THE DOCUMENTARY

I first met Will Hechter at his home when I was invited to participate in planning a fundraiser for the Israel Museum in Jerusalem. The vehicle they were using was the premiere of a movie to be shown at one of the major theatres. Will and his wife Linda and eight ladies in attendance were enthusiastic about the project. I was familiar with the museum because I had visited it a few years earlier and thought it was a good cause. I contributed $5,000.

I saw Will a few years later in Forest Hill Village. We had a conversation over coffee and talked mostly about baseball. Even though he was from Winnipeg, far from any professional team, I found him very knowledgeable about the major leagues and we talked about some of the many great Jewish players.

I suggested to Will that we create a poster of an All-Star Jewish team and donate it to various Jewish organizations for use as a fundraiser. He thought it was a good idea but he had a better one: to do a documentary honouring some of the great Jewish baseball players both current and past.

I agreed. We made a plan to contribute $50,000 each and raise the balance through others in the Jewish community. We assumed that it would take close to a million dollars to complete the project and for that we needed a budget.

We both knew that Ken Burns was the best documentary maker in the field and travelled to his facility in Walpole, New Hampshire. The Ken Burns people were just as enthusiastic about the project as we were. We paid them $15,000 and received a detailed budget of just under $1 million. It was a wonderful experience to meet them where they did all of their work. At the time they were working on a project for PBS on the National Parks of the U.S. I am sure their enthusiasm for our project stemmed from their award-winning documentary series on baseball, which ran for ten weeks on TV.

It was obvious to everyone that some high-profile Jewish baseball players, both former and current, should be interviewed. We both agreed that four good people who also should be approached were Billy Crystal, Carl Reiner, Mel Brooks, and Larry King. All of them grew up in the New York area, a hotbed of baseball.

At about the same time, Will was busy hiring an alternate director because the Ken Burns people were too busy to take on the project immediately.

I knew the four celebrities would be very hard to reach and received scores of charitable requests every month. I decided to take our request out of the ordinary. Along with a letter, I sent each of them a gold pack of Jewish baseball cards, which had

been offered by the American Jewish Historical Society for a $500 donation. They were numbered 1-500. (They are currently selling on eBay for $1,000.) I knew Larry King had young boys and I could picture him going through the cards with them and telling them about the golden years of baseball in New York.

I FedExed the letters and the cards to all of their agents. As I expected, I received no immediate response. I followed up with phone call after phone call to all four of them. In the case of Billy Crystal, I went to New York to speak to his agent, at my own expense.

Finally I got some results. I was told that the letter and the gold box were in Larry King's hands and that he liked them and would participate with CNN's permission, which he did receive. The FedEx to Carl Reiner sat in his lawyer's office for three weeks. I was upset that he had not received it. He finally did and accepted the invitation. However, in the end he did not appear in the documentary because his wife passed away in the interim and he asked to bow out.

The plan was to put the money in a not-for-profit entity, have a grand opening fundraiser in both Toronto and New York, and then distribute the documentary to

That's Will Hechter and me on the right, with some of Ken Burns' people in Walpole, N.H.

many organizations to use as their fundraiser. We set out to raise the balance of the money and met with success. I approached Miles Nadal and received a pledge of $50,000 for starters and a commitment from him to help us further. Will approached a few others, also with some success. I felt very optimistic that we could reach our goal of $1 million.

However, at this point Will had a change of heart. He said he wanted to be executive producer and didn't want "to be beholden to anyone." He wanted to finance the whole project himself. I remember telling him he could even call himself the president of the United States and that would be okay with me.

About this time he hired a director who was not happy that I was contacting anybody and asked me to desist. I said that the letters had already been sent as Will and I had decided and while I would not approach anyone else, I did want to follow through on the four celebrities because of all the time, effort, and money I had spent.

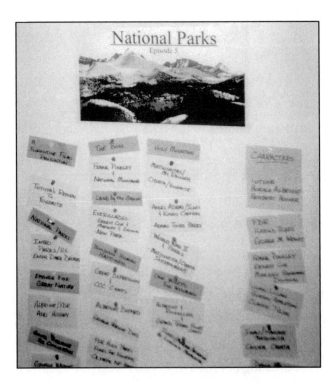

Plans for the documentary on the National Parks.

I knew Mel Brooks would be a particular problem. However, also I knew that Allan Slaight was a friend of Mel and had a place in the same complex on Fisher Island in Miami where he lived. I asked Mr. Slaight, who was in Toronto at the time, to send the package to Mel Brooks. He did that for me and refused to take the money for the FedEx. I never heard from Mel Brooks even though a few years earlier we had presented him with a certificate making him an honorary member of our group, The Knights of the Round Bagel. (He and Carl Reiner autographed certificates for all the members of our group.)

After seeing Billy Crystal's agent twice in New York and receiving lots of promises, I decided to leave that task to the director to follow up. Crystal never did participate.

I called anyone who had made pledges and told them Will did not need their money and would be financing the whole project himself. I called Miles Nadal and told him we did not need his pledge of $50,000.

Obviously, my $7,500 share of the $15,000 that was paid was an expense of the project so I asked for the money back. For some reason that I cannot fathom, Will refused to return the money. In other words, he would be writing off my $7,500 in his not-for-profit entity. I thought that was neither proper nor fair and on principle I went to Small Claims Court for satisfaction. The judge agreed with me and ordered Will to give me the money. I donated the $7,500 to help send some needy kids to a Jewish summer camp.

Later I found out that he did not finance the project himself but solicited hundreds of thousands of dollars from others in the Jewish community. To my knowledge, he never approached Miles Nadal for money.

I have been associated with many people as a partner over the years in business but was never so disappointed in a person's integrity as with Will Hecther's. I had spent many hours with Will on this project and helped him to sort out some of his personal problems. To say I was disappointed in his conduct would be an understatement.

To his credit, Will did complete the documentary. I was at the opening in Toronto and loved it. It was everything I thought it would be and I felt proud to have had a role in it.

Mal Coven
39 Avenue Road, Suite 514
Toronto, Canada M5R 2G2
Tel: 416-513-0101   Fax: 416-934-1943

PERSONAL & CONFIDENTIAL   June 26, 2007

Miles S. Nadal
Chairman & CEO
MDC Partners
45 Hazelton Avenue
Toronto, Ontario M5R 2E3

Dear Miles:

Wow! Our chance meeting at the Bagelworld last Sunday and your enthusiasm for the project that Will Hechter and I have initiated will not only raise millions of dollars for the Miles Nadel JCC but will produce a classic documentary that will generate income for the Miles Nadel JCC for years to come.

In addition, we believe that the publicity from our documentary with the name Miles Nadel JCC prominently displayed in connection with the film will lift its profile much like the 92nd Street 'Y' in Jewish circles all over North America. We will produce a classic that will be shown for years to come, updated from time to time at Jewish events so future generations will know the prominent contribution that Jews have made to every phase of the American national pastime.

As you know, we have contacted the Ken Burns people. We outlined to them the general subject of "JEWS IN BASEBALL" culminating in the selection of an all-time Jewish All-Star team. With great enthusiasm they agreed to take on the project in spite of the heavy load they have. It will take 1½ years to produce the film.

Will and I would like to meet with their people some time in July. They are proposing initially a $15,000 fee for the research and development phase, similar to paying an architect to draft blueprints before a structure is built, to cover their work from July 2007 through November 2007. They will put together their own "YourStory" contract detailing their responsibilities. During this period the full contract for the actual project will be developed.

They have told us the completed film will cost approximately $1.5M. Will and I will commit to raising half a million including our contribution but, as I told you on Sunday, we need you as an anchor sponsor for the balance to do that.

Frankly, I might be able to exceed our figure with this vehicle to the direct benefit of the Miles Nadel JCC but only with your commitment as an anchor.

Your commitment for the million dollars can be paid out over the next 18 months. With that commitment, we will get the fundraising started as soon as possible. Obviously, all net proceeds from this film will go to the Miles Nadel JCC.

The income will come from many sources for many years, some right after the film is completed, on an ongoing basis for years to come, in part from the following: PBS, HBO, Cineplex, tabletop books and licence income from t-shirts, sweatshirts and caps. All this just for starters.

We envision the culmination of the completion of the film ... a black tie fundraiser at Roy Thomson Hall, red carpet and all with sports and other celebrities, both Jewish and not, from the Commissioner of Baseball to the Mayor of NY, from Andy Kofax to Bob Feller, George Wills to Tim Russet, from Billy Crystal to Robert Merril. The affair will attract publicity all over U.S. and Canada as both sports news and entertainment news. Can you picture a similar premiere in New York, LA, Miami, Chicago?

As you know, controversy creates ratings and, among other things, we plan either live or taped after each showing of the film a round table of sports writers and/or other baseball celebrities to debate the merits of our All-Star team versus other world champion teams, i.e., 1946 Red Sox, 1958 Yankees, etc. There will be lots of room for argument and discussion.

Miles, we will keep you informed on an ongoing basis. The following is a list of the things they will explore in the initial stage July 2007 to November 2007.

1.   Finding staff, defining roles and procedures
        (i)   (1) Director
        (ii)   (2) Producers
        (iii)   (2) Associate Producers
        (iv)   Production Assistant(s)
        (v)   (1) Editor, (1) Sound Editor
        (vi)   (2) Assistant/Associate Editors (picture and sound)
        (vii)   (1) Location Scout
        (viii)   (1) Accountant

2. Finding a writer, getting him/her started
   (i) Oversee writer's creative direction through multiple drafts
   (ii) Research potential on-camera interview subjects

3. Finding our film's "angle" or approach to the topic

4. Developing a detailed budget, timetable
   (i) Contact potential cinematographers for project
   (ii) NOTE: Budget will exclude fees/rights for visuals, music
   (iii) NOTE: Budget will exclude writer's salary
   (iv) Salary disbursement-schedule for YourStory staff
   (v) Developing, negotiating and signing project contract

5. Travel and miscellaneous expense reimbursement process

6. Timetable and outline of filmmaking process

7. Exploratory of archives/libraries that will provide visual elements

8. Exploratory of rights and clearances on:
   (i) Visual images
   (ii) Music
   (iii) Story elements

9. Compile list of necessary equipment upgrade expenses for project.

The actual project will commence upon signing a formal contract no later than November 2007. They then need to have a rough draft of a script from a writer before they actively engage in Pre-Production. The project will be broken up into the following sections: Pre-Production, Production, Post-Production, and Finishing. They will provide a detailed breakdown of each section as part of the Research and Development, as well as an approximate timeline.

WE NEED A RESPONSE FROM YOU before we can pin down the date for our July meeting with Burns' people.

Thanks again for your enthusiasm for this documentary.

Sincerely,

Mal Coven

cc   Will Hechter

MAL COVEN

38 Avenue Road, Suite 514, Toronto, Ontario, Canada M5R 2G2
Tel: (416) 513-0101   Fax: (416) 934-1943

Fax #:	(416) 960.9555	Date: 7/18/07
Attention:	MILES NADAL	
Company:	MOC PARTNERS	
Cover Page plus	page(s)	
Re:	DOCUMENTARY "JEW IN BASEBALL"	

THANK YOU FOR YOUR PLEDGE TODAY

OF 50,000K TO SUPPORT THE MAKING

OF THE DOCUMENTARY "JEWS IN BASEBALL"

THE NET PROCEED OF WHICH WILL BENIFIT

THE JEWISH COMMUNITY CENTERS OF

GREATER TORONTO. YOU HAVE KICKED

OFF WILL HECHTER'S + MAL COVEN'S DRIVE

TO RAISE 1.5MILLK. FOR THIS PROJECT

MANY THANKS   REGARDS

                     MAL

Mal Coven
39 Avenue Road, Suite 514
Toronto, Canada M5R 2G2
Tel: 416-513-0101   Fax: 416-934-1943

April 28, 2008

PERSONAL & CONFIDENTIAL

Miles S. Nadal
Chairman & CEO
MDC Partners
45 Hazelton Avenue
Toronto, Ontario M5R 2E3

Dear Miles:

I told you this verbally but, for the record, I am putting it in writing.

My partner in the documentary "Jews and Baseball" decided last Fall to fund the whole million dollar project himself through his own charitable foundation. He does not want to seek any outside funding there for any pledges made are no longer valid. That includes mine and yours.

He has hired a writer and director and has commenced filming. Of course, we wish him good luck with the project. Obviously, because it is through his own charity he will have complete control of who benefits. As you know, my idea was to have the Miles Nadal JCC beneficiary of the proceeds from the film. I doubt if that will be the case now.

Separately, I guess if I bump into you now in the Bagel World you will be eating a white egg omelette and a whole wheat bagel.

Great to hear of your successful diet. Keep it up.

Regards,

Mal Coven

MAL COVEN

38 Avenue Road, Suite 514, Toronto, Ontario, Canada M5R 2G2

Tel: (416) 513-0101   Fax: (416) 934-1943

Fax #: (416) 964-8868   Date: June 16, 2008

Attention: Will Hechter

Company:

Cover Page plus   0   page(s)

Re: _____

Will:

I thought I would put in writing some of the things we agreed upon these past several weeks.

You invited me to participate again in "Jews and Baseball" on a consulting basis. After some thought I accepted under certain conditions. You accepted those conditions. They are as follows:

1.   I have no financial investment obligation.
2.   I will receive no compensation for my services and will pay any expenses incurred, i.e., ... etc.
3.   I ask to be present only in order to meet some of the personalities to be interviewed *Only when possible* not all, but the ones I choose.

As you know, I believe a strong focus should be on the All-Star team. If I am satisfied with them, *THAT* can you use my name on the film as a consultant.

As a consultant I will be, and have been, already making some suggestions to you about promoting the film. I will be doing it on an ongoing basis either verbally or in writing. I hope I can be helpful and make a meaningful contribution. *OK By Hechter except note on 3*

Mal

Mal Coven
39 Avenue Road, Suite 514
Toronto, Canada M5R 2G2
Tel: 416-513-0101   Fax: 416-934-1943

June 15, 2008

PERSONAL & CONFIDENTIAL

Miles S. Nadal
Chairman & CEO
MDC Partners
45 Hazelton Avenue
Toronto, Ontario M5R 2E3

Dear Miles:

I wanted to keep you informed about what turns out to be a happy situation. After suing and collecting $7,500 from my associate in the "Baseball and Jews" documentary project, he has asked me to come back as a consultant with none of my money invested in it. As you may remember, he wants to finance the whole project himself through his charitable foundation. That's fine with me and I am sure with you.

I agreed to come back so I could have some influence to make sure that the major part of the proceeds would go to Miles Nadal JCC. He has hired a director and writer, both well-known and exceptionally talented. He has already spent over 200K and has been filming for a few months. I will keep you informed because I know you will be interested.

Regards,

Mal Coven

MAL COVEN

June 22, 2008

PERSONAL & CONFIDENTIAL

Mr. Larry King
c/o John Ferriter
Wm. Morris Agency (WMA)
151 El Camino Drive
Beverley Hills CA 90212 USA

Dear Larry:

It is only a coincidence but Bobby Woolf was a schoolmate and friend from the time he came from Maine at both Boston Latin School and Boston College.

I am acting as an unpaid consultant for a documentary "Jews & Baseball" currently being filmed. We have retained Peter Miller as director. Peter has worked with Ken Burns, most recently co-directing "The War" an eight-part series that appeared on PBS recently. We have also retained Ira Berkow as our writer. Ira wrote sports for The New York Times and has written a dozen books on baseball and sports. At the request of Hank's son, Ira finished the Hank Greenberg book that Hank was doing before he died. The film is being produced by Will Hechter who runs a hedge fund in Toronto. It is being financed through a charitable not-for-profit foundation. All proceeds from the film will be for the benefit of Toronto JCC and JCCs in the New York and Los Angeles areas.

This charitable project started with an idea from the American Jewish Historical Society (AJHS) on 16th Street in New York. They document everything Jewish from the plight of Russian Jews to having just received the papers and pictures of the 2nd Avenue Deli for posterity. They have been doing this since the late 1800's.

38 AVENUE ROAD, SUITE 514
TORONTO, ONTARIO, CANADA M5R 2G2
TEL.: (416) 513-0101
FAX: (416) 934-1943

Our dream is a black tie premiere at our Roy Thomson Hall, maybe at the Toronto Film Festival, or around that time with baseball celebrities galore for the benefit of the Toronto JCC. We would repeat the same in New York and Los Angeles for the benefit of their JCC. Please help us in this worthwhile endeavour.

Sincerely,

Mal Coven

PS   I am also enclosing a few articles written on Jews and baseball that you might find interesting.

MAL COVEN

July 11, 2008

<u>**PERSONAL & CONFIDENTIAL**</u>

Mr. Billy Crystal
c/o Cindy Berger
PMKHBH
161 6th Avenue
IOR
New York, NY 10013

Dear Billy:

I am acting as an unpaid consultant for a documentary "Jews & Baseball" currently being filmed. We have retained Peter Miller as director. Peter has worked with Ken Burns, most recently co-directing "The War" an eight-part series that appeared on PBS recently. We have also retained Ira Berkow as our writer. Ira wrote sports for <u>The New York Times</u> and has written a dozen books on baseball and sports. At the request of Hank's son, Ira finished the Hank Greenberg book that Hank was doing before he died. The film is being produced by Will Hechter who runs a hedge fund in Toronto. It is being financed through a charitable not-for-profit foundation. All proceeds from the film will be for the benefit of Toronto JCC and JCCs in the New York and Los Angeles areas.

This charitable project started with an idea from the American Jewish Historical Society (AJHS) on 16th Street in New York. They document everything Jewish from the plight of Russian Jews to having just received the papers and pictures of the 2nd Avenue Deli for posterity. They have been doing this since the late 1800's.

They did something very unique that I am sure you would like to know about. They published a set of the **149 Jewish major league baseball cards** of players through 2003 and followed it up with three sets of approximately 60 cards 2004-8. They sold $1.9 million worth of cards. The Gold Edition numbered 1 to 500 sold for $500, Silver for $200, and a black and white set for $100. I am enclosing all that they have produced for you and/or your kids.

38 AVENUE ROAD, SUITE 514
TORONTO, ONTARIO, CANADA M5R 2G2
TEL: (416) 513-0101
FAX: (416) 934-1943

Separately, I am enclosing a card of your namesake. Did your great-greats come from Odessa? If so, we know how you acquired your baseball skills.

"Jews & Baseball" is an educational film that will show the immense contribution Jews have made to all facets of our national pastime. We hope to sell it to PBS or ESPN and subsequently distribute it to Jewish organizations and Jewish Film Festivals all over North America.

Included in the film is an all-time Jewish All-Star team. I am enclosing some of their cards separately. I am sure many of them you are familiar with. There were great players in the first half of the 20th century. A surprise is Buddy Myers. You see we have Lou Boudreau at short stop because his mother was a Jew. That is good enough for the ultra-orthodox. It's good enough for us.

The following is the team we have selected:

1st base	Youkillis (Red Sox)
2nd base	Buddy Myers (Senators)
Shortstop	Lou Boudreau (Indians)
3rd base	Al Rosen (Indians)
Right field	Shawn Green (Blue Jays)
Centre field	Sid Gordon (Giants)
Left field	Hank Greenberg (Tigers)
Catcher	Harry Danning (Giants)
Pitcher	Sandy Koufax (Brooklyn)
Pitcher	Ken Holtzman (Cubs)
Manager	Moe Berg (Red Sox coach)

I am also enclosing these cards separately.

We have already filmed eight interviews with some of the players or a close relative, also Marvin Miller, the labour lawyer. Shortly we have scheduled Theo Epstein, GM of the Red Sox and the owner of the Mets, Fred Wilpon, both of whom have agreed to be filmed.

Billy, as a super baseball fan, we would like to interview you for the film. There is no question your interview will be a great asset to the film. Billy, this is a first-class project whose budget will run well over a million dollars. Obviously we would film it at your convenience at a location you choose.

Our dream is a black tie premiere at our Roy Thomson Hall, maybe at the Toronto Film Festival, or around that time with baseball celebrities galore for the benefit of the Toronto JCC. We would repeat the same in New York and Los Angeles for the benefit of their JCC. Please help us in this worthwhile endeavour.

Sincerely,

Mal Coven

PS   I am also enclosing a few articles written on Jews and baseball that you might find interesting.

PPS I have a dream. For my 80th birthday I will see Billy, Mel Brooks, and Carl Reiner on Larry King's show talk about growing up in New York with Giants, Yankees, Dodgers. I have or will be shooting for that.

Copy: Cara Maslin

MAL COVEN

PERSONAL & CONFIDENTIAL

Carl Reiner   July 15, 2008
c/o George Shapiro
Shapiro West & Associates
141 El Camino Drive, Suite 205
Beverley Hills CA 90212 USA

Dear Carl:

As a charter member of the "Knights of the Round Bagel", I am committed to honesty and integrity. You and Mel were knighted in the year 2000 - certificate enclosed.

I am enclosing the following Golden Package as a bribe or attention-getter – take your choice - but for a noble cause.

Anti-Semites be damned. They will say we've taken over our national pastime. Curling is the only sport still sacred.

I am acting as an unpaid consultant for a documentary "Jews & Baseball" currently being filmed. We have retained Peter Miller as director. Peter has worked with Ken Burns, most recently co-directing "The War" an eight-part series that appeared on PBS recently. We have also retained Ira Berkow as our writer. Ira wrote sports for The New York Times and has written a dozen books on baseball and sports. At the request of Hank's son, Ira finished the Hank Greenberg book that Hank was doing before he died. The film is being produced by Will Hechter who runs a hedge fund in Toronto. It is being financed through a charitable not-for-profit foundation. All proceeds from the film will be for the benefit of Toronto JCC and JCCs in the New York and Los Angeles areas.

This charitable project started with an idea from the American Jewish Historical Society (AJHS) on 16th Street in New York. They document everything Jewish from the plight of Russian Jews to having just received the papers and pictures of the 2nd Avenue Deli for posterity. They have been doing this since the late 1800's.

38 AVENUE ROAD, SUITE 514
TORONTO, ONTARIO, CANADA M5R 2G2
TEL: (416) 513-0101
FAX: (416) 934-1943

They did something very unique that I am sure you would like to know about. They published a set of the 149 Jewish major league baseball cards of players through 2003 and followed it up with three sets of approximately 60 cards 2004-8. They sold $1.9 million worth of cards. The Gold Edition numbered 1 to 500 sold for $500, Silver for $200, and a black and white set for $100. I am enclosing all that they have produced for you and/or your kids.

"Jews & Baseball" is an educational film that will show the immense contribution Jews have made to all facets of our national pastime. We hope to sell it to PBS or ESPN and subsequently distribute it to Jewish organizations and Jewish Film Festivals all over North America.

Included in the film is an all-time Jewish All-Star team. I am enclosing some of their cards separately. I am sure many of them you are familiar with. There were great players in the first half of the 20th century. A surprise is Buddy Myers. You see we have Lou Boudreau at short stop because his mother was a Jew. That is good enough for the ultra-orthodox. It's good enough for us.

The following is the team we have selected:

1st base	Youkillis (Red Sox)
2nd base	Buddy Myers (Senators)
Shortstop	Lou Boudreau (Indians)
3rd base	Al Rosen (Indians)
Right field	Shawn Green (Blue Jays)
Centre field	Sid Gordon (Giants)
Left field	Hank Greenberg (Tigers)
Catcher	Harry Danning (Giants)
Pitcher	Sandy Koufax (Brooklyn)
Pitcher	Ken Holtzman (Cubs)
Manager	Moe Berg (Red Sox coach)

We have already filmed eight interviews with some of the players or a close relative, also Marvin Miller, the labour lawyer. Shortly we have scheduled Theo Epstein, GM of the Red Sox and the owner of the Mets, Fred Wilpon, both of whom have agreed to be filmed.

Carl, we have put a lot of blood, sweat and money in this educational film that will be shown for years to come.

We're after a "four bagger" - Crystal, King, Reiner and Brooks - all New Yorkers, all fans, to do a short interview. As I write, this same package is in the hands of Larry King and Billy Crystal. To get this package to Mel Brooks would be impossible for me but not for you. Please do it for me.

In my 80th year, my dream is a black tie premiere at our Roy Thompson Hall in conjunction with Toronto Film Festival or around that time with baseball celebrities for benefit of Toronto JCC. We would repeat the same in New York and Los Angeles for benefit of their JCC. Please help us in this worthwhile endeavour.

Sincerely,

Mal Coven

PS   I am enclosing a piece written by the late Chuck Weir that tells you more about Jews and baseball.

Enclosures: Chuck Weir on "Jews and Baseball"
Knights of Round Bagel certificate
Hartman letter
Word hotdog

MAL COVEN

Mel Brooks   July 17, 2008
c/o Allan Slaight
Slaight Communications
1102 – 2 St. Clair Avenue West
Toronto, Ontario M4V 1L6

Dear Mel:

Allan Slaight was kind enough to deliver this letter and package to you for me.

As a charter member of the "Knights of the Round Bagel", I am committed to honesty and integrity. Mel, you were knighted in the year 2000 - certificate enclosed.

I am enclosing the following Golden Package as a bribe or attention-getter – take your choice - but for a noble cause.

Anti-Semites be damned. They will say we've taken over our national pastime. Curling is the only sport still sacred.

I am acting as an unpaid consultant for a documentary "Jews & Baseball" currently being filmed. We have retained Peter Miller as director. Peter has worked with Ken Burns, most recently co-directing "The War" an eight-part series that appeared on PBS recently. We have also retained Ira Berkow as our writer. Ira wrote sports for The New York Times and has written a dozen books on baseball and sports. At the request of Hank's son, Ira finished the Hank Greenberg book that Hank was doing before he died. The film is being produced by Will Hechter who runs a hedge fund in Toronto. It is being financed through a charitable not-for-profit foundation. All proceeds from the film will be for the benefit of Toronto JCC and JCCs in the New York and Los Angeles areas.

This charitable project started with an idea from the American Jewish Historical Society (AJHS) on 16th Street in New York. They document everything Jewish from the plight of Russian Jews to having just received the papers and pictures of the 2nd Avenue Deli for posterity. They have been doing this since the late 1800's.

38 AVENUE ROAD, SUITE 514
TORONTO, ONTARIO, CANADA M5R 2G2
TEL: (416) 513-0101
FAX: (416) 934-1943

They did something very unique that I am sure you would like to know about. They published a set of the 149 Jewish major league baseball cards of players through 2003 and followed it up with three sets of approximately 60 cards 2004-8. They sold $1.9 million worth of cards. The Gold Edition numbered 1 to 500 sold for $500, Silver for $200, and a black and white set for $100. I am enclosing all that they have produced for you or anyone that might enjoy them.

"Jews & Baseball" is an educational film that will show the immense contribution Jews have made to all facets of our national pastime. We hope to sell it to PBS or ESPN and subsequently distribute it to Jewish organizations and Jewish Film Festivals all over North America.

Included in the film is an all-time Jewish All-Star team. I am sure many of them you are familiar with. There were great players in the first half of the 20th century. A surprise is Buddy Myers. You see we have Lou Boudreau at short stop because his mother was a Jew. That is good enough for the ultra-orthodox. It's good enough for us.

The following is the team we have selected:

1st base	Youkillis (Red Sox)
2nd base	Buddy Myers (Senators)
Shortstop	Lou Boudreau (Indians)
3rd base	Al Rosen (Indians)
Right field	Shawn Green (Blue Jays)
Centre field	Sid Gordon (Giants)
Left field	Hank Greenberg (Tigers)
Catcher	Harry Danning (Giants)
Pitcher	Sandy Koufax (Brooklyn)
Pitcher	Ken Holtzman (Cubs)
Manager	Moe Berg (Red Sox coach)

We have already filmed eight interviews with some of the players or a close relative, also Marvin Miller, the labour lawyer. Shortly we have scheduled Theo Epstein, GM of the Red Sox and the owner of the Mets, Fred Wilpon, both of whom have agreed to be filmed.

Mel, we have put a lot of blood, sweat and money in this educational film that will be shown for years to come.

We're after a "four bagger" - Crystal, King, Reiner and Brooks - all New Yorkers, all fans, to do a short interview. As I write, this same package is in the hands of Larry King, Billy Crystal and Carl Reiner.

In my 80th year, my dream is a black tie premiere at our Roy Thompson Hall in conjunction with Toronto Film Festival or around that time with baseball celebrities for benefit of Toronto JCC. We would repeat the same in New York and Los Angeles for benefit of their JCC. Please help us in this worthwhile endeavour.

Sincerely,

Mal Coven

PS   I am enclosing a piece written by the late Chuck Weir that tells you more about Jews and baseball, along with some other baseball writing.

Separately, because Son of Frankenstein received poor critical acclaim, I had to drag Barbara kicking and screaming to see it last week in New York. The hell with the critics - she loved it and I loved it, the whole audience loved it – 3 or 4 standing ovations, hooting and yelling with delight. You've probably heard this before but I had to tell you anyway.

Enclosures: Chuck Weir on "Jews and Baseball"
              Knights of Round Bagel certificate
              Hartman letter

MAL COVEN

July 31, 2008

Peter Miller
Willow Pond Films
801 West End Avenue
New York, NY 10025
USA

Dear Peter:

In 2007 Will Hechter and I were initially equal partners in the documentary "Jews and Baseball". I think it is important for you to know the circumstances of my leaving and returning to the project in Spring of 2008.

This project, "Jews & Baseball" started with a conversation and meeting with Will and I in 2007. It was initiated because of the success the American Jewish Historical Society (AJHS) had in selling $1.9 worth of Jewish baseball cards.

Will and I decided we would make a documentary and would each invest an equal amount of money and raise the balance. We proceeded to do that in 2007 and received, including our own pledges, $350K. At some point Will decided he would finance the whole project himself through a not-for-profit charity and became executive producer. At this point we had a falling-out and I withdrew from it under those circumstances. Will proceeded, as you know, to hire you and Ira and commenced making the film.

Some time in early spring 2008 Will asked me to rejoin the project, probably for two reasons. First, I was born and bred in Boston, having grown up in the era of Ted Williams and the Boston Braves. As you can easily realize, like most kids I lived and breathed baseball but probably, more importantly, I had a high profile and great respect in the Jewish community in Toronto, was very close to many potential financing participants, either corporate or individual, and had the ability to raise additional funds if necessary.

38 AVENUE ROAD, SUITE 514
TORONTO, ONTARIO, CANADA M5R 2G2
TEL: (416) 513-0101
FAX: (416) 934-1943

I agreed under certain circumstances. I wanted to be able to input some of my thoughts re "Jews and Baseball." I wanted to be listened to even though I did not have, nor did I want to have, any authority.

I am writing to you directly so you will know some of my thinking and the reasons for it.

Enclosed is a piece written by the late Chuck Weir, a well-known writer in Canada, as a favour to me. In my opinion, it captures the essence of the project. I understand you are not too enthusiastic about having a Jewish all-star team as part of the project. However, Will has told me that would fall more to the writer.

I feel strongly that an all-star team is very important as a marketing tool for the film. We picked players, some high profile, some not, but all excellent players deserving of the honour because of their record. Others may not agree with our selection. That is good. Controversy is an important marketing tool. We want people to argue the merits whether they be sports writers, sport talk show, or just fans.

Since we now have Larry King and Carl Reiner on board at this writing, and potentially Billy Crystal and Mel Brooks, I can picture them reminiscing about these players in their youth growing up in New York.

Now I would like to speak to my efforts on behalf of – I call them my 'four bagger' – King, Crystal, Reiner and Brooks.

I was told after I initiated my letters that you objected to anyone contacting them but yourself. I assume you wrote or emailed them to invite them into the project.

My guess is they get scores of requests for charitable appearances for various fundraisers. Also, I assumed these four, unlike the baseball people, would be very difficult to reach personally by me.

As I am retired from my original business I though I could be helpful. I have both the time and resources. I thought I would take my request out of the norm. As you see by the letters sent to Larry King and the other three, I have sent them all the Jewish baseball cards $500 Gold Box and all the subsequent cards sold by the AJHS. I also enclosed Weir's piece on "Jews and Baseball" to give them a sense of the project and a certificate given to Brooks and Reiner in 2000 making them honorary members of our group, "Knights of the Round Bagel". It was autographed by them for us.

In the case of Larry King, I followed up with numerous phone calls and FedExs to John, Darcy, and Brian to make sure King personally got my package. I knew if he did he would go through the cards with his kids and reminisce about some of the old NY players. I know he did that. I felt this would take a giant step in convincing him to participate (we would have his kids on our side).

With Crystal, his same package in addition contained separate cards of the all-stars so he could review their records. Luckily, also a card of Bill Crystal, a player from the 20's, originally from Odessa, Russia (who might even be related).

To summarize, I was trying to perk their interest in the project and I thought that would be helpful to you.

Today I received final confirmation from Cindy Berger that the package has been received personally by Crystal. As his daughter is being married, he has not looked at it as yet.

Getting my package in Mel Brooks' hands was difficult until I remember that he was a friend and neighbour of Allan Slaight (Slaight Communications) on Fisher Island. Allan was kind enough to send it to his residence without divulging it. I have recently followed up with a FedEx letter.

Peter, I have seen some of your work and loved what I saw. I had followed Ira's column in <u>The Times</u> for years and was always a fan of his. You both have great names in the industry. However, having some or all of the brand names of King, Crystal, Reiner and Brooks will help to make a sale to the likes of ESPN, PBS or HBO and assure large proceeds for the JCCs.

Again, to summarize, hopefully my four letters, 60-odd phone calls and 30-odd FedEx's have made a positive contribution.

Sincerely,

Mal Coven

As this is a Canadian-sponsored finance project, a piece about Goody Rosen. A pretty darn good player for Brooklyn (not a star) might be appropriate. He was the pride of Toronto when he played. I guarantee he will get a big cheer at the Toronto premiere by the many who knew him so well.

Copy: Ira Berkow

MAL COVEN

John Ferriter   August 8, 2008
Wm. Morris Agency (WMA)
151 El Camino Drive
Beverley Hills CA 90212 USA

Dear John:

It's been a month now since I actually spoke with you about our documentary "Jews &
Baseball" and the possibility of Larry King participating in an interview. You encouraged
me and I thank you for that. I tried to take it out of the norm assuming you get scores of
requests over the period of a week (maybe even daily) by sending, at my expense, all of the
Jewish baseball cards the American Jewish Historical Society had printed, also background
material on the documentary itself and general information on Jewish contribution to our
national pastime. Happily, it seems the material made an impression on Larry and his kids
and he agreed to participate. We sent similar letters and material to Carl Reiner, Billy
Crystal and Mel Brooks.

At this writing, Carl Reiner has accepted our invitation, Billy Crystal has the package but
has not looked at it, I am told, because of his daughter's wedding. Mel Brooks has it but to
date we have not heard from him.

John, I have spent a lot of time, effort and expense to reach these four guys and I want to
tell you it was not easy. I was a retailer, not in the entertainment business.

I did this on my own - although the director, Peter Miller, was not happy about it, to put it
mildly - because I believed so strongly about the project.

I would appreciate a note from your office, if not from Larry, I guess a sort of a thank-you
note for the cards and a recognition that my efforts helped in getting Larry to participate.
Thank you in advance.

Sincerely,

Mal Coven

PS   The letter will go into my file with my accomplishments in my 80th year.

38 AVENUE ROAD, SUITE 514
TORONTO, ONTARIO, CANADA M5R 2G2
TEL: (416) 513-0101
FAX: (416) 934-1943

MAL COVEN

December 29, 2008

Cara Maslin
P.M.K. H.B.H.
622 3rd Avenue
New York, NY 10017

Dear Cara:

Thank you for your holiday note. I must tell you I was very disappointed you did not keep your promise to tell me that Billy Crystal had agreed to be filmed. His is the last interview to be done. I knew he would go along. I hope the material I sent him (gold box of Jewish baseball cards) and the background material on "Jews & Baseball" helped.

The trailer will be ready for my 80th birthday at the Four Seasons in April. Billy is in good company with Larry King, Fred Wilpon, the baseball Commissioner, and a dozen or so other Jewish baseball celebrities. Sandy Koufax gave us his first interview in 25 years because he wanted to be a part of this for posterity. You see, being tenacious gets results.

How about making amends for your unkept promise - a note from Billy thanking me for the gold box of cards would be great.

Separately, I came back from Washington recently. I was invited to the annual dinner of the N.I.A.F. (National Italian American Foundation) as we are doing a fundraiser for them with Italian American major leaguers. It is similar to what we did for the American Jewish Historical Society (AJHS). I sat with Gina Lollobrigida, Barbara Sinatra and Yogi Berra, among others. It was great fun.

..2/

38 AVENUE ROAD, SUITE 514
TORONTO, ONTARIO, CANADA M5R 2G2
TEL: (416) 513-0101
FAX: (416) 934-1943

Also, our new start-up venture, Lola's Cupcakery, is opening in Fort Lauderdale in January. We have started catering already and are overwhelmed with orders.

We will, at some point, be looking for a PR person for both the documentary and Lola's Cupcakery. As you may remember, we will be doing a premiere for the documentary in Toronto, New York and L.A.

I am enclosing a few things you might find interesting.

Best regards to you and to Starr,

Mal

P.S. The finger puppets are to make sure you remember me.

Enclosures: Lola package
              Finger puppets
              Business cards

MAL COVEN

August 16, 2008

PERSONAL & CONFIDENTIAL

Michael R. Bloomberg
Mayor, New York City
City Hall
New York NY 10007 USA

Dear Mayor Bloomberg:

I am associated with a documentary "Jews & Baseball" currently being filmed. All of the proceeds of the film will be donated to the 92nd Street 'Y' as well as Jewish community centres in Toronto and Los Angeles.

Although it originated in Toronto, New York and New Yorkers will have a huge presence. Larry King and Carl Reiner have agreed to participate and at this writing we are waiting to hear from Billy Crystal and Mel Brooks, all originally New Yorkers. Many of the players or their relatives already have been, or have agreed to be, filmed. Names like Harry Danning, Sid Gordon, Sandy Koufax, Hank Greenberg are either from New York or played there. Fred Wilpon has also agreed to be interviewed on film. I am sure these and many of the players being honoured are familiar to you.

As a former Bostonian of the Ted Williams era, sad to say only Kevin Youkillis and Theo Epstein will be included.

We have retained Peter Miller as director. Peter has worked with Ken Burns, most recently co-directing "The War" an eight-part series that appeared on PBS recently. We have also retained Ira Berkow as our writer. Ira wrote sports for <u>The New York Times</u> and has written a dozen books on baseball and sports. At the request of Hank's son, Ira finished the Hank Greenberg book that Hank was doing before he died. The film is being produced by Will Hechter from Toronto. It is funded through a charitable not-for-profit foundation. All proceeds will go to the aforementioned community centres.

..2/

38 AVENUE ROAD, SUITE 514
TORONTO, ONTARIO, CANADA M5R 2G2
TEL: (416) 513-0101
FAX: (416) 934-1943

This charitable project originated with an idea from the American Jewish Historical Society (AJHS) on 16th Street in New York. I am sure you are familiar with their work. The AJHS marketed Jewish major league baseball cards and raised $1.9 million with the endeavour.

"Jews & Baseball" is an educational film that will show the immense contribution Jews have made to all facets of our national pastime. We hope to sell it to PBS or ESPN and subsequently distribute it to Jewish organizations and Jewish Film Festivals all over North America.

The stories from Larry King and Carl Reiner growing up with baseball in New York, the interviews with former players or their relatives, the input of others - from Sandy Koufax to Fred Wilpon - will make this film both entertaining and educational. It is obvious the focus on New York will be very prominent.

Our goal is to have premieres in Toronto, New York and Los Angeles. We envision Roy Thomson Concert Hall in Toronto and similar locations in New York and Los Angeles as a fundraisers for the aforementioned community centres.

Can't you picture 3,000 or more at the premiere singing "Take Me Out To The Ballgame" in English and Yiddish (written by Tin Pan Alley Jews). Mandy Potemkin will sing along either in person or on film.

To date we have raised $500K in Toronto towards our budget for the film of $1 million needed to complete it. Any support from New York City in any way would be most helpful.

I strongly feel that this documentary will not only be a great benefit to the 92nd Street 'Y' but also to New York City. I am enclosing some background material on "Jews & Baseball" and a set of Jewish baseball cards from AJHS which jump-started this worthwhile endeavour.

Sincerely,

Mal Coven

Enclosure: Baseball cards

25

AL GREEN'S 75TH BIRTHDAY

ONE would think that Bagel World would not be an appropriate venue for such a celebration as Al's 75th birthday party. However, David and Barry, Al's sons, decided to take the place over one evening, putting tablecloths on the tables and adding a small band to make it more festive.

My first reaction was, "My G-d, how can you ask ladies to go downstairs to use those washrooms? They're worse than some of the ones I've seen in Eastern Europe."

I decided to remedy the situation. I rented a portable commode usually used on work sites and had it placed on the sidewalk in front of the restaurant for the use of the ladies.

I blew up two huge posters that I adapted from a sculpture magazine, put the Green name next to the Rodin name, and decorated the commode with them. To make it more dramatic, I had my housekeeper Julie sew a cover for the commode with a fabric and bow and had an unveiling during the party.

I'm not sure any of the ladies ever used the commode, but we sure had a lot of laughs at the unveiling.

MAL COVEN'S SPEECH

ON BEHALF OF

THE KNIGHTS OF THE ROUND BAGEL

ON THE OCCASION OF

AL GREEN'S 75TH BIRTHDAY

JANUARY 25, 2000

THE BAGEL WORLD

LADIES AND GENTLEMEN:

MY NAME IS MAL COVEN AND I HAVE DEPUTIZED MYSELF TO SPEAK ON
BEHALF OF A GROUP THAT'S BEEN KNOWN TO FREQUENT THIS
LUXURIOUS BISTRO. OUR GROUP'S NAME IS WORLD-RENOWN AND GOES
BACK TO THE DAYS OF KING ARTHUR. WE GO BY THE NAME "THE
KNIGHTS OF THE ROUND BAGEL".

SPEAKING TO SUCH AN ILLUSTRIOUS GROUP AS THIS, I FEEL VERY HUMBLE
INDEED, AND I THINK THAT IS VERY APPROPRIATE BECAUSE WE ARE
GATHERED IN A VERY, VERY HUMBLE PLACE, AND I REPRESENT A VERY
HUMBLE GROUP, THE KNIGHTS OF THE ROUND BAGEL. (NOT TO MENTION
ANY BY NAME BUT A FEW OF US ARE NOT SO HUMBLE.)

VERY SADLY, SOME OF MY FELLOW KNIGHTS CANNOT BE WITH US AS
THEY HAVE DEPARTED: IAN AND PHIL HAVE DEPARTED TO WEST PALM,
LEO TO LONGBOAT, AND MOE TO MEXICO.

BEFORE MOE LEFT, HE GAVE ME SOME GREAT ADVICE FOR TONIGHT. HE
SAID, "MAL, THINK, THINK, THINK OF *SOMETHING*." SO THIS IS WHAT WE
HAVE COME UP WITH.

AL, FROM THIS DAY FORTH, YOUR NAME WILL BE FOREVER ASSOCIATED
WITH THE BEST IN YOUR ART FORM. WE SUSPECT THAT PEOPLE THE
WORLD OVER WILL COME TO SEE THIS *OBJET D'ART*. THE NAMES
ADORNING THIS PIECE WILL FOREVER BE INTERTWINED.

SECURITY GUARD

UNVEIL!

AL'S PRIVATE PRIVY

FOR THOSE THAT CANNOT SEE THROUGH THE WINDOWS, THESE TWO
POSTERS ADORN THE PRIVY.

BY THE WAY, THESE ORIGINAL POSTERS WERE DONE BY THE

CHINESE/JEWISH POSTER MAKER

KINKO

GREEN, RODEN & KINKO

HAPPY BIRTHDAY, AL!

26

THE KNIGHTS OF
THE ROUND BAGEL

I registered the name *Knights of the Round Bagel* because I thought it was so appropriate for a group I belonged to that had breakfast five days a week at 7 a.m. for close to 20 years at the Bagel World. Miriam, a waitress there, served us in her unique way, usually at the table next to the coffee machine. That was an important location because we could get refills of coffee on a self-serve basis if necessary.

The original Knights, in alphabetical order, were: Alan Blackstein, Mal Coven, Leo Goldhar, Al Green, Phil Litowitz, Ian Roher, Al Sandler, Mendy Sharf, Sid Silverberg, and Moe Smith. Our conversations run the gamut from golf to the stock market to new business investments to fishing.

Among the group were five developers, two retailers – one of whom turned to developing – a toy importer, and a roofer. In season, golfing usually monopolized the conversation, with various members usually lamenting their performance the previous weekend. That was not very interesting to me because I retired after one game in the 1950s with Jay Long, Larry Blackman, and Benny Diamond when
Δ325

I struck another golfer with a ball that went astray. Fortunately – for him and me – after being hit in the testicles and rolling on the ground for ten minutes, he recovered sufficiently to resume his game.

It was not easy to get a word in during those golf conversations but I did my best. There was a lot of interest in Biway before I retired and to some degree in some of my original projects after I retired. Jokes were plentiful, particularly from Al Green. Every day he opened his black book into which he had written punch lines to remind himself of his recently learned jokes.

Whenever a beautiful lady came to the register to pay, the flow of our conversation was seriously interrupted.

In season, fishing was also a topic. That was Mendy's bag, in particular. I never could quite understand he attraction of spending hours in a boat catching fish and then throwing them back into the lake. Mind you, I did enjoy our outings many Julys at Leo Goldhar's cottage. It was quite usual for eight of us to go out in three boats looking for the catch of the day. We followed Mendy's direction for the best place to anchor that morning and the results most often produced only a handful of fish. After fishing, we all enjoyed a sumptuous barbecue served by Leo and Sala. The group grew to 30 or so for the barbecue.

The breakfasts at the Bagel World were very important to me because they got me out of the house by 6:30 a.m. When I was not at Biway, I usually drove back to my office at home, talking on my car phone with Barbara, Maxine, and Joanne.

Our group from time to time dined together – at times with the ladies – at Lee Gardens on Spadina. Al Sandler was influential there and we received first-class food and service. On one occasion the boys got together at Al's cottage, where he served his world-famous bouillabaisse. On that occasion Mendy told me never to buy a cottage, listing for me the pitfalls of ownership. He was wasting his breath because I never intended to buy one.

One of my special memories is one of my birthday celebrations with the Knights of the Round Bagel. The guys gathered at my home on Old Forest Hill Road to be greeted by a bus that whisked us away to Harold Kamin's "Gentlemen's Club." The highlight of the evening was not the food.

Moe Smith was a wonderful gentleman who would literally give you the shirt off his back if you asked. On the occasion of his 50th wedding anniversary with Mildred, each of us put in $1,000 to send them for two weeks to Pritiken. Moe was very heavy. Unfortunately it only helped him for a short time.

It was at one of the Bagel World breakfasts that I persuaded Al Green to create a sculpture as an award called the Corky, to honour the A-Hole of the Year 2000, an event I describe earlier in this book.

I still go to the Bagel World for breakfast but it's not the same. Some of the boys still come anywhere from 7 to 9 in the morning. They are still my friends and I see many of them from time to time.

I have new friends that I sit with. Among them are Gloria and Stan Gold and Sam Frydrych. Also Bernie Bedder, my old neighbour on Brantley Crescent, who always tests me on my knowledge of baseball in the 1940s and 1950s.

Mal Coven

Mel Brooks
c/o William Morris Agency
1325 Avenue of America
New York, NY 10019

January 9, 2001

Dear Mel:

The Knights Of The Round Bagel need your help!

Lest you have forgotten, you are an Honorary Member (certificate enclosed).

We must find someone worthy of this year's Corky Award (sculpture enclosed) for the Asshole Of The Year (A/Hole if you prefer).

In Canada we have lots of shmucks but alas, no assholes.

WE NEED YOUR HELP.

Do you have any A/Holes down there?

The Corky Sculpture was struck by a famous Canadian (Al Green) from an idea by a genius (me). It was decided a large cork was fitting (no pun intended) for a large A (hole) more so than a wine keg.

WE NEED YOUR HELP!

Enclosed certificate only given to Jackie Mason (in absentia) for the A/Hole Of The Year 2000 and the accompanying celebration.

What about a venue for this potential black tie affair? What do you think?

Regards,

Mal Coven

P.S. The Slaights know who I am

...officer visited him last Saturday, the State Department spokesman, Richard Boucher, said.

Another Chinese-born American, Li Shaomin, was detained in February, and two Chinese with American resident status, Gao Zhan and Qin Guangguang, are also being held.

Rural Unrest

...ance once and for all.

On Saturday they arrested Mr. Su, considered a ringleader. On Sunday at 4 a.m., at least 600 officers of the local police and the People's Armed Police, an anti-riot force affiliated with the army, arrived at the village edge in trucks and vans. The officers had been told that all of Yuntang village was a "criminal gang," witnesses later said.

Armed with rifles, pistols and electric prods, the officers ran around ...dblock and started breaking ...es, waking the rest of the ... front of the primary ... the officers confronted ... of hundreds, according to wit...es, and at 4:20 a.m. they opened fire. By some accounts, they began by firing low, at the legs, but when farmers started fighting back with rocks and sticks, they shot to kill.

Two men died and a third was paralyzed, and a total of 18 wounded villagers are now recovering in two local hospitals.

The deaths were confirmed by a to... ', who added, shaking his ... se taxes in 1998 were too high.

The police occupied the village for the day, detaining three more people but releasing them later.

Now the residents of Yuntang feel they are living in a virtual state of siege, with ...e watching their roadway, ...n in a back room and a ...comrade in jail. They await the decisions of the provincial government, and have sneaked out a written plea for atten-'...'.. higher authorities in Bei-

This winter Prime Minister Zhu ... gan to reduce the crushing tax ...s on farmers, proposing to ... on pilot projects in Anhui ...vince in which all extra fees were abolished and farmers pay a single ...ax, with total tax burdens considera-...y reduced.

The idea is popular, but no one has ...answered the obvious problem it ses: how to make up the enormous ...ortfall in fu... for local govern-...ment, which, corru... ractices aside, must also build ro... s and schools and pay teachers and the police.

Other points of view
on the Op-Ed page
seven days a week.
The New York Tim...

---

positions they held Sunday before Bangladeshi troops occupied a strip of land in Meghalaya. Despite the announcement, a local Indian police official reported ...at minor skirmishes were continuing. At least 11 Indian soldiers have been killed; the Bangladeshi toll is not known. *Celia W. Dugger (NYT)*

JAPAN: APPEAL TO 'RICH JEWS' A candidate for prime minister said Japan should try to attract "rich Jews to help solve the country's problems of repeated economic recession and dwindling population." Economy Minister Taro Aso, a contender in Tuesday's vote by the Liberal Democrats, added, "This might be arbitrary and biased, but I think the best country is one in which rich Jews feel like living." Mr. Aso asserted that his remarks were not offensive, saying: "Japanese cannot distinguish between Jews, Italians or Spanish. But by the same token, foreigners cannot tell the difference between Japanese, Vietnamese, Chinese and South Koreans." *Howard W. French (NYT)*

VIETNAM: PARTY LEADER MAY STEP DOWN The leader of the Vietnamese Communist Party, Le Kha Phieu, said he was ready to step aside for a younger man, if the conditions were right. Asked if he expected to remain in the post of party secretary general, Mr. Phieu, 70, said. "It depends, but I think I have reached the age and if the conditions are right, then the conditions should be created for a younger person." A senior Vietnamese government official said that the National Assembly chairman, Nong Duc Manh, 61, would replace Mr. Phieu. *(Reuters)*

AFRICA

ETHIOPIA: 39 DIE IN STUDENT CLASHES At least 39 people were killed in clashes this week in Addis Ababa between students and security forces, hospital officials reported. University students are on strike over what they say are repressive educational policies. The Education Ministry has closed the university indefinitely. *(Agence France-Presse)*

BURUNDI: COUP FAILS All the junior army officers who tried to stage a coup on Wednesday have surrendered. Military officials said President Pierre Buyoya's Tutsi-led government was still in charge, though the coup attempt exposed how vulnerable he is as he tries to negotiate peace with Hutu rebels. *Ian Fisher (NYT)*

World Business Briefing, Page W1

MAL COVEN

Satoshi Hara   April 23, 2001
Consul General
Consulate General of Japan
Suite 3300, Royal Trust Tower
P.O. Box 10, 77 King Street West
Toronto, Ontario M5K 1A1

Dear Sir:

We note with much interest Economy Minister Taro Aso's desire to attract wealthy Jews to help solve your country's economic problems.

I am writing you on behalf of eight businessmen interested in possibly pursuing an investment of time and money in Japan. Our expertise is development and construction of apartments, condos, commercial, both retail and industrial; also with expertise in retailing and manufacturing.

We would like you to provide a sponsor and a guide through the intricacies of Japan's commerce and culture. A one-week orientation would be needed to help us get properly focused.

As we are all of the Jewish faith, will you please find the locations of synagogues in Tokyo and anywhere we might be travelling.

Sincerely,

Mal Coven

On behalf of:

Leo Goldhar, First Professional Management
Sid Silverberg, Dominion Roof
Ian Rohr, Rortan Ventures
Phil Litowitz, Durberry Homes
Mendy Scharf, Wycliffe Development
Mal Coven, Darob Limited
Al Sandler, Wycliffe Ltd.
Moe Smith, Smitty Transportation

c.c. Taro Aso

38 AVENUE ROAD, SUITE 514
TORONTO, ONTARIO M5R 2G2
TEL.: (416) 513-0101
FAX: (416) 934-1943

DON'T MISS THIS EXCITING EDUCATIONAL EVENT!

Coven Invitational
Floating Poker* Seminar

October 15, 1992 at 1:00 PM   17 Old Forest Hill Road

Light lunch will be served

*L*ecturers include:-
Prof. L. Simpson on "Penny Poker"
Prof. R. Jacobson on "Hearts"
Prof. S. Mandel on "War"
Prof. A. Fish on "Fish"

*E*ligibility:
● *mares 60 years or older*
● *non-winners of $5000 lifetime*
● *carrying weight over 160 lbs.*
● *no geldings*

The small print: We do not guarantee the appearance of any of the above but will do our best to get them there. Admittance is proof of UJA contributions of $10 or more during past two years. Please call Mal Coven at 484-4407 to reserve your place at this extraordinary sporting event!

*Approved by Hoyle

Mal Coven

YOU ARE INVITED

ON

THURSDAY JULY 27, 1995

AT

7:30 pm

TO

"JULIE'S CHINESE DINER"

HOMECOOKED AT

COVEN'S

17 OLD FOREST HILL ROAD

NO SHRIMP
NO PORK
NO VALET PARKING
NO DATES

WINE BY SHARE

17 Old Forest Hill Road
Toronto, Ontario
Canada M5P 2P6

(416) 484-4407

✳ REGRETS ONLY
484-4407

Knights of the Round Bagel

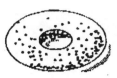

You are cordially invited to partake in a **Super Duper Evening** at

CENTRO'S

on Tuesday August the 8th, 1995

Cocktails: 7:00pm
Dinner: 8:00pm

Dress Code: *what ever you are wearing*

Appetites: *have belly empty*

Bladder: *fully cleared up for fill up*

Wine by Mendywood Sharf

SHOW UP OR ELSE.....

Regards,

Moe Smith

⇧ ⇧ ⇧ ⇧ ⇧ ⇧
FEED DOCUMENT THIS DIRECTION
**IMPORTANT
FAX MESSAGE**

TO _MAL COVAN_
COMPANY _____
FAX NO. _485 9652_
FROM _____
NO. OF PAGES _2_
RE _____

Y2K
ONCE IN A MiLLENiUM
FiSHiNG DERBY

THURSDAY, July 27, 2000

@: Goldhar's Cottage

SPECIAL ENTERTAINMENT & PRIZES:

FEATURING. POLISH WINE!!!

To: Mal Coven   Fax: 934-1943

Fish-off time: 10:30 am

Lights out: WHEN SALA SHOWS UP!

1st Prize: PENAL IMPLANT installed by Doctor "Shaky" Schacht ...

2nd Prize: PAIN treatment by Doctor Marvin Roebuck ...

3rd Prize: LIFETIME supply of Energizer batteries for a new dildo if
                            prizes 1 and 2 are not successful!

Program:
10:30 am to 12:00 pm	Fishing
12:00 pm to 2:00 pm	Lunch Onboard
2:15 pm to 2:16 pm	Clean & Gut Fish
2:20 pm to 5:00 pm	Tennis. Drinks. Movies and Whale Watching
5:30 pm to 6:00 pm	Cocktails and Lies
6:30 pm to ???	Dinner & Entertainment

New Rules - Anyone who catches a fish will be barred from next years Derby!

P.S.   Under 65's must have a fishing licence

R.S.V.P.   Cindy by July 21st. 2000   at (416) 753-7630 Tel
                                                           (416) 753-7641 Fax

Dear Mal

<u>TO ALL B.B.'s</u>

SUBJECT: BOUILLABAISSE & FISH DINNER

TIME & PLACE: THURSDAY, AUGUST 31st at 5:00 p.m., SANDLER'S COTTAGE

Dear Mishpucha (Yo all) - <u>MEN ONLY</u>

     I have tried to accommodate everybody but its almost impossible,
5 different dates were put forward and it was not possible to get everyone,
at the same time. The August 31st date Thursday, appears to be okay, at
least as of this fax date.

     I need at least 8 chevra to make it work.

     It has been suggested that some may want to play golf at National
Pines, and them come to the cottage at around 4-5 p.m. (GREAT IDEA). It
allows cottagers to remain up for the long weekend, also fish is freshest
on Thursday. If I can get 8 yes' it's a go. If not, we'll do it in 1996.

     Please fax my office - 905-881-9697 or phone 905-881-3040, and
leave message with Sheri - <u>PLEASE ADVISE EARLIEST</u>!

                                       Thanks, Al

The Toronto Blue Jays cordially invite you to a brunch
honouring 2011 Hall of Fame Inductees

Roberto Alomar & Pat Gillick

Sunday July 24, 2011
9:00 AM - 11:15 AM

. . . .

FENIMORE ART MUSEUM TERRACE
5798 STATE HIGHWAY 80
COOPERSTOWN, NEW YORK

R.S.V.P. TO MAGGIE CARPENTER AT
MAGGIE.CARPENTER@BLUEJAYS.COM

NATIONAL BASEBALL HALL OF FAME

INDUCTION

ALOMAR · BLYLEVEN · GILLICK

20 11
NATIONAL BASEBALL HALL OF FAME

27

THE TORONTO BLUE JAYS

I have been a Blue Jays fan from day one. I have corresponded with the club frequently, offering suggestions from songs to hot dog stands. Below are some letters to and from Paul Godfrey and others. One was to ask Paul to make Michael Florence a scout for Australia; another was a condolence letter from Dr. Lee Rubenstein of Cleveland after Toronto lost four games in a row.

Of course, throwing out the first ball with some grandchildren in attendance was special. Just recently, through the good graces of Paul Chapnick and Paul Beeston, I was invited to a brunch at Cooperstown, the day Roberto Alomar and Pat Gillick entered the Hall of Fame.

A few other thoughts about the Blue Jays.

One of the delights of going to see a Blue Jays game is the food, in particular the kosher hot dogs at the Olde Spadina Ave. stand. I always stop there to eat one of their delightful hot dogs.

(Once I visited the stand with my grandson Daniel. As a growing boy he had two. I decided to follow his lead. It took me 24 hours to recover.)

In 2009 I was shocked to find the stand had literally been moved to left field from its prime location. Instead of long lines, there were very short ones. Obviously they were suffering financially.

As a season's ticket holder, I received a questionnaire from the Blue Jays by email. I seized upon this as a chance to voice my disapproval.

Throwing out the first ball, in Rogers Stadium, 2002.

Being very new with computers it took me close to an hour to fill the question-naire out. When I pressed the send button I found out the questionnaire was not "live" yet. I was furious. Furious enough to call Paul Beeston to lodge an official complaint.

I thought I would get his voicemail, but, lo and behold, Paul picked up the phone himself. The first words that came out of my mouth were "the computer."

"I don't know anything about computers," Paul said.

I continued with my tale of woe. He listed very sympathetically as he was himself a kosher hot dog fan. He said he would see what he could do to resolve the situation.

The bad news was he could not do much. The good news was that the long lines at the Olde Spadina Ave. stand seemed to return. I guess, like me, other customers got used to the long walk to the stand at left field.

Pure Mal Coven, I guess. If I see an injustice, I try to rectify it. I did not succeed in this case, but I didn't let it pass and tried my best.

⌒

On one occasion my son-in-law Tim Gofine was using my baseball tickets and had just settled in to watch the game when the usher came down with another gentleman with tickets for the identical seat numbers. This didn't upset Tim. Of course he didn't move – this was obviously a mistake by the Blue Jays.

I wasn't upset either, when I heard the story from Tim. However, I decided to make the most of it and complain to the Blue Jays office. I thought they should know about it. When I spoke to the Blue Jays their rep was very apologetic and said he would make up for it by letting me throw out the first ball in an upcoming game.

Of course I accepted. What an unexpected pleasure! I went down to a game a few weeks later with my son David and my grandchildren at the time, Daniel, Miriam, and Nomi.

I hadn't thrown a ball in many years, so a few days earlier I went to see David so I could prepare for this great and unexpected pleasure. I asked him to get a glove and throw a ball around with me so I wouldn't make a fool of myself by throwing ball inaccurately.

David delivered a very low blow.

"Dad," he said, "I don't need a glove to catch your throws."

I wanted to make sure that my throw would reach the catcher. I remembered a pitch that was thrown by Rip Sewell. The pitch was called a euphus ball. It went way up in the air in a huge arc and then down. He actually threw this pitch in games. One of those occasions an All-Star game. In that particular game the American League was ahead 9 to 0. Sewell threw it to Ted Williams, who stepped out of the batter's box and hit it out of the park for a home run.

A friend of mine was a photographer for the Blue Jays and took four pictures of me winding up and throwing the first euphus ball since that game in 1941. I have all of this documented in my sports memorabilia room, showing me winding up and throwing that ball. I also have one of those pictures made into a baseball card inserted in my frame of 150 Jewish baseball players under the title Most Valuable Player.

Paul V. Godfrey, C.M.
President and
Chief Executive Officer

October 23, 2000

Mal Coven
38 Avenue Road
Suite 514
Toronto, Ontario
M5R 2G2

Dear Mal:

Thank you for your recent letter. I will discuss your idea of a Blue Jays song
with our promotion and marketing departments.

I appreciate your input and thank you for writing to me.

Yours sincerely,

Paul V. Godfrey

PVG/jcs

TORONTO BLUE JAYS BASEBALL CLUB
ONE BLUE JAYS WAY, SUITE 3200, TORONTO, ONTARIO, CANADA M5V 1J1
PHONE 416-341-1430 • FAX 416-341-1435 • www.bluejays.com

Toronto Blue Jays Baseball Club
One Blue Jays Way, Suite 3200,
Toronto, Ontario, Canada M5V 1J1
Phone: 416 341 1000
www.bluejays.com

November 10, 2006

Mr. Michael Florence
103 Vesta Road
Toronto, Ontario
M5P 2Z8

Dear Michael:

It has been brought to my attention that you are going to Australia for a month to visit your son and his family.

I also understand that being a dedicated baseball fan and someone who attends most of the Blue Jays home games, that you may be interested in doing some work for the ball club as an unofficial scout while you are "down under".

I'm sure that you will be hard-pressed to keep busy while you're on vacation and I thought that you could see some baseball games either at the high school, college or minor league level. You may be aware that they did enter a team in the World Baseball Classic and because the game is now a worldwide sport, it is important that our reach be as far and wide as possible.

Please find enclosed some of our scouting check-lists . Of course, this assignment is without remuneration but, who knows, you may find the next Roy Halladay on your trip.

Sincerely,

Paul V. Godfrey
President and Chief Executive Officer

Paul V. Godfrey
President and
Chief Executive Officer

November 17, 2006

Mr. Mal Coven
38 Avenue Road
Suite 514
Toronto, Ontario
M5R 2G2

Dear Mal:

I was pleased to do the letter for Michael Florence and your gift, although certainly not necessary, was very much appreciated.

I sincerely hope that the Club's acquisition of Frank Thomas doesn't end the same way as Casey's poem.

And, yes, I do remember Chuck Connors – he was one of my favourites.

All the best,

Paul V. Godfrey

PVG/jcs

Paul V. Godfrey
President and
Chief Executive Officer

August 27, 2007

Mr. Mal Coven
38 Avenue Road
Suite 514
Toronto, Ontario
M5R 2G2

Dear Mal:

Many thanks for sending me the very cute photo of your grandchildren.

My guess is that Randy Levine probably receives a lot of mail and is just acknowledging your communication without putting too much thought into his response.

However, working for Steinbrenner must kill whatever sense of humour one has.

Best wishes,

Paul V. Godfrey

P.S. – *I would suggest that you buy Blue Jays caps for the kids next time you're down at the Rogers Centre..!*

TORONTO BLUE JAYS BASEBALL CLUB
One Blue Jays Way, Suite 3200, Toronto, Ontario Canada M5V 1J1
Phone: 416-341-1430 • Fax: 416-341-1435 • www.bluejays.com

Paul V. Godfrey
President and
Chief Executive Officer

May 25, 2007

Mr. Mal Coven
38 Avenue Road
Suite 514
Toronto, Ontario
M5R 2G2

Dear Mal:

It was great to speak to you the other day and I hope that your project we discussed is a great success. I'm sure there will be great public interest in such a film. Many thanks for sending me the collection of Jewish Major League Baseball cards. They make a great topic of discussion, especially in the world of baseball trivia.

I hope that you and your family are well and I look forward to speaking to you soon.

Yours sincerely,

Paul V. Godfrey

PVG/jcs

TORONTO BLUE JAYS BASEBALL CLUB
One Blue Jays Way, Suite 3200, Toronto, Ontario Canada M5V 1J1
Phone: 416-341-1430 • Fax: 416-341-1435 • www.bluejays.com

Mal Coven
39 Avenue Road, Suite 514
Toronto, Canada M5R 2G2
Tel: 416-513-0101   Fax: 416-934-1943

April 27, 2008

PERSONAL & CONFIDENTIAL

Mr. Paul Godfrey
President
Toronto Blue Jays
One Blue Jays Way
Toronto, Ontario M5V 1J1

Dear Paul:

Thank you for dropping in on my birthday party at Rogers Centre a couple of weeks ago and joining in on "Take me out to the ballgame." It was very kind of you to do that. Next year is my 80th so I'll have to do something to top that.

I really can't hold it against you but I lost a steak dinner bet that Frank Thomas would hit 20 home runs. I have to check the wording of my bet. I'm not sure if the 20 meant Blue Jays' home runs only.

Separately and seriously, I no longer have any connection with the documentary "Jews and Baseball." My former partner in the project decided to fund it himself to the tune of $1 million. He also decided that he did not want to seek any outside funds. He has hired a writer and director and has started to do some filming. Of course I wish him the best of luck with the film and hope it will be a big success. Miles is off the hook on the 50K pledge he made for it.

Regards,

Mal Coven

PERSONAL & CONFIDENTIAL

Mr. Paul Godfrey   October 12, 2008
President
Toronto Blue Jays
One Blue Jays Way
Toronto, Ontario M5V 1J1

Dear Paul:

I received the news of your resignation with mixed emotion. Of course I did not want you to vacate your position because my direct contact with the Blue Jays operation evaporated. I've got no one to advise on trades, etc. I am also assuming my friend Michael Florence lost his position as honourary scout for the Blue Jays in Australia. On the other hand, I know since your first job working for Jimmy Kay you have accomplished much. During my time after moving from Boston you had a successful career as Metro Chairman and followed that as a successful publisher of The Sun.

Nothing is perfect in this world. Although you didn't win any pennants, you organized the floundering Blue Jays front offices, put in place good people there and on the field. I predict that in the next two years they will be on top of the heap again because of your efforts.

Paul, remember, it's in some ways a game of chance. If six games went the other way you would be in the playoffs. With the Jays pitching they would look good in any short series. Too bad you can't hit 30 home runs with 100 RBIs and bat 300.

Good luck and good health.

Mal Coven

P.S.   What do you think of this suggestion? Triple A team in North York, "North York Metros" or some such name. if the Harold Green Theatre can get 800 subscribers, I think you could get 2,000 season ticket holders. To get 15 or 20 guys to put money into it would be easy in my opinion (me included). I think it would be great. See Hall of Fame magazine and some of the things done to promote baseball in minors.

October 17, 1991

Dear Mal –

   I was deeply saddened to hear about
our recent losses (4) At this time of sorrow,
may your faith give you strength and may
the caring of others give you comfort. Also, a
new manager wouldn't hurt either.

Sincerely

Lee

P. S. I don't care what you guys are saying.
I had nothing to do with this.

LEE RUBINSTEIN, M.D., INC. — MT. SINAI MEDICAL BUILDING • 26900 CEDAR ROAD
TELEPHONE 831-3474 • BEACHWOOD, OHIO 44122

AUGUST 16, 1991

MAL COVEN
ASST. 2ND VICE-PRESIDENT
  IN PARTIAL CHARGE OF
    MARKETING
BINI WORLD-WIDE ENTERPRISES
BILL BUCKNER DRIVE
TORONTO, CANADA

DEAR MAL,

    I APOLOGIZE FOR NOT WRITING SOONER. I'M REALLY ENJOYING THE BOOK YOU SENT ME. I'VE ONLY READ THROUGH CHAPTER 35 SO I DON'T KNOW WHAT THE HECK IS COMING UP IN CHAPTER 36 THAT YOU FOUND SO INTERESTING.

    ANYWAY, I DECIDED TO TURN ALL MY PENT-UP SPORTS ENERGY INTO ROOTING FOR THE BLUEJAYS. I HOPE TO GIVE THEM THE SAME KIND OF GOOD LUCK I'VE BROUGHT TO THE INDIANS, BROWNS, CAVALIERS AND THE CHALLENGER SHUTTLE. BY THE WAY, I HAVEN'T FOLLOWED THEM (TORONTO) FOR THE LAST COUPLE OF WEEKS. HOW'RE THEY DOING?

    HOPE TO SEE YOU SOON. LOVE TO BARBARA
THANKS AGAIN

                                  Lee

PAUL BEESTON, F.C.A.
President

December 13, 1991

Mr. Mal Coven
17 Old Forest Hill Rd.
Toronto, Ontario
M5P 2P6

Dear Mal:

Thank you for your letter, hat, button and threat.
In reviewing the list, certainly Doctor Lyons is a
threat, but he is the only one. It is our
intention if the Terminator is traded to retain the
services of Ms. Moira Lasch to defend our rights.

Please govern yourself.

                    Yours very truly,

                    Paul B.

SC:

NATIONAL✳POST

May 4, 2009

Mr. Mal Coven
38 Avenue Road
Suite 514
Toronto, ON
M5R 2G2

Dear Mal:

You are an amazing man. I was thrilled to participate in your 80th birthday, but I'm sorry that I wasn't there for most of the evening. Your friends said many wonderful things about you. It was a warm and touching party and you should be very proud.

Continue to be the "idea guy" that you are. Thanks for sending me the cartoon.

Yours sincerely,

Paul V. Godfrey

National Post – 1450 Don Mills Road, Toronto, ON M3B 2x7 Canada
T: 416-383-2433 • F: 416-383-2463 • E: pgodfrey@nationalpost.com

NP nationalpost.com | FP financialpost.com

MAL COVEN

September 14, 2010

Mr. Paul Beeston
President
Toronto Blue Jays
1 Blue Jays Way, Suite 3200
Toronto, Ontario M5V 1J1

Dear Paul:

Here is a great idea for The Blue Jays.

Everybody sings "Take Me Out To The Ballgame" – add a second stanza with words on the big screen. Sing it to yourself and have some fun.

Separately, don't forget – a better location for the kosher hotdog stand next year.

Regards,

Mal

Enclosure: Song lyrics

38 Avenue Road, Suite 514
Toronto, Ontario, Canada M5R 2G2
Tel: (416) 513-0101
Fax: (416) 934-1943
malcoven@rogers.com

With Joyce and Paul Chapnick in Cooperstown at the induction of Alomar and Gillick into the Baseball Hall of Fame.

At the ballpark with the Blue Jays mascot are my grandchildren Miriam (left), Daniel, and Nomi.

28

MAL COVEN, PRANKSTER

OBVIOUSLY there is still a little boy in me. Witness the many pranks I play on some of my friends.

Leonard Simpson and his wife Micki Moore were driving up from their home on Williams Island in North Miami to Palm Beach to have lunch with Barbara and me at Ta-Boo on Worth Avenue.

There are only two gas stations in Palm Beach. I went to one of them with a huge bottle of Evian water and told the attendant I would be returning with a friend in need of gas. I prepped him on his part in my prank, leaving the Evian water with him.

I returned to the gas station with Leonard later, telling him that I needed to fill up my car.

The attendant played along very nicely. Cradling the bottle of Evian water as if it were fine wine, he approached me and said, "You need water in your radiator, sir. Will this do?"

"Are you nuts?" Leonard said to me.

"In Palm Beach we only put Evian water in our cars," I said.

~

Another prank I am very proud of is one I pulled on George Hartman many years earlier in Toronto. I picked him up at his home to go to a Blue Jays game. This was in the 1990s when the Blue Jays won two World Series and appeared in many other playoffs.

George was a rabid fan and always went to the game with a baseball glove. In my mind only young kids did that. George said that he never went to a game without his baseball glove.

"How many balls have you caught?" I asked.

"Not one," he replied.

In about the fifth inning George had to go to the men's room. I told him I'd hold his glove for him.

As soon as he was gone I ran to the stands and bought an authentic American League baseball and brought it back to our seats. I let all the people near our seats in on the gag.

When George returned I yelled, "I caught it – and what a beautiful catch it was!"

The others around us were still high-fiving me.

I did eventually tell him the truth and gave him the ball.

—

I had been working with David Milne, who was helping me design both the Biway's $5Max store and its logo. David is the principal of one of the foremost design companies in North America. He was recommended to me by Joe Mimram of Joe Fresh fame. Being recommended by Joe helped bring the price down to fit my budget.

As I left a meeting with David he asked me if I liked maple syrup. I said I did. I still had some left over from bottles Morris and Judy Fish sent me from time to time from their farm in Stukely, Quebec. Nevertheless, I said I would take some.

The syrup he gave me was in a mailing cylinder that looked as if it contained a bottle of wine. The top of the cylinder bore a maple leaf. The only writing on the package were the words "Use Irresponsibly."

I assumed that he was giving the same gift to his many clients as a holiday gift. That gave me an idea.

I put a small red sticker over the message so it now read "Use responsibly."

My good friend Dr. Paul Chapnick was a man of expertise in many areas. Not only was he a fine oral surgeon, but he taught at the University of Toronto, was a noted art collector, a baseball buff, and most importantly for my purposes, a wine connoisseur.

Earlier I had related a story to him about a call I had made to Dan Doucette, leaving a message congratulating him on being appointed manager of the Baltimore Orioles baseball team. I had met Dan when we were both involved in the Israel Baseball League.

Just after that I received a return call from someone I thought was Dan thanking me for thinking of him. When I asked him for his email address, he said it was "pchapnick." Paul had played a trick on me and I promised to return the favour and to beware.

The maple syrup was the opportunity I had been waiting for. I invited Paul for coffee at Aroma in Forest Hill Village. I produced the cylinder and told him I had been given this bottle of fine Canadian wine worth well over $100.

"As I am not a wine drinker and you are, I want you to have it," I said, recommending that he give it to one of his wine expert friends who might better appreciate it or use it himself.

He thanked me and took it home.

I received a call from him later that morning. It seems he had decided to consume it himself with his wife Joyce.

I wish I could have seen him when he realized it was maple syrup.

He tried to save face by saying he was putting it on his pancakes for breakfast.

Tom Bodkin
Assistant Managing Editor
Design Director

The New York Times

620 Eighth Avenue
New York, NY 10018

E bodkin@nytimes.com

Mr. Mal Coven   October 19, 2007
38 Avenue Road, Suite 514
Toronto, Ontario
Canada, M5R 2G2

Dear Mr. Coven,

Mr. Sulzberger passed your suggestion on to me.

Let me begin by saying how delightful it is to hear from a dedicated reader, and thanking you for your suggestion.

I agree that a smaller format New York Times has appeal, for all the reasons you cite.

Two big British papers, The Times of London and the Independent, did exactly as you suggest; they sold tabloid versions of their papers alongside their broadsheet. Both have now eliminated their broadsheet.

We have considered the tabloid format many times over many years, and have created several prototypes of products in that format.

There are, though, some significant barriers to presenting the entire New York Times as a tabloid. One is the shear volume of content we provide. On a busy weekday our paper contains as many as 120 broadsheet pages divided into 8 thematic sections (Sunday is even bigger). There's no way to divide a tabloid into multiple sections. Retaining the same content would take a 240 page tabloid. That would be a very thick paper and navigating to subjects of interest would be cumbersome at best.

And then there's advertising. It would be difficult to get an advertiser to pay the same for tabloid page as a broadsheet page.

That said, we continue to study different formats for different products.

Thank you again for you interest and thoughtful proposal.

Best,

cc: A.O. Sulzberger Jr.

29

THE NEW YORK TIMES

I have been reading the *New York Times* since a Boston Latin School teacher made it mandatory.

You can see by the following correspondence that I am very free with my advice. These letters tell you something about me and the *Times*.

MAL COVEN

October 9, 2007

Mr. Arthur Sulzberger Jr.
Publisher
The New York Times
620 8th Avenue
New York, NY 10018 USA

Dear Mr. Sulzberger:

I am enclosing a "To Whom it May Concern" letter from an executive of a large financial
company as a way of introducing myself.

Many years ago in my freshman year at Boston Latin School (oldest public school in North
America founded in 1635), my Civics's instructer made it mandatory to read <u>The New York
Times.</u> I have kept the habit until this day even though I now live in Toronto.

Since retiring the business I founded, I have developed numerous original projects and original
ideas – mostly not-for-profit, many successful – that have given me great personal satisfaction.
In some cases I have appointed myself non-paying consultant to a few large corporations. In
many cases they have followed on my suggestions.

I have one for <u>The New York Times.</u>

The struggle for a hard copy newspaper readership is well documented. My suggestion is that
you test a tabloid edition to <u>The New York Times</u> to run simultaneously with the broadsheet.
Same news, same copy but in tabloid format.

38 Avenue Road, Suite 514
Toronto, Ontario, Canada M5R 2G2
Tel: (416) 513-0101
Fax: (416) 934-1943

MAL COVEN

Even though tabloids are usually known for sensational content, there are several successful exceptions, i.e., Barrons. There is no doubt that tabloids are more easily handled and are a great convenience, particularly for commuters. Many newsstands present tabloids in a different location therefore you would get another kick at the can when potential new readers go to tabloid areas. I feel that you just might convert some of those tabloid readers to The New York Times. How many remains to be seen. You presently print tabloid format in your book review section so the tabloid version is not new to you. I am assuming, perhaps wrongly, that the incremental cost would be small. Obviously the layout would be somewhat different but not substantially. I have taken the trouble to mock-up a version for you to see. Also, my personal opinions is that the tabloid version would stay around longer and have additional readership in reception areas, offices, etc.

If my theory is correct, there would be substantial upside in readership with probably a relative downside in cost.

An afterthought as I am writing this: tabloids like Now in Toronto and Phoenix in the US and also the one in New York (the name skips my mind) do attract a younger audience. This may be an additional plus.

Sincerely,

Mal Coven

P.S. As this is a seriously thought-out proposal, I would appreciate your comments. If perchance you did use it, I would appreciate a donation to the Miles Nadal Jewish Community Centre in Toronto.

Enclosures: George Hartman letter
            2 mocked-up of the New York Times tabloid

38 Avenue Road, Suite 514
Toronto, Ontario, Canada M5R 2G2
Tel: (416) 513-0101
Fax: (416) 934-1943

MAL COVEN

February 10, 2009

PERSONAL & CONFIDENTIAL

Mr. Arthur Sulzberger Jr.
Publisher
The New York Times
620 8ᵗʰ Avenue
New York NY 10018 USA

Dear Mr. Sulzberger:

I recently read with much interest the <u>Chicago Tribune</u> plan for a weekday tabloid edition. I am enclosing both my original letter to you dated October 9, 2007 and Tom Bodkin's reply to it.

I think another look at my suggestion might prove to be of some value.

First, I would like to address Tom's reason for rejecting the idea. His reasoning was as follows:

- The experiment in London did not prove to be successful.
- There was a barrier to presenting <u>The Times</u> because of the number of pages involved.
- The advertiser would not go along with the rate needed, or words to that effect.

I would respond in this way. The argument about London trying unsuccessfully does not carry much weight as each city has its own peculiarities, perhaps even more so London and New York.

..2/

38 AVENUE ROAD, SUITE 514
TORONTO, ONTARIO, CANADA M5R 2G2
TEL: (416) 513-0101
FAX: (416) 934-1943

As to the barrier to presenting the weekly <u>New York Times</u> because of the number of pages, I respond in this manner. The tabloid edition – let's call it "<u>New York Times Limited Edition</u>" – would be sold in the New York City market only in the tabloid area on New York newsstands. It would be a limited edition appealing to the tabloid reader. The latter is a quick reader, a headline reader. The focus would be on New York City and State news. I could picture selected columns, selected editorials and selected sports, obviously New York teams. I am sure there are many other things that would fit into the profile of the limited edition.

This limited edition, sold only on newsstands, could attract new advertisers, relatively small retailers or other small businesses that cannot afford the full <u>New York Times</u>. How much additional circulation this would engender and how much it would take from the other tabloids I don't know. Potentially, there could be a big upside with a relatively small downside expense for this experiment.

I would be delighted to hear your comments or some other appropriate person.

Sincerely,

Mal Coven

Enclosures: Hartman letter
                Copy of letter dated Oct. 9, 2007
                Copy of letter from Tom Bodkin

Arthur O. Sulzberger, Jr.

February 12, 2009

CHAIRMAN
The New York Times Company

PUBLISHER
The New York Times

620 Eighth Avenue
New York, NY 10018

212-556-3588
asulz@nytimes.com

Dear Mr. Coven,

    Thank you for writing me again. At this moment the idea of a New York Times tabloid is still not one we are embracing. But we continue to look at it as the world around us is so rapidly shifting.

                Sincerely,

Mr. Mal Coven
38 Avenue Road
Suite 514
Toronto, Ontario
M5R 2G2
Canada

MAL COVEN

May 20, 2009

PERSONAL & CONFIDENTIAL

Mr. Arthur Sulzberger Jr.
Publisher
The New York Times
620 8th Avenue
New York NY 10018 USA

Dear Arthur:

It's me again (now that you know my age, the salutation is not inappropriate).

This one will be brief. I have given and received several leatherette-bound personalized 18" x 12"-sized complete New York Times edition on the day I was born (April 8, 1929). You are probably aware it was printed by "Historic Newspapers", 11 North Main Street, Wigtown, Wigtownshire, Scotland DG8 9HN and distributed by Acorn, a mid-West catalogue house. Why are you not offering and selling it as you do other merchandise (sports, etc.)? Obviously there is a licensing agreement there. But it belongs in *your* newspaper and on *your* website.

My background is retail. I know a good item when I see it.

Sincerely,

Mal Coven

Enclosures: Historic Newspaper insert

38 AVENUE ROAD, SUITE 514
TORONTO, ONTARIO, CANADA M5R 2G2
TEL: (416) 513-0101
FAX: (416) 934-1943

Mal Coven

November 7, 2007

Mr. Tom Bodkin
Assistant Managing Editor
New York Times
620 8th Avenue
New York NY 10018

Dear Mr. Bodkin:

Thank you for your October 19th letter in response to my suggestion that, as a test, you print a tabloid in addition to your broadsheet. Perhaps I should stick to innovative retailing ideas where I have had much success. On second thoughts, I am going to take one more "kick at the can" so here goes.

Like many of your readers, I find countless obituaries exceptionally interesting. They contain little-known information about the person. I think a book could be marketed containing the most outstanding ones. The following are some ideas on how this could be done:

1. Publish every five years or possibly each decade
2. Broken down by categories:
    -   science notables
    -   political figures
    -   sports figures
    -   war figures/heroes
    -   general human interest figures, etc.

Please pass this idea onto whom it may concern. Obviously I would appreciate a response.

Sincerely,

Mal Coven

c.c.   Mr. Sulzberger

38 AVENUE ROAD, SUITE 514
TORONTO, ONTARIO, CANADA M5R 2G2
TEL: (416) 513-0101
FAX: (416) 934-1943

MAL COVEN

December 6, 2011

Arthur G. Sulzberger Jr.
Chairman & Publisher
The New York Times
620 8th Avenue
New York, NY 10013

Dear Arthur:

I am enclosing copies of correspondence I have had with your people and yourself. You were kind enough to respond to me personally to my suggestion that you run a tabloid in New York as well as your broadsheet that would only report on New York City news, sports, etc. It is only to refresh your memory.

The purpose of this letter is twofold: one is a complaint about your relatively new Week In Review. I can only speak for myself and my wife and several of my friends who are dissatisfied in one particular change. Most of the news, particularly it seems in these trying times, are not exactly uplifting. The only oasis was the second page of the old review that contains the political cartoons and quotes from the late evening comedian. Frankly it was the first thing we would go to for a laugh and/or a smile. There is something missing on Sunday morning in Toronto.

I am also enclosing a piece written by Barry Rubin, a well-known writer on Middle East affairs. It is an educated man's opinion but to anyone who has an interest in the wellbeing of Israel it is scary. I would appreciate your comments.

Wishing you good health along with the New York Times.

Sincerely,

Mal Coven

P.S.   My autobiography will be published this spring. It traces my life from Boston to the present. I am enclosing some comments from a few people to whom I have sent excerpts. They are obviously complimentary.

Enclosures: Past correspondence
             Barry Rubin article
             Biography comments

38 AVENUE ROAD, SUITE 514
TORONTO, ONTARIO, CANADA M5R 2G2
TEL: (416) 513-0101
FAX: (416) 934-1943
malcoven@rogers.com

Can you believe it?
Mal Coven is gonna be 80!!!

So we're having a very special birthday party
for a very special guy, and it wouldn't
be the same without you.

Now here's the catch. Instead of gifts
would you please bring along a toast,
or a song, or a poem, or a limerick — Hey,
we'll even accept sincere speeches —
anything at all to let Mal know how
you feel about him. O.K.?

Saturday, April twenty-fift
seven-thirty o'clock

Four Seasons Hotel
"Windows"
21 Avenue Road, Toronto

Black tie welcome

RSVP
barbaracoven@sympatico.ca
or fax 416.413.1918

Please park at 38 Avenue Road

30

MY 80TH BIRTHDAY PARTY

A few selected mementos from a wonderful party that Barbara put on for me when I turned 80. Among them is a note from Barbara, one of our longest-standing friends, and another from Irv and Elaine Bloomberg. Irv came from his sick bed to attend.

MAL'S 80TH BIRTHDAY
WITH LOVE FROM BARBARA COVEN

Good evening and welcome to Mal's 80th birthday party!

Mal so loved his 65th bash that it was difficult for him to wait 15 years to celebrate his big 8-0 milestone.

Perhaps you already know that Mal finds *any* wait a problem. He can't wait in traffic, in line for a movie or for a meal. He has one new original idea after another and he starts often at 4 a.m. writing proposals, business plans and letters. Mort Zukerman, Ben Cammarata of TJ Maxx, Marvin Traub, Punch Sulzberger, Barbara Walters, Billy Crystal, Larry King and Paul Godfrey to name just a few have all received information and ideas from Mal.

In the film Frost/Nixon, Nixon says to Swifty Lazar: "Never retire, Mr. Lazar. To me the unhappiest people in the world are retired. They have no purpose. What makes life mean something is purpose, a goal; a battle; a struggle."

Mal has never retired. To name a few Coven enterprises over the years we include:

- Majestic Electronics
- My First Car
- Puppets
- Israeli Baseball League
- Jewish Baseball Cards
- Blue Jay Heroes Cards
- The Terminators
- Heritage Plaques
- Marketplace for Catalogues
- Jewish Baseball Film
- Italian Baseball Cards
- Lola's Cupcakes

All have been original ideas.

To me Mal is a constant surprise with each new idea - and he always has new ideas or a new enterprise. I am astonished by his creativity, enthusiasm and diligence. Mal makes things happen!

I have been with Mal over 25 years and in that time he has grown and blossomed before my eyes into the amazing Mal that we know, love and celebrate tonight.

And if you are here, it's because *you* are special. As family and friends you know that Mal is always there for you with great kindness, generousity, and kibitz.

If "you" are blessed to be in Mal Coven's life, you are fortunate indeed. And because you are all in his life — "he" is blessed and fortunate indeed.

Dinner will be served and then you will have *your* opportunity to roast, toast and say what's in your heart.

First I call upon Mal's blessing and dividend David to make a toast.

For Mal's 80th

Mal(y), Mal(y),

This is your birthday, true.

We have known you

Even when you were blue.

You never come empty handed,

A treasure you'll always find.

And you look sweet,

Whenever we meet,

No matter what you do!!!

Mal(y) Mal(y)

This is your birthday true.

We have known you

When BIWAY was brand new.

Your ventures and your photos

Your cupcakes all yummy, too.

You'll always be, a friend to we

No matter what you do.

With our love
Judy + Audrey

An original cartoon by Gary Clement
as a gift in celebration of my 80th birthday.

Dear Zaida,

Happy birthday! Let the celebrations begin! Now that your birthday has arrived, we wanted to let you know how much we appreciate you, learn from you, and love you.

You have influenced the people we are becoming and the way we experience life. We look up to your generosity- giving tzedakah to the community and sharing with your family and friends. Your enthusiasm and zest for life pervade everything we do with you. Visiting galleries, travelling, and enjoying Friday night meals together are just a few of our favourite activities that we share with you. Your spirit of seeking knowledge and your constant entrepreneurial endeavors always inspire us.

Tonight is the start, the kick off of your birthday celebration. With family and friends we are celebrating you. We are celebrating the memories we have shared and the many memories that we will continue to create with you.

As your gift, we have decided to capture these memories through film. We will make a film about your life, and highlight your involvement in your family, community, and the world around you.

We are so excited to celebrate your 80th birthday with you!

Love,
Robin, Tim, David, and Victoria
Miriam, Nomi, Daniel, Isaac, Sam, Ruby, and Pearl

<u>FOR MAL ON HIS 80th BIRTHDAY</u>

FORTY FIVE YEARS AGO, MAL AND HIS PARTNERS GAVE US A BREAK.

REFLECTING ON THOSE YEARS OUR ASSOCIATION WAS NOTHING LESS THAN GREAT.

HIS SUGGESTION ON KLACKERS WE DID TAKE

THIS ADVICE FOR SURE WAS NO MISTAKE.

MAL IS NOW 80 YEARS YOUNG AND QUITE DESERVING

HE LOOKS SO GOOD IT'S QUITE UNNERVING.

MAL IS A GUY WHO IS WITTY AND CHARMING

AND SOMETIMES HE CAN BE A BIT ALARMING

IN BUSINESS AND IN PLAY MAL CERTAINLY DOES NOT MISS A BEAT

A NICER GUY THAN HIM, YOU WOULD NOT MEET,

AS YOU CAN SEE, OUR RELATIONSHIP AND FRIENDSHIP HAS LASTED FORTY-FIVE YEARS.

DON'T YOU AGREE, TONIGHT, THIS DESERVES HONORABLE MENTION AMONGST ALL MAL'S PEERS.

LET'S RAISE OUR GLASS AND PROPOSE A TOAST

HERE'S TO MAL COVEN, **THE MAN WHO'S THE MOST**!

LOVE,
IRVING AND ELAINE BLOOMBERG

April 11, 2003

Dear Daddy:

The truth is that there is no present that I could buy
for you that would express how much I love you and
what a wonderful father I think you are.

You have always encouraged me to do the things that
are important to me and have not only given me
financial support, but more importantly the confidence
to pursue my passions.

You have taught me how to look beyond my own needs
as a parent, and to encourage my children to do the
things that they want to even though I am sometimes
afraid to let go.

Our trip to Israel is so greatly appreciated- we could all
really use the break and are so excited to spend time
with friends and family in a place that is so important
to all of us.

Thank you for letting us go- in spite of the security
situation in Israel and around the world. We will miss
you at the seder but look forward to being together
next year. Happy Birthday!

Love
Robin

PART SIX

AND IN CONCLUSION

Dear Malcom

FROM RIVER'S SON
MAX

UPDATE AROUND 1998

Thankyou for the great tickets!

We were 3 rows back from Vince carter.

The game went to overtime 114 to 118 for the other team.

I touched a players hand and almost caught his jersey.

from:

32

ENTREPRENEURIAL TIPS

FOR TEENS

I have always liked to talk to young people, particularly those in their teens and 20s. Lately it seems my Biway background and the writing of my autobiography have resonated with them. Actually, it seems that I naturally come forward with advice whether people in this age group ask for it or not.

A case in point is a conversation I had this past winter with a teenager employed at our condo in Florida. I asked José what he wanted to do in the future.

Something to do with health care, was his response. A doctor, perhaps even a nurse.

I suggested he was wasting his time as a car jockey and would be much better off in the long run if he worked at a hospital even though the pay might not be as good.

That is the same advice I would give to any young entrepreneur. It is the same advice that was given to me after I was rejected from Filene's executive training program. My cousin told me I would be better off inside looking in than outside looking in. It's a good strategy to take any job with the company or in the field you want to go with.

José quit his job a week later. I am told he is working at the Mount Sinai Hospital in Florida.

Making a good impression on adults is very important for young entrepreneurs and it is very important to start at a very young age. My advice to any such who are reading this book is to make a personal calling card for yourself. Wherever you go, whoever you meet, give it to that adult at some point in your conversation. Believe me, any adult will be impressed and will remember you for it. This connection may prove fruitful to you one day in the future when you're applying for a position or wish to meet someone who may hold the keys to your future.

You want to be an entrepreneur? Start young. Go to Costco where they buy and sell merchandise at a very low price with a markup of 10%. Make a list of staple items, canvass houses door to door, put a 10% mark-up on your items, and tell your customers you will deliver once a month. They are still getting a bargain whether they shop at Costco or not.

Build a route that way and add more items to your list and take off the poor selling ones. Leave your card for calls for additional items. Pick a number for a minimum order. You have come up with a new idea – always follow it through. Good ideas are a dime a dozen; they're not worth a damn unless you follow through on them.

Make a point to do little favours for people. Don't wait to be asked. Also, give little gifts of appreciation no matter how inexpensive. It is the thought that counts. The goodwill that it will bring you over time is immeasurable. It will help you get a foot in the door and could well lead to something even better. People remember these things. Build the reputation of being a giving person, starting when you're young age or at any age. This will give you a competitive advantage, for sure.

When you have met an adult of interest, make sure you ask him for his card, too. Follow through with a note telling them how glad you were to make their acquantance. Goodwill built over a long period is invaluable.

If you should meet an adult in a field or company you are interested in, volunteer as an intern to observe and work for no pay. You will create more goodwill even if they turn you down.

33

UNUSUAL CORRESPONDENCE

I have several hundred letters in my files that I have written for various reasons. This is quite a contrast to three letters I wrote during my 28 years at Biway.

I am including several in this book and the replies I received. Some are letters bearing suggestions that I thought might be helpful to their receivers. Some contain ideas and tips I sent to retailers so I could keep in touch with the retail scene. Some were sent to persuade executives to adopt one of my original concepts, some were just to lend a hand to a friend or an acquaintance, and still others were just to get my feelings off my chest.

Corresponding with people has been an important part of my retirement. Many of the responses I have received are special to me. The ones I cherish the most are thank-you notes. They range from one written by an eight-year-old boy who was thrilled to go to a Raptors game to a member of the Knights of the Round Bagel whom I helped send on a two-week holiday for his 50th anniversary.

Moe Smith

September 21, 1995

Mr. Mal Coven
17 Old Forest Hill Road
Toronto, Ontario
M5P 2P6

Dear Mal,

How does a man measure a friend, it certainly is not by his stature nor his wealth. I would like to tell you that I am probably the richest man in the world. To have a friend like you and all the boys of our bagel group. The gift regarding my health is one that words cannot express.

So rather then give you a thousand reasons of thanks, I close to say you have touched my heart deeper than I could explain my life is far richer than ever before, so in closing from Mildred and myself no need to say more except

thank you

From us with all our love,

Moe

Feb 23, 1986

Dear Mr. Coven

I want very much to tell you how much my daughter and I appreciated your kind and generous act today!

We were both looking forward to the performance and were disappointed when we saw the "sold out" sign — then you came in.

Your great seats made it a thrilling day for us.

Thanks again. Hope to see you again.

Lou Birenbaum

BATSHEVA AVERY

----

660 BRIAR HILL AVENUE, SUITE 206, TORONTO, ONTARIO 787-3176

MAL COVEN
115 COMMANDER BLVD.
SCARBOROUGH, ONTARIO.

OCTOBER 17, 1986.

DEAR MAL:

PLEASE FIND ENCLOSED A CHEQUE FOR THE AMOUNT YOU GENEROUSLY
INVESTED IN MY RECORD PROJECT.

ALTHOUGH WE CONTINUED TO RAISE FUNDS, WE FELT IT WOULD BE A
WISER COURSE OF ACTION TO PURSUE A LABEL TO PRODUCE THE RECORD.
WE ARE IN THAT PROCESS NOW.

I WOULD LIKE TO TAKE THIS OPPORTUNITY TO THANK YOU FOR YOUR
SUPPORT AND YOUR ENCOURAGEMENT. YOU REALLY ARE A LOVELY MAN.

I WOULD ALSO LIKE TO WISH YOU AND BARBARA ALL THE BEST IN THE
NEW YEAR. YOU ARE IN MY THOUGHTS.

SINCERELY,

Batsheva
BATSHEVA AVERY

Babson College

Babson Park
(Wellesley)
Massachusetts
02157-0901

617/235-1200
FAX 617/239-5614
TELEX 948069
Cable BABCOL WELL

February 21, 1990

Mr. Mal Coven
17 Old Forest Hill Road
Toronto
Canada M5P2P6

Dear Mal,

    I want to thank you for taking the time to talk to me,
considering the fact that you have not seen me in about ten years.   I
also want to thank you for being so very nice to my mother.

    On Tuesday I called our Development Office to let them know I had
talked with you. They wanted to know if they could contact you
directly to discuss the best way to approach the Fingolds. Babson has
a Corporation member who lives in the Toronto area, Neil Landy, and he
would be the person to make contact with the Fingolds; unless you feel
it would be a better idea for Babson to send me to meet with them
also. In any case, I will not give out your telephone number until I
talk with you next week.

    As for my background:

        1989 - present Director of Intramurals, Babson College

        1982 - present Men & Women's Varsity Swimming Coach,
                        Babson College

        1974 - 1989   Athletic Director & Science Teacher,
                        Tenacre Day School

        1978 - present Director, Tenacre Day Camps

        1978 - 1988   Swimming Coach, Wellesley High School

    Once again, I want to thank you for your time and effort for even
considering helping Babson College in its attempt to set up a meeting
with the Fingolds.

                        Warmest Regards,

                        Rick Echlov
                        Office: (617) 239-5297
                        Home: (508) 655-0497

RE:m

DANIEL K. INOUYE
HAWAII

PRINCE KUHIO FEDERAL BUILDING
SUITE 7325, 300 ALA MOANA BOULEVARD
HONOLULU, HI 96850
(808) 546-7550

United States Senate

ROOM 722, HART SENATE BUILDING
WASHINGTON, DC 20510
(202) 224-3934

September 26, 198(

Mr. Mal Coven
President
The BiWay
115 Commander Boulevard
Scarborough, Ontario MIS 3M7

Dear Mr. Coven:

Thank you for your thoughtful letter of September 23rd
regarding my recent remarks on Israel. I appreciated your
gracious comments and welcomed the opportunity to meet with
members of your UJA mission from Toronto.

Please be assured of my continued support as we work
together to secure peace and stability for Israel in the
years ahead.

Aloha,

DANIEL K. INOUYE
United States Senator

DKI:dcl

Paul V. Godfrey, C.M.
President and
Chief Executive Officer

November 6, 2001

Mr. Mal Coven
38 Avenue Road
Suite 514
Toronto, Ontario
M5R 2G2

Dear Mal:

It was great to see you the other night at the Baycrest Gala. When I finish my search for a new General Manager of the Club, I would be pleased to speak to Adam Cooper. Please tell him that I will contact him in early December.

Thank you for your ongoing sup

Yours sincerely,

Paul V. Godfrey

PVG/jcs

TORONTO BLUE JAYS BASEBALL CLUB
ONE BLUE JAYS WAY, SUITE 3200, TORONTO, ONTARIO, CANADA M5V 1J1
PHONE: 416-341-1430 • FAX: 416-341-1435 • www.bluejays.com

Time Inc. Magazines

Sports Illustrated
Time & Life Building
Rockefeller Center
New York, NY 10020

212-522-1212

January 17, 1992

Mal Coven
3100 South Ocean Blvd.,
Apt. 504N,
Palm Beach, Fla. 33480

Dear Mr. Coven,

I enjoyed our conversation the other day and look forward to meeting you in person. I have enclosed a sampling of my clips as well as a resume.

Regarding a visit to Toronto: Early March might be ideal as my mother will also be in town. Please let me know if this suits your schedule.

DAVID ORRICK MODELL

Sincerely,

Michael Jaffe

Michael Jaffe

Mal,

Thanks for the article
I enjoyed it.

David

Allan H. (Bud) Selig
President & Chief Executive Officer, Director

October 27, 1994

Mr. Mal Coven
17 Old Forest Hill Road
Toronto, Ontario, Canada   M5P 2P6

Dear Mr. Coven:

Thank you for your very interesting letter.

I appreciate your comments and suggestions relative to
the labor situation and I have sent your letter on to our
Player Relations Committee for their consideration.   We
do need a change in our economic system to preserve
baseball for future generations and I assure you we will
do everything we can to get this work stoppage resolved
in an expeditious and meaningful manner.

Your letter was very constructive and I thank you for
taking time to write to me.

Sincerely,

Allan H. Selig
Chairman, Executive Council
Major League Baseball

AHS:sr

Milwaukee Brewers Baseball Club <> County Stadium <> P.O. Box 3099 <> Milwaukee, Wisconsin 53201-3099 <> (414) 933-4114

Les Ventes TransContinentales Inc.
TransContinental Sales Inc.
6650 RUE ST. URBAIN, MONTREAL, QUEBEC, CANADA H2S 3G9

TELEPHONE: (514) 273-9581
TELEX: 055-60956
CABLE: CONTRANS
FAX: (514) 270-1267

SPRING
1996

Dear Mel,

    This Malcolm Lester is lucky to have a friend like you. You certainly have gone all out.

    I hope Malcolm makes it, so that your efforts are not in vain.

        Regards

                    Dan

Mal Coven

August 28, 2000

To: Tim Russert

Fax: 202-885-4674

Re: Your conversation with William Safire on the new wave of greetings (pun intended) from handshake, to bearhug, to air kiss, to Sammy Sosa finger and heart.

Mr. Safire referred to days past when Ted Williams tipped his cap. Any Bostonian – and millions of others too – know *Ted Williams* never tipped his cap in his whole career. I don't even think the last at bat when homered (check with Wills). I hold you as an accessory after the fact.

Your shows are super.

Regards,

Mal Coven

SUITE 514
THE PRINCE ARTHUR
38 AVENUE ROAD
TORONTO, ONTARIO
M5R 2G2

TEL: (416) 513-0101
FAX: (416) 934-1943

Mal Coven

September 12, 2000

Ms. Jennie Backus
Democratic National Committee

By Fax: 202-863-8063

Dear Jennie:

This is from a former Bostonian living in Toronto.

Experience is and should be an issue in the election.

I remember well Senator Hatch, Republican, running for the nomination speaking of Bush in a sound bite on TV. "Let him come back in eight years when he has enough experience to be qualified."

How would that sound in a Gore commercial?

Please send to whom it might concern.

Good Luck.

Mal Coven

SUITE 514
THE PRINCE ARTHUR
38 AVENUE ROAD
TORONTO, ONTARIO
M5R 2G2

TEL: (416) 513-0101
FAX: (416) 934-1943

To : Mal Coven

From : Ruth Berger

FAX - 1 - 416 - 934 - 1943

September 18, 2000

Dear Mal

As promised, the wee article from yesterday's Ottawa Citizen on our efforts for the Terry Fox run. Thanks for your generous support! And thanks too for the invitation to pop by on Saturday evening. It will be great to see you, Barbara and so many of the gang from the cruise.

Here's that story I told you on the phone about Jackie Mason. As you know, I have done a lot of ad production over the years and a dear friend in the business is Max Villeneuve from Montreal who heads Chrysler Canada's french language ads. Max is half Scottish, half French and half Iriquois - but Jewish in his heart. When we were doing a shoot for the federal Government a few years back, we would keep ourselves in stitches between takes (it can take several days to produce the footage for a 30 second ad - hurry up and wait, like in the movie business) doing Jackie Mason routines. After a deadly impression, Max told me the following:

His wife is from a prominent Chinese family in Mauritius - a prosperous island in the Indian Ocean. In fact, I think his wife's family owns half the island but that is another story. Anyway, Max sent his wife's relatives the tape of Jackie Mason's Broadway show and they just loved it. They memorized the tape! So now you have a lot of Chinese people running around Mauritius doing Jackie Mason shticklech!!!!

See you Saturday.

Ruth

Running for the memories

Many in annual Terry Fox event also honouring friend

BY DAVID REEVELY

In today's Terry Fox runs across Canada, hundreds will run not only for Terry's memory, but for Gerry Berger's, too.

Mr. Berger, a lifelong civil servant who worked on everything from the Auto Pact to the Calgary Olympics to the 1994 Commonwealth Games in Victoria, died two years ago of esophageal cancer. But the firm for which he worked after he left the public service, Government Policy Consultants, is sponsoring hundreds of Mr. Berger's former co-workers.

His widow, Ruth, and their grown children, Lisa and Michael, will be running and walking the 10-kilometre courses in Ottawa and Toronto.

"All the money that we and the GPC people raise, they match," Mrs. Berger says. She and her children have raised more than $5,000 this year. She has cheques and good wishes from other people in the Olympic movement — Dick

Ruth Berger will be in today's Terry Fox run to honour her late husband, Gerry, who died of cancer two years ago.

Pound, the Montreal lawyer and International Olympic Committee vice-president, sent $100.

"My feelings, making the calls, have gone from excruciating to extreme gratitude," she says. She pauses, and her jaw clenches for a moment. "All the people he worked with and the friends he made, they haven't forgotten."

The Bergers and the GPC runners wear buttons with Mr. Berger's photo, taken just before his second and last run, in 1997. "You can see how thin he was," she says. "And there's no

hair under his cap any more."

Mr. Berger walked the course that year, rather than running it, "but he finished," says his widow.

Ann Stanton-Loucks, chairwoman of the Ottawa run, says 46 companies are sponsoring their employees in corporate challenges. She hopes to raise $300,000 this year, with about 6,000 runners, walkers, cyclists and skaters registered.

GPC gives trophies to the employee who raises the most pledge money and to the one who completes the course quickest. "There should be a third trophy," Mrs. Berger smiles. "Gerry was a fierce runner. He'd run summer, winter, whenever ... but he was slow. There should be a trophy for the one who takes the longest but still finishes."

She says her husband joined the Terry Fox campaign in 1996, after working with Rick Hansen — who pushed his wheelchair around the world — on the Commonwealth Games two years before.

"He got very involved in fighting for disabled athletes after that," says Mrs. Berger. "It's amazing now to see how it all got tied together."

Mal Coven

January 12, 2001

Bert Tansky
President & CEO
Neiman Marcus
1618 Main Street
Dallas, Texas 7520

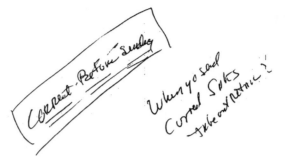

Dear Bert:

I am writing this letter at the suggestion of a close friend and former associate at Filenes, Hal Leppo. Hal worked for and with me at Filenes before I moved to Toronto. I started a discount chain and ended up with stores pretty much across Canada.

I was frustrated when a very dear friend showed me an original item she developed herself away from her usual business. My own opinion is it's a big winner at both retail and catalogue. It's original and never been done before. It's for upscale America. Unbelievably, she can't get a callback from Saaks or Neiman (and she's no shrinking violet).

If there is any way she could just get a showing I think you would be doing yourself a favour as well as her. It probably would go into small leather goods department or sunglass department.

Her name is

> Naomi Alexandroff
> trading under Naomi A
> 1321 Sherbrooke Street West, Suite D60
> Montreal, Canada H3G 1J4
>
> Office: (514) 284-3697
> Fax: (514) 284-2272

Many thanks.

Mal Coven

THE PRINCE ARTHUR
38 AVENUE ROAD, SUITE 514
TORONTO, ONTARIC
M5R 2G2

TEL: (416) 513-0101
FAX: (416) 934-1943

MAL COVEN

March 28, 2001

Richard Peddie
President
Toronto Raptors
Air Canada Centre
40 Bay Street, Suite 400
Toronto, Ontario
M5J 2X2

Dear Richard:

First, thanks for a good season. I'm an eternal optimist. I bet $20 on the Raptors to win it all in Las Vegas.

Richard, I want you to do yourself - not me - a favour. Enclosed is a resume of a super kid. He is currently doing his MBA at Western majoring in Marketing. He is looking for something challenging this summer, May through September or some part thereof. As you can see by his resume, he has done work for American Hockey League, among other fine things. Money is not an issue. One interview and you would know why you would be doing yourself a favour.

Best wishes,

Mal

38 AVENUE ROAD, SUITE 514
TORONTO, ONTARIO M5R 2G2
TEL.: (416) 513-0101
FAX: (416) 934-1943

MAL COVEN

March 28, 2001

Paul Godfrey
President & CEO
Toronto Blue Jays
1 Blue Jay Way
Toronto, Ontario M5V 1J1

Dear Paul:

I'm going to do you another favour. Enclosed is a resume of a super kid. He doesn't pitch but he is currently doing his MBA at Western majoring in Marketing. He is looking for something challenging and is available this summer, May through September or some part thereof. As you can see by his resume, he has done some great things including work for American Hockey League. One interview and you would know why you or your son would be doing yourselves a favour.

Wishing you good health and good pitching.

Regards,

Mal

P.S. Money is not an issue

38 Avenue Road, Suite 514
Toronto, Ontario M5R 2G2
Tel.: (416) 513-0101
Fax: (416) 934-1943

MAL COVEN

October 11, 2001

Ms. Sovannil Binn
Time Inc.
Time Life Building
Rockefeller Center
New York, NY 10026-1393 USA

Dear Ms. Binn:

I thank you for your September 7th reply to my letter of complaint re: "Classic Jazz Collection", copies of which were sent to the six most senior executives in your company.

It appears, however, that you have neither addressed nor investigated my main concern, namely, the deception of the voice-over commercial and the physical impossibility of reading the one-second disclaimer on the top of the screen.

It also appears you have not viewed it personally as you promised to do as you have not even commented on that, except to say you are an honest and trustworthy company. Ms. Binn, I don't waste time and money to get back a few dollars.

If I do not get a satisfactory reply to what I believe is an obvious deception, I will be forced to rewrite the six senior executives of your company and show them our correspondence and complete lack of progress.

Ms. Binn, on behalf of the thousands of people who were deceived as I was, I will not be satisfied until this matter has been dealt with fairly.

Yours sincerely,

Mal Coven

38 AVENUE ROAD, SUITE 514
TORONTO, ONTARIO, CANADA M5R 2G2
TEL.: (416) 513-0101
FAX: (416) 934-1943

Heather M. Reisman
PRESIDENT

468 King Street West, Suite 500
Toronto, Ontario M5V 1L8
416-364-4499
fax: 416-364-0355

January 25, 2002

Mr. Mal Coven
38 Avenue Road
Suite 514
Toronto, Ontario
M5R 2G2

Dear Mal,

It was good to chat with you this afternoon. Thanks to you and your pal for the goodies. I hope you enjoy these books – I think they would go great with mandelbroit.

Best personal regards,

Encl.

!ndigo
Books Music & more
www.indigo.ca

SPEAKER'S OFFICE

הכנסת
KNESSET

Jerusalem, July 10, 2002
1 Av, 5762

Mr. Mal Coven
38 Avenue Road, Suite 514
Toronto, Ontario M5R 2G2
Canada

Dear Mr. Coven,

The Speaker of the Knesset, MK Avraham Burg, has asked me to thank you for sending him your plan for resolving the Israeli-Palestinian conflict.

Sincerely yours,

Revital Poleg
Senior Adviser and Chief of Staff

A ⚫ Kruger Company

Thursday, October 07, 2004

Mal Coven
38 Avenue Road, Suite 514
Toronto, ON M5R 2G2

Mr. Coven,

Thanks very much for contacting Scott Paper Limited with your proposal to sponsor the
swan boats at the Stratford Festival.

While the proposal that you have provided is intriguing, we will decline participation at
this point in time.

Nevertheless, if the Stratford Festival decides to go ahead with your idea, feel free to
contact us. If the Festival can provide a more specific sponsorship proposal indicating
the cost of the program and the benefits to Scott Paper including brand presence, number
of consumer impressions and promotional opportunities, then we would gladly review it.

Best of luck and, once again, thanks very much for thinking of Scott Paper and White
Swan.

Regards,

Patrick Leu

CC: Mario Gosselin, Nancy Marcus

MAL COVEN

July 14, 2008

PERSONAL & CONFIDENTIAL

Richard Deluce
Chief Executive Officer
Porter Airline
Toronto City Centre Airport
Toronto, Ontario
M5V 1A1

Dear Richard:

I still use BiWay stores as an introduction even though we sold it to Dylex in 1990.

I am delighted to tell you that Barbara and I have taken Porter to NY at least six times and we have only good things to say.

- The access to the airport is first-class ($12 taxi ride)
- The people serving are always bright and cheerful even at 6:30 a.m
- The lounge is quiet and peaceful with great amenities
- One hour before flight time is a great time saver
- The box meal on board is perfect for 1-1/4 hour trip as is the choice.

To summarize, everything is either premium or first-class. But having been a retailer of some note, I must tell you that you have made one mistake. If everything is premium, you should be charging a premium fare for all the things I have listed. I bet nobody ever put that in the suggestion box. I hope to see you again on a future flight. You're a hands-on guy, my guess is you're down there frequently.

Good luck.

Mal Coven

38 AVENUE ROAD, SUITE 514
TORONTO, ONTARIO, CANADA M5R 2G2
TEL: (416) 513-0101
FAX: (416) 934-1943

Mal Coven

39 Avenue Road, Suite 514
Toronto, Canada M5R 2G2
Tel: 416-513-0101   Fax: 416-934-1943

April 27, 2008

PERSONAL & CONFIDENTIAL

Mr. Galen G. Weston
Loblaws
1 President's Choice Circle
Brampton ON L6Y 5S5

Dear Galen:

My letter of April 24 told you of my concern of your clothing departments in your store at Dufferin & Steeles. I stand by everything I said about that store.

However, I was informed Saturday that your store in Milton is your new prototype. In my professional opinion - and in two words - it's first-rate. I was very impressed.

It is everything that I would want it to be. Space allocation, ease of shopping, good merchandise assortment. You don't have to take a back seat to anyone and no question in my mind you can compete successfully with WalMart, Zellers or The Bay.

On the basis of what I saw, the future is very bright after you've straightened out your distribution problem. I spoke frankly before and am doing the same in this letter.

Sincerely,

Mal Coven

PS I am putting my money where my mouth is and buying additional stock. I will try and say hello after the year-end meeting.

Copies to Allen Leighton
        Galen Weston

MAL COVEN

August 6, 2008

Michel Lacoste
Chairman & CEO
Lacoste S.A.
8 rue de Castiglione
75-001, Paris, France

Dear Sir:

You see by the enclosed letter I had been a successful retailer in Canada for many years starting with one store in 1962 and subsequently selling our chain in the '90's. Part of our success was due to innovative thinking.

The purpose of this letter is to be helpful to Izod and the Lacoste brand. In North America it is stylish to wear tops outside of the belt. This is true with crew necks, collar knits and also woven sport shirts. The knits are worn approximately four inches below the belt line. Pockets are still accessible and the garment hangs loose. It is more comfortable and convenient. Younger men don't want the bother of tucking in their shirts.

Mature men, 50's, 60's or so, have followed that lead and copied the style but for a logical and different reason. If you have a paunch, it is much more flattering to have the t-shirt hang loose rather than tight around the waist under the belt. Snug fit around the waist is not flattering. Unfortunately, a large population of mature men are in that category.

Lacoste knits, of which I have 15 or so, of course are very generous in length and have to be tucked in or they look like miniskirts. Obviously that is done purposely so they don't ride up under one's pants. I have cut mine down to approximately four inches below the belt. The enclosed pictures show both ways.

..2/

38 AVENUE ROAD, SUITE 514
TORONTO, ONTARIO, CANADA M5R 2G2
TEL: (416) 513-0101
FAX: (416) 934-1943

My suggestion to you is that you do a range of "Lacoste shorties" to take advantage of this trend. It is not a fad but an important trend. Also, they should be a touch more generous in the waist.

As for Izod, why not go with the trend and have a short version. Access to the pockets would be easily accessible. The back length should be an inch or so longer than the front for both Lacoste and Izod.

The only remuneration for this suggestion is a letter for 'bragging rights' and one Lacoste knit if you adopt my suggestion, size 7, shortie.

Sincerely,

Mal Coven

Enclosures: 4 pictures
              Hartman letter

MAL COVEN

June 17, 2008

<u>PERSONAL & CONFIDENTIAL</u>

Lynne Mooney Teta
Headmaster
The Boston Latin School
78 Avenue Louis Pasteur
Boston MA 02115 USA

Dear Lynne:

I thought I would put some of my random thoughts in a more formal way.

When doing a promotion in our retail business we were always looking for a "handle" for a promotion or even an advertisement. Boston Latin School has a "handle" for your 375-year anniversary but a subtext for the part of the celebration that we have been discussing also needs a "handle", I strongly believe.

A hundred Boston Latin School heroes of the last one hundred years is a very good one. It is something to hang your hat on.

I was thinking of dividing the heroes into classifications: medicine, politics, academics, arts, music, law, science, military service, church service, and I am sure others. These come to the top of my mind.

I also think that having the students involved in some meaningful way is very important, and also using it as an educational tool in some way, I am sure you will agree, is important. In my fax to you, I outlined some possibilities. Voting in some way. Declamation could also be useful. I am sure you can think of others.

38 AVENUE ROAD, SUITE 514
TORONTO, ONTARIO, CANADA M5R 2G2
TEL: (416) 513-0101
FAX: (416) 934-1943

The awards that I have suggested I think have merit, i.e., gold, silver boxes. If handled properly can raise a lot of money for some specific goal. A special scholarship or renewable plan. There are dozens, I am sure.

At an appropriate time I would be honoured to sit in on any meeting that you might be planning to contribute whatever I can.

Sincerely,

Mal Coven

P.S. As you probably surmise, I do not email. Faxes and letters are my bag.

Mal Coven
39 Avenue Road, Suite 514
Toronto, Canada M5R 2G2
Tel: 416-513-0101   Fax: 416-934-1943

June 17, 2008

PERSONAL & CONFIDENTIAL

Innes vanNostrand
Vice-Principal
Office of Advancement
Upper Canada College
200 Lonsdale Road
Toronto, Ontario M4V 1W6

Dear Innes:

Thank you for giving me an hour of your time last week. I enjoyed the meeting immensely. It was the first time I had been on the campus and was exceptionally impressed with the whole scene. I hope the 1,100 or so students there appreciate what they are a part of.

I think some of the things we kicked around, if properly done, can raise a lot of money (well into six figures). If and when you are ready, I would be happy to sit down with you again and see if we can crunch some numbers that are mutually beneficial.

Sincerely,

Mal Coven

UPPER CANADA COLLEGE

200 Lonsdale Road
Toronto, Ontario
Canada M4V 1W6
TEL 416 488 1125

www.ucc.on.ca

Mr. Mal Coven
38 Avenue Road
Suite 514
Toronto, ON M5R 2G2

October 8, 2008

Dear Mr. Coven:

I wanted to thank you for contacting Upper Canada College with your idea about creating cards featuring outstanding UCC alumni.

Innes van Nostrand and I were certainly intrigued by the concept. We think it has some promise. However, we are concerned that we wouldn't have a large enough market to warrant a cost-effective print run. Furthermore, in the short term, we just don't have the resources to handle the research, writing and photo collection required to execute the project.

I've kept a photocopy of a couple of the cards, for reference. Should we decide to pursue this initiative over the next year or two, a representative of UCC will be in touch with you.

It was a pleasure meeting you.

Sincerely,

Julia Drake
Director of Communications

P.S. My colleague, Sandi Laine, says "hello"!

MAL COVEN

May 6, 2009

PERSONAL AND CONFIDENTIAL

Mr. André Cointreau
President & CEO
Le Cordon Bleu
8 rue, Léon Delhomme
75015 Paris, France

Dear Mr. Cointreau:

I am not a real estate agent but a former successful retailer who developed a 249-store chain in Canada (see Hartman letter enclosed). I am writing this to help a dear friend, Nadia Brandler. Nadia owns a unique 100-year-old property at 81 St. Nicholas Street, formerly an RCMP stable, in downtown Toronto. Fourteen years ago she renovated 8,000 square feet (4,000 on each floor) and opened an international make-up school, "Complexions". She had a similar school in London. It trains students to do make-up and special effect masks for the movie and theatre industry. It is exceptionally successful to this day.

She recently renovated the balance of the property into two additional stores, each one 2,400 square feet. One has been rented to a French franchise "Benit", a unique exercise business, also very successful. The store in the centre behind the wrought iron gate in the picture is for lease. I suggested to her that she contact Le Cordon Bleu because of the two neighbouring businesses and its unusual thriving location adjacent to Toronto's elite stores, upscale high rise condominiums and other notable institutions such as the Royal Ontario Museum, University of Toronto and Queen's Park (seat of the Ontario government). In my opinion, it would be a good location for an upscale cooking school such as yours. Just north of this area, approximately two miles, are scores of luxury homes in the Forest Hill and Rosedale areas. Several of their residents have visited your Paris school.

..2/

38 AVENUE ROAD, SUITE 514
TORONTO, ONTARIO, CANADA M5R 2G2
TEL: (416) 513-0101
FAX: (416) 934-1943

I understand from Sylvie Sofi Alaroon that, unlike USA which is franchised, the only location in Canada in Ottawa is corporate owned. That is the reason I am contacting you directly.

You may not be aware of many things about Toronto so I will tell you something about our beautiful thriving city. You see by the photograph the Four Seasons is moving from their current location two short blocks away. They are building both a new hotel and a condominium residence. Both buildings have over fifty floors, both locations are a few short blocks from 81 St. Nicholas Street. Metro Toronto has a population of over four million and attracts half of the 200,000 immigrants yearly. It is a growing and vibrant community. The houses a few blocks away range from $1.5 million to $10 million. The many new high-rise condos sell for from $800 to $1,300/square foot The latter is the highest average price in Canada. It is the fourth largest TV market in North America and you see by the aerial photo that Bloor Street, adjacent to 81 St. Nicholas Street, is home to every international retailer in USA and Europe.

Whether or not you are interested in locating a school at 81 St. Nicholas Street, I would appreciate a reply to this proposal as soon as possible.

Sincerely,

Mal Coven

P.S. If 2,400 square feet is not sufficient for your needs, an additional 2,400 square feet could be built on now or in the future.

c.c.   Sylvie Sofi Alaroon
        Ottawa Culinary Arts Institute

Enclosures: 4 photographs
              2 brochures
              Hartman letter

The National Ethnic Heritage Foundation
38 Avenue Road, Suite 514
Toronto, Ontario Canada M5R 2G2
Tel (416) 513-0101
Fax (416) 934-1943
www. nehf.org
1@ nehf.org

PERSONAL AND CONFIDENTIAL

Mr. Jay Schottenstein   May 27, 2009
President & CEO
Retail Ventures
1800 Moler Road
Columbus, Ohio 43207 USA

Dear Jay:

I am enclosing the first few samples of the 100 Italian baseball heroes that we are doing for the
National Italian American Foundation (NIAF). As you know, we want to look into doing the
three DiMaggio brothers in glass. The idea came to me when you mentioned doing Sandy
Koufax Caro in glass. We want to do the DiMaggio brothers for presentation at their annual
dinner in Washington in November. The Sandy Koufax will have to wait until we have an
appropriate venue. That will be when the baseball documentary is completed, the beginning of
2010. Most of the filming has been done but there are other issues that will take several months,
I am told.

The Italian project, with which I am intimately involved, is being done through our not-for-
profit entity, National Ethnic Heritage Foundation.

Please put me in touch with the right person so I can get started with the DiMaggio project.

Regards,

Mal Coven
Chairman

Enclosure: Baseball cards

NATIONAL ETHNIC HERITAGE FOUNDATION
57 W 75ᵗʰ Street 2B, New York, NY 10023
herbertklein@nehf.org   www.nehf.org
917-400-9799

The Office of the President   March 26, 2010
The White House
1600 Pennsylvania Avenue NW
Washington, DC 20500

Dear Mr. President:

Children need heroes and role models. We at the National Ethnic Heritage Foundation (NEHF) have plans for creating a new set of "Heroes cards", using a proven trading card format, to inspire children to set their sights higher by painlessly learning about currently successful African Americans in education, writing, research, science, art, medicine, business, politics, military, public health, and more. We do not necessarily exclude pop culture or sports, but the focus is on demonstrating what a good education can yield. Our "Heroes" card set, and possible related posters are easy for children to relate to, are inexpensive, have a long, useful life, and are ideal for classroom use.

The National Ethnic Heritage Foundation (www.nehf.org) is a small, young, 501(c)3 non-profit organization with an ambitious ethnic and child-oriented educational mission and highly experienced pro bono management.

Our "Heroes" heritage cards are a proven tool to get the message to an impressionable young audience. Kids love cards. The enclosed samples were made and successfully distributed for the American Jewish Historical Society in 2003, and the latest for the Sons of Italy Foundation in 2009.

We are considering investing in a new set of cards honoring 100 African American heroes. We would like to get them out by the millions to inner city schools and churches, and other organizations that can place them where they can do the most good. This task is larger than we can do ourselves.

We seek blessing and encouragement from an administration that prides itself on improving education. We need to meet people who can provide advice and guidance in the selection of the honorees and the distribution of the cards. Ideally, someone from your staff can introduce us to related educational private or public agencies that can help with the distribution and needed fundraising.

Thank you for any help you can provide,

POSTMEDIA/NETWORK

January 24, 2011

To Whom It May Concern:

Re: Mal Coven

I have known Mal Coven for many years. He is an accomplished businessman with an unbelievable vision for undertaking projects that conclude with success. He is creative, hard working and very goal-orientated.

Mal's role as a mentor would be of great benefit to those undertaking a business start-up or the restructuring of a exciting business that needs a new vision and creative approach or simply some wise words about operational direction.

Mal is truly an individual who can grasp many problems and ultimately seeks the right solution.

Yours sincerely,

Paul V. Godfrey
President and Chief Executive Officer

1450 DON MILLS ROAD   POSTMEDIA NETWORK INC.
TORONTO, ONTARIO M3B 2X7   /POSTMEDIA.COM

MAL COVEN

PERSONAL

Heather Reisman, CEO
Indigo
468 King Street West
Toronto, Ontario M5B 1L8

March 14, 2011

Dear Heather:

Perhaps you remember me, a founder of the BiWay stores. When you were my neighbour at 38 Avenue Road I sent you a welcoming gift of *mandelbrot* and you were kind enough to send me two books, one of which was Kirk Douglas's book on aging. I did not take that personally as you couldn't know my age (now 82). I approached you on two of my many original projects I developed since selling BiWay to Dylex, namely, "Marketplace for Catalogues" and Pinky Puppets, both of which your company wrongly (from my point of view) rejected.

I have always prided myself in being able to spot great items and the enclosed are two. Consider one a gift in return for the second book you sent me. The other is to show to the appropriate buyer at Indigo. It comes in a small display stand and is selling exceptionally well, retailing at $5. It comes in assorted patterns, appealing to ladies, is quite well designed, ideal at the cash register. It has been sold as high as $10 (hint). I have not found the original source but I am sure your people can. In Florida it is distributed by H.D. Smith Company (954-977-8188).

Separately, I guess I want to get on the good side of you as I am writing my autobiography, tentatively titled "The Nine Lives of Mal Coven and/or BiWay Remembered." It will contain a dozen of my original projects since retiring from BiWay plus twelve good pieces of advice for potential teenage entrepreneurs. Two of my original projects are current and very much alive and proceeding nicely.

I am available for coffee with you 24/7 if you would care to know more about them.

Best regards,

Mal Coven

Enclosure

PS   I always take advice from people I respect. Colin Powell's advice to a large group of young people is as follows: 1. Be kind to the people you work with and those that serve you; 2. Always write thank-you notes; 3. Small gifts to show your appreciation is always helpful. I try to follow his advice.

38 AVENUE ROAD, SUITE 514
TORONTO, ONTARIO, CANADA M5R 2G2
TEL: (416) 513-0101
FAX: (416) 934-1943
malcoven@rogers.com

!ndigo
Books & Music Inc.

March 17, 2011

Mr. M. Coven
38 Avenue Road, Suite 514
Toronto, ON
M5R 2G2

Dear Mr. Coven,

Firstly, thank you for your letter and the two lights. I will forward them to the appropriate buyer to see if this is something we wish to carry. It was thoughtful of you to think of us.

Secondly, regarding writing your biography I can put you in touch with the Category Manager who buys biography. He will be able to provide some guidance on potential publishers etc.

Yours sincerely,

Navraj Sagoo
Executive Assistant to H. Reisman

chapters.indigo.ca

468 King Street West, Suite 500, Toronto, Ontario M5V 1L8   416-364-4499   fax: 416-364-0355

EPILOGUE

WRITING this book has been a great joy because it has given me a chance to look back on my life and realize how fortunate I have been.

A percentage of my good fortune was the result of my determination to succeed; another percentage was the result of pure chance.

Driving to see Jerry Levinson in Montreal to give my 1953 Dodge convertible an airing changed my life. On that trip I met my future wife, Miriam Fish, and soon after that her brother, Morris (Moishe) Fish. As mentioned earlier in this book, when Moishe persuaded me to take some freshly caught fish to his mother Zlata in Val-David, he used the words, "Fish are lucky" to persuade me. He sure was right about that.

Later, if Miriam hadn't convinced me that the original Biway store must still be available because it could not be sold as quickly as we had been told, there would never have been a Biway.

Being introduced to Barbara by Judy and Aubrey Golden has brought me 27 years of love and happiness with Barbara.

My children Robin and David are happily married to Tim and Victoria. Robin is an executive at the UJA office and David has found his calling teaching in the U.K. They have brought my grandchildren Miriam, Nomi, Daniel, Isaac, Sam, Ruby, and Pearl into my life.

I have had a very fulfilling life, and, most important, peace of mind.

ACKNOWLEDGMENTS

EVEN though I wrote this book by hand, it never could have been accomplished without the help of four people.

I dictated my handwritten manuscript to Patricia Starr, who typed most of it on a computer. The balance was done with the help of Bernice Lester of Letter Perfect; all of the letters I have written were reproduced by her. She has had 20 years of experience reading my handwriting. Special praise to my Barbara, who spent many hours editing, particularly during the final stages of the book. She spotted things that even my esteemed publisher had not discovered. My publisher, Don Bastian, put the finishing touches on the book, and became a good friend in the process.

Acknowledgment also goes to Vishala of Forest Hill Photos, who printed all the pictures for the book, and to Josefina Motton in the Prince Arthur office who supplemented my computer knowledge.

INDEX

Locators in italics refer to scanned documents or picture captions